Persona Studies

Persona Studies

An Introduction

P. David Marshall, Christopher Moore, and Kim Barbour

WILEY Blackwell

This edition first published 2020
© 2020 John Wiley & Sons, Inc.

The right of P. David Marshall, Christopher Moore, and Kim Barbour to be identified as the authors of this work has been asserted in accordance with law.

Registered Office(s)
John Wiley & Sons, Inc., 111 River Street, Hoboken, NJ 07030, USA

Editorial Office
111 River Street, Hoboken, NJ 07030, USA

For details of our global editorial offices, customer services, and more information about Wiley products visit us at www.wiley.com.

Wiley also publishes its books in a variety of electronic formats and by print-on-demand. Some content that appears in standard print versions of this book may not be available in other formats.

Library of Congress Cataloging-in-Publication data applied for

9781118935040 (hardback); 9781118935057 (paperback)

Cover Design: Wiley
Cover Images: © FeelPic / Getty Images, © Semmick Photo / Shutterstock

Set in 10/12pt Warnock by SPi Global, Pondicherry, India

Printed in the United States of America

V10008781_031419

Contents

About the Authors

P. David Marshall, PhD, is a professor and holds a Personal Chair in New Media, Communication and Cultural Studies at Deakin University in Melbourne, Australia. He has published widely in the area of public personality systems with his most recent books entitled *Celebrity Persona Pandemic* (2016, University of Minnesota Press), the coauthored *Advertising and Promotional Culture: Case Histories* (2018, Palgrave Macmillan), the coedited *A Companion to Celebrity* (2016, Wiley) and *Contemporary Publics* (2016, Palgrave Macmillan).

Christopher Moore, PhD, is a senior lecturer in digital communication and media at the University of Wollongong, Australia. His research in game studies has examined the affective dimensions of first-person video games and the role of screenshots and virtual items in the expression of gamer persona. He is a coeditor of the journal of *Persona Studies* and published work on machinima and adaptation in *Understanding Machinima: Essays on Filmmaking in Virtual Worlds* (Bloomsbury, 2013). He is the coeditor of the collection in *Critical University Studies, Zombies in the Academy: Living Death in Higher Education* (2013, Intellect) and the edited collection *Enchanting David Bowie: Space | Time | Body | Memory* (2015, Bloomsbury).

Kim Barbour, PhD, is a lecturer in the Department of Media at the University of Adelaide. Her research looks at online personas and particularly focuses on the use of social media, and her dissertation "Finding the Edge: Online Persona Creation by Fringe Artists" was the first long-form study in the field of persona studies. Barbour's work has been published in *Celebrity Studies, First Monday, TDR,* and *The Drama Review,* as well as the edited collections *The Digital Academic* (2018, Routledge), *Making Publics, Making Places* (2016, University of Adelaide Press), and *Media, Margins and Popular Culture* (2015, Palgrave Macmillan). In 2014, she co-founded the online open access journal *Persona Studies,* and continues in the role of managing editor.

Acknowledgments

This book has a rich and collective history in its formation. The authors wish to thank the many people who have been instrumental in building and engaging in this emerging discipline of persona studies. All our colleagues who have been involved in developing the related journal and the many people who have listened as we have developed the key ideas contained in this book – we are indebted to you and your support. We would also like to thank the Persona Celebrity Publics (PCP) research group and the emerging Fame and Persona Research Consortium (FPRC) where we trialed some of these approaches and how they intersected across disciplines. Our respective departments and colleagues at Deakin University, the University of Wollongong, and The University of Adelaide continue to support our research and writing. In particular, we would like to mention our appreciation of the work of Sharyn McDonald, Katja Lee, Lucy Moore, Glenn D'Cruz, and Rebecca Hutton. Wiley has also been very supportive in getting this book through all the stages to publication and we would like to thank in particular Elisha Benjamin and Catriona King. We would also like to acknowledge some of our colleagues from different parts of the world who have been particularly valuable in allowing our ideas to grow and develop: Brigitte Weingart, Bethany Usher, Barry King, Jason Karlin, Sandra Mayer, Helle Haastrup, Nete Kristensen, Stephen Moestrup, Gianni Guastella, Richard Smith, Joshua Greenberg, Celia Lam, Samita Nandy, Jackie Raphael, Tama Leaver, Annik Dubied, Brian Cowan, and Jing Xin.

David: I would like to thank my wonderful children Erin, Zak, Julia, and Paul for all their patience. I would like to convey a very special thank you to my beautiful wife, Sally, who is always so helpful, supportive, and loving. I love you and always will.

Chris: I am exceptionally fortunate to be a part of two wonderful teams who have contributed to this book, both the excellent and adventurous academics, Kim and David, and my patient and endlessly supportive family, Xavier, Harriet, and Lucy. My work on this book would not have been possible without the love and dedication of my wonderful wife, Lucy, who is the greatest of collaborators. Thank you.

Kim: Thank you to my wonderful mentors (David and Chris), and my family for demonstrating a generous, inclusive, and fulfilling intellectual life is not just possible but desirable and rewarding. Most importantly, endless gratitude to my partner Richard and daughter Abigail for their continual love and support.

Introduction

A Short History of the New Public Self

The odd paradox of research is that when one claims that something is new, it is the easiest statement to make and the hardest to prove. Every day, we are inundated with new information that claims something is profoundly different, whether an event which will change the course of history, a new miracle cure/drug for some human ailment has been developed, or maybe another herald-like prophecy that predicts the end of the Earth. Perhaps this appeal to the new has accelerated with the way our attention is captured through online searches and drawn to images and proclamations that present "the most amazing," "the most unbelievable," and "the most outrageous" which dwarf newspaper head-lines of the past and make us feel that we are perpetually seeing the world through the ocular lens of a Ripley's Believe it or Not tourist museum or a continuously updated *Guinness Book of Records.*

Nonetheless, new things and new practices do emerge; they may not be as dramatically different from the past as we might imagine, but sometimes change is both real and present. This book explores something we perceive as quite a fundamental change in the way that we negotiate ourselves through life. What we argue is that increasingly we are engaged in the production of a public self. On one level, this seems an absurd position to take. After all, are we not producing a public version of ourselves every time we walk outside and move into the public world of a street or hop on a bus or train? Our claim in this book is that this has expanded in some interesting and intriguing ways for us and that this production of a public self is actually connected to our techniques of presentation when we walk outside, but is put into different registers and modes. If we think of our various media forms as extensions of our cul-ture – and specifically extensions of how we conceive of what is public – then any display of ourselves through different media is a formation of a public self. These mediated versions of public selves have defined our public sphere in various ways for more than two centuries and perhaps with less intensity for centuries prior. Collectively, we have read newspapers and magazines which

•

Persona Studies: An Introduction, First Edition. P. David Marshall, Christopher Moore, and Kim Barbour.

have described the exploits of others. With more twentieth-century technologies such as film, television, and radio, this description has become deepened, intensified, and made more representationally complete for us to construct not only a public sphere that makes sense and coheres, but also a collection of public individuals that we can identify, discuss, and critique in a relatively new way as if they are known to us.

What is now distinctly different is that collectively but in individualistic ways we negotiate a much-shifted media and communication scape that produces quite different constitutions of public activity. In a sense, online culture, mobile media, and game culture which move between these spaces have produced an elaborate reconfiguration of what constitutes public and private space and activity. These changes have developed partly through what could be described as the "**mediatization**" of the contemporary moment. What we mean by mediatization is connected to the recent research on this area (Couldry 2014; Ess 2014; Lundby 2009, 2014), where different thinkers have expressed how various aspects of contemporary life – for example, politics and culture – are now seen through the lens of media which provides a form of legitimation and privileging of certain narratives and shared experiences. Our particular application of mediatization is to express how the formation of the contemporary self is now constructed and displayed through technologies and forms of expression that resemble media forms. In other words, we communicate through printed text, through images, through video and audio in a way that re-constructs our identity through these various signifying systems. Playing games, texting, teleconferencing, video streaming and participating in Twitter, YouTube, Tumblr, Flickr, Pinterest, WeChat, and Reddit and a host of other forms of connecting and communicating with others has produced an environment where individuals are collectively producing very elaborate versions of themselves. We will explore this development of mediatization further in Chapter 2 when we introduce the concept of **intercommunication,** which identifies the blending of media and communication as well as the highly mediated blending of different types of interpersonal communication.

To capture this constructed, fabricated, produced, and presented public self that goes beyond our past notions of a public personality or celebrity and becomes an elemental part of literally billions of people worldwide, we were drawn to a word and concept that expresses the very sense of the artifice of identity. The idea of **persona** best articulates this new technologically mediated but naturalized identity that we inhabit individually and collectively. Although the term persona has a long history of use that we expand upon considerably in Chapter 1, it is perhaps useful in this introduction to identify what persona is not, and thereby get closer to its value in understanding the way in which we engage and use online culture.

First of all, *persona is not the individual.*

It has all the appearances of being an individual, but it is in fact the way an individual can organize themselves publicly. Persona is a projection and a performance of individuality. This form of projection and performance is destined for some type of audience, some community and some collective. Thinking about how the collective is somehow part of this fabricated performance of individuality, identifies the second distinction that needs to be made about persona.

So, second, *persona is not a collective.*

This may seem an obvious point, but the distinction is important. Persona, in its appeal to a collective formation, embeds in its fiber the indexical signs of the collective itself. Persona then is essentially a way to negotiate one's self into various collectives. Thus a politician produces a persona that is an attempt to embody the cultural meanings of what his/her electorate might think of as, yes, a good politician, but also the accouterments of ethnicity and identity and status that will strengthen that appeal. The construction of persona individualizes this appeal to a particular collective. The complexity of this persona work is carried out by an individual in most cases, but as with politicians that are supported by political parties this persona work may be actually part of the job and responsibility of a campaign manager or press agent or secretary. For the other billions who are constructing online personas via social media platforms, this work – for, as we identify throughout this book, this has become a serious component of everyday labor that may or may not generate some sort of income or compensation – has become so normalized that it has blended into the flows of everyday life. In Chapter 2, and our final three chapters that provide exemplifications, we explore this kind of **industrialized agency** that particularly online persona expresses: where a contemporary individualized value is cultivated pandemically and relentlessly. In interesting and complex variations, a persona can inhabit a collective sense of self where a professional identity or a way of involving oneself in the games industry produces a formation of a persona across a shared group of people. Also, in some ways, contemporary persona identifies a new comfortability with inhabiting some configuration of a *commodified self.* This new constitution of public identity is often linked to celebrity.

And this insight underlines our third significant negative distinction: *persona is not synonymous with celebrity.*

This differentiation between the use of celebrity and persona is important for a number of reasons. First of all, it has to be acknowledged that celebrities have been and still are one of the best ways to understand something like persona. They are an array of familiar figures that we have given collective identity monikers such as stars, superstars, icons, cultural leaders, and political leaders along with a host of other variations of these terms. Celebrity identity is also fundamentally attached to media forms. The collective knowledge we have about our famous people is dependent on their mediatization: we see them on screens, we recognize their voices and mannerisms through similar technologies and we see them conveyed to us through third parties such as interviews and features in magazines or magazine-like online fora. Moreover, celebrities are some of the best incarnations and examples of "industrialized agency," a term that we are linking to the activity of persona construction and maintenance that millions upon millions produce and reproduce in daily rituals of online behavior.

But the differentiation between the concept of celebrity and persona is useful to understand. Persona, as a practice and as a formation of the public self, articulates a larger understanding of this move to mediatization, one that has become clearly more pervasive through the technological affordances of identity construction, sharing and "broad" and "narrow"-casting that are now the commonplace and everyday features of social media use. Celebrity, despite its high visibility, is a *subset* of persona: in so many ways it articulates and expresses persona; but it needs to be underlined that persona goes well beyond the structures and experiences of celebrity. Celebrity is a particular formation of persona, one that from the now extensive analysis of its meaning can be seen as very much connected to various powerful media forms that have similarities to online culture but clearly some historical differences.

As we explore this space of difference between celebrity and persona, we now arrive at another negative proposition about persona. *Persona cannot be completely understood as a contemporary and online phenomenon*: it has clear precursors in public identity formation.

The public personas of celebrity, for instance, have served as powerful precursors of online personas. From the early persona studies research, one of the important values of celebrity is to see them as pedagogical tools for millions on how to structure a strategic public identity (Marshall 2006, 2010). The previous two centuries have provided models of the relationship of media to public individuals that are valuable sources for our understanding of persona. In the nineteenth century, as Stephen Gundle's (2008) work has revealed, the reporting and visibility of prominent individuals via newspapers and magazines originally helped produced the twentieth century's relationship to glamor. Glamor itself can be read as an outward depiction of the self for public display and its movement from film and fashion celebrity icons in the nineteenth and twentieth centuries into how individuals determined their own public comportment actually identifies the transformation of the public self, outside of the strictures of class and social position.

Delving further into precursors of the particularities of contemporary persona helps us shift from saying *what persona is not* to a more affirming and positive sense of *what persona actually is* and what this form of investigation allows us to explore. What is essential about persona is that it *implies an interplay between the understanding of public and private.*

This exploration of where persona fits into the spectrum of public and private is nuanced by investigating it historically. Persona is a Latin word and its precursor, *prosopon*, identifies that it was also a term employed in Ancient Greece and we analyze this in much greater detail in Chapter 1. What needs to be identified here from ancient history is that there has always been a play between what is depicted in the outside world – what we might call publicly – and what is somehow kept in more private spaces. As Hannah Arendt's work has underlined, Ancient Greek culture separated their domestic (oikos) sphere with different rules, orders, and etiquette quite markedly from what is presented in public (Arendt 2013 [1958]). The ancient Athenian citizen (it is always important to underline that this citizen was universally male and of course excluded other members [such as slaves] of the Athenian community) performed a public role and produced a relationship to politics and strategy that was quite distinctive and separate from the private world of the household – the domestic sphere as it was thought at that time. In other words, there was something discontinuous in the understanding of the personality of the individual from public to private and this was entirely acceptable (Arendt 2013 [1958], pp. 28–30).

A cautionary reading of how individuality itself was thought of in different epochs and eras and the ways these differences were instrumental in transforming the public stage of self-presentation is necessary. Collective configurations of dress styles – a public display of the self – in different historical and cultural settings may have depicted gender, ethnic, group, job, title, and social position differentiations. Through these techniques the public presentation of the self was often behind the guise of collective identities. One can read the traditional ethnic garb as fragments and regularly used components that became, by the nineteenth and twentieth centuries, ways in which the emerging nation and nation-state could express its collective identity. The relationship between collective and individual identity is complex and informs and layers our understanding of public and private.

Persona as a research focus aims to deepen understandings of the shifts and transformations of the relation between public and private as it is articulated through public displays of the self. The individual, through their constructed and displayed persona, serves as a complex mediating device that moves between the public and the private. What is fascinating in the current way in which online and social media persona is managed today is that we can actually observe, collect, and analyze these various ways that the personal develops, reforms, and reconstitutes over time. We can see the manner in which the intimate, the private, the quasi-public, and the **micro-public** of friends develops, a term that will be unpacked in detail in Chapter 4. We can also discern the interconnections that produce an even wider public through the elaborate network of sharing and exchanging that sometimes builds millions of viewers/users/sharers that can on occasion establish the significant power of an individual persona. YouTube stars such as JennaMarbles and HolaSoyGerman, among many thousands of others, embody through their personas this new form of celebrity-like behavior.

This spectrum of public identity is a wonderful way in which people engage with others in the contemporary moment. However, this genuine beauty of pandemic persona work – what we could call the spread of both a new formation of a persona articulated through public personalization and a celebration of individuality in new collective formations – does have some more conflicting consequences. So, personas are produced through corporately owned platforms which require particular types of personalized information in order to become or remain profitable. In this book, we call the owners of Facebook, Instagram, Twitter, Tumblr, and other social media platforms part of the **intercommunication** industry. With a certain brilliance, these companies have set up a way in which individuals can have the sense of sharing with others, but also generate massive amounts of data about themselves that these corporations can legally mine, analyze, and directly share with other interested corporations. As companies,

1) they have moved successfully into the territory of interpersonal communication as phone companies have done for more than a century;
2) they have augmented this with the capacity to collect, organize and shape the flow and connection of that interpersonal communication by providing the pathways for more mediated feeds that are structured into this flow of communication; and
3) they have worked to highly target the individual and algorithmically associate them with an array of further feeds that are essentially paid messages or what the **legacy media** industry would call advertising.

As much as persona is imbricated in these very sophisticated intercommunication industries, it is equally valid to realize that as individuals construct their personas, they are increasingly aware that their data has been organized and shared for economic gain. As researchers in this area, we see one of the key storylines of this book is that the study of persona is designed to assist groups and individuals in the ways that they can negotiate and strategize their online persona.

To both research persona and to aid in the strategies toward strategically and tactically constructing personas, we have embraced a few related research traditions as well as connected to the kinds of public/collective personas that have been privileged as public identity markers over the last few centuries. As much as this last sentence is filled with our new (but nonetheless very important) jargon, it identifies that we consider "action research" incredibly valuable in the future development of persona studies. Action research has been advanced and promulgated in education studies in particular as a way for researchers to both conduct research and to help the subjects of their research toward better practices. As you will see in Chapters 5–8, we have explored a number of professional and recreational identities and how they are reconstructed into personas online. Our interventions in these various activities is specifically designed to be useful and ultimately applied by individuals and professional associations as their professions become reconstituted by the work of online culture and the parallel work and transformations of the intercommunication industries which are always part of contemporary persona making.

Connected to this work on making groups and individuals more aware of their persona work, our study of persona is also designed to familiarize researchers with how we can both conceptualize the kinds of labor – emotional, tactical, collective, strategic, economic, esthetic, and design work – that persona entails. As Chapter 6 explores, the techniques of phenomenological and online "listening" (Crawford 2009) can be an effective way to make sense of the substantial amount of work individuals put into their online personas. Similarly, but with a different emphasis, our approach to persona highlighted in Chapter 7 is also to develop visual graphics of how individuals and groups connect and this visualization identifies the tangible evidence of how online persona works.

Investigating persona is complicated. Our book acknowledges this complexity. First, it does so in terms of an awareness of how the historical constitution of persona is essential for understanding the contemporary online transformation. Second, it privileges the ways that persona's strategic and public individuality is in constant negotiation with the economic structures that now shape it in new directions in online and social media contexts. And third, we acknowledge the equally significant understanding that constructing personas is relational with others' efforts at constructing personas. Persona as a meaning system is dependent on what could be called **prosopographic** relations (Marshall, Moore, and Barbour 2015). **Prosopography** is derived from history of place and persons and literally means study of "an individual's life/career" from a close study of the "collective biography" (OED Online 2018) It is a study of the personal through various ways dress, documents, comportment, and objects established the relations of power and influence within a particular community or village. In a sense, our current work on persona is to investigate the strategies and the relational significance of strategies in the contemporary moment – with a full acknowledgment and genuflection to the millennia of persona construction in different contexts and structures of both communication and power.

This has been an exciting book to research and write and, we hope, an equally exciting book to read. Its subject matter identifies a transformation that builds from human history and its structure of public comportment, and translates that into the highly mediatized and screen-oriented contemporary and pervasive public persona. Each of the chapters has a clear objective in its revelation of persona and the value of persona studies. Given the relative newness of the intellectual project, there is a particular logic in reading the chapters sequentially as the early chapters conceptually inform our applications in the later chapters. To give you a sense of this logic, this introduction will try to identify the significance of each chapter and their relationship to each other from beginning to conclusion.

Chapter 1 works through how persona can be conceptualized and draws primarily on how past research and historical work can inform this contemporary configuration of public identity. It begins with a reading of the contemporary way in which strategic public identities have been built and expressed in online culture. We acknowledge a cultural studies approach around both tactic and strategy and how this "art of making do" (Fiske 1989, pp. 25–29) describes the way individuals working in new collective and sharing configurations develop strategic and publicly directed personas.

From a cultural studies' inspired approach, the chapter then integrates key words and concepts into the investigation of the meaning and significance of persona. To make sense of these contemporary iterations, we move back in time and theory and integrate first the value of the ancient Greek and Roman meaning and deployment of the concept of persona and identify how this mask of identity is a useful path to explore our contemporary information and communication-technology rich present.

The chapter then works through the related central theoretical traditions and key thinkers that have used persona directly – such as Jung – and others such as Freud who have implied the divides between different levels of identity formation. We also acknowledge the imagistic movement around persona that emerged at the beginning of the twentieth century in literary movements associated with Ezra Pound, and to a lesser degree T.S. Eliot, as writers attempted to produce entities to express internal meanings of the self outwards.

Central to our use of persona is its connection to performance studies, specifically how the everyday was reconfigured by Erving Goffman (1959) into an expression of presentation. Important terms such as "frame," "frontstage," "backstage," and many others express the sociological dimension of our persona work and construction as a collective reading of the public self that is connected via Goffman to the social theories around symbolic interactionism. The chapter concludes by extending and linking Goffman's approach to the emerging presentational media and cultural regime that is shaping a wider dimension of the personalization of presentation. Some of these personalization processes are linked to notions of individuality and public expression that have developed in particular ways for the last forty years and longer: celebrity culture, we argue has served as a pedagogical resource for the shaping of this wider and now online presentation of the self publicly.

As much as Chapter 1 integrates the historical and theoretical antecedents of persona studies into the contemporary moment, Chapter 2's focus is specifically on an interpretation of how online culture is forming this new generative development of a mediatized public identity that is literally coursing through the technological and communication veins of the world's many diverse cultures. Entitled the "Contemporary Significance of Persona," it highlights certain recent analytical frames to interrogate the widespread phenomena.

Other concepts and terms circulate around and inform our work, but perhaps none is more central to the explorations in this chapter and beyond than the relatively new term directly derived from our work on persona, *intercommunication*. This term captures both the industrial quality of how people are organized into platforms and applications through social media use and the multiple levels of media, communication, and exchange that contemporary online culture siphons through the individual user. Intercommunication also provides the pathway for the chapter to explore the surveillance culture that is produced by these same platforms and their multiple redeployment back into economic, advertising, and marketing models of identity and exchange. Certain theorists are integrated into this study of the contemporary concept of persona including situating Foucault's work on the panopticon (1979), Deleuze's "societies of control" (1992), McLuhan's now dated but reinvigorated notion of the "global village" (1989), along with the recent scholarship of Alice Marwick through her exploration of status and influence in Silicon Valley and microcelebrity (2013), and Alison Hearn and Stephanie Schoenhoff's provocative critique of the "influencer" culture (2015).

Chapter 3 – entitled "Intercommunication and the Dimensions and Registers of Persona" – provides an expanded toolkit for the investigation and analysis of persona. It first explicates persona via intercommunication into specific elements – that online and intercommunicatively constructed persona is an individualized, **interpersonal**, **indexical**, and internetworked aggregated entity that is shaped by this particular industrial model as well as by the activities of social media participants. From this basis, Chapter 3 then works through the registers of persona – in other words, the prominent patterns with which people present and perform their public identities online. We have grouped these under professional, personal, and intimate registers. Augmenting this analysis are the five dimensions of persona, the first four of which are the **public**, the **mediatized**, the **performative** and the **collective** dimension of persona. The fifth dimension of persona for analytical purposes is what we have labeled the ugly neologism, **VARP**, which stands for the **value, agency, reputation, and prestige** dimension, an essential component that through its monitoring and internalization of value shapes billions and their constructing their public identities online.

In Chapter 4, we focus on the collective constitution of public persona particularly as it has manifested itself via digital networks. Persona, as we have tried to define it, is the movement of the individual into the collective, but intriguingly persona is neither individual nor collective. This chapter works through the new logics of this identity and the differing and transforming possibilities for individuals as they negotiate identities that generate value for an elaborate intercommunication industry that is also actively generating personas. As much as for us as players and participants in the various social media platforms as it is for the corporations who have provided the platforms for our forms of play and public identity construction, persona is a "quasi-object" and not a subject: this form of object – borrowing from Latour (2005) for this insight and extension in our understanding of persona – produces forms of mediation in the social. The individual can produce "micro-publics," but it always has to be acknowledged that this form of production of the public self is also generating other versions of the public self that are used for quite different, but sometimes related directions. The data of the public self is something that the individual can attempt to monitor their use – what is called sous-veillance (Mann 2004) – and also work to intervene in that form of monitoring. The complex combination of our willing acceptance of self-monitoring through social media and wearable applications is a fascinating reconstruction of what our new collectivized self can be, and how our data produces multiple personas for different social and economic ends. The desire to make oneself into what is called a microcelebrity is a prominent way in which some individuals attempt to play in this space of identity for their apparent gain, while others work to block, hack, and transform the produced identities. Our persona work is realizing that these forms of public display of the self are data clusters, sometimes aggregated, sometimes linked to audience-like micro-publics, sometimes sold, sometimes visualized for different ends and goals, but always identifying the wider activities and engagement that persona identifies and our research into its quasi-object status reveals.

Chapter 5 is our "methods" chapter as it charts the techniques that we have privileged and employed in our own studies of persona. As you might expect, some of the concepts and terms that we have used in the previous chapters that established the theoretical and conceptual dimensions of Persona Studies reappear and are situated in our move toward application. Our hope is that these analytical approaches can be adopted by others as they move into exploring persona in more detail.

Given the nature of persona – that it is something that we all employ for our negotiation into more visible and apparently public worlds – the chapter first acknowledges there is a need to see some of our work inspired by "auto-ethnography." Our approach expands from this base of insight and acknowledges the values of ethnographic techniques, but what we privilege is an approach to persona construction that is self-reflexive. To capture that direction, we have called our technique of engagement **first person action research** where through deep analysis the exploration of the managed persona of the researcher provides the entry into the layers of digital construction, the connection to friends and followers, and the cross-connection with the interconnection of networks and webs that reflect back on how we as individuals would like to manage our online selves better and with greater clarity. This method in our work has also been linked to **interpretative phenomenological analysis (IPA)** (Smith, Flowers, and Larkin 2009) where open acknowledgment of active interpretation of actions by both researcher and subject is developed in the deep description and is the basis of our close study in Chapter 6. Our use of IPA is naturally with quite small samples and is located first within a deep understanding of the *context* of any individual's activities in constructing persona. Second, our IPA work integrates a reading of online activity and its persona creation that goes beyond observation into what Crawford (2009) calls "listening" – a combination of text, image, deployment, and the interactions that occur through and by individuals online. From that processual and interpretive foundation, this IPA method moves to in-depth and unstructured interviews that assist our interpretation of what the individual is attempting to construct through their persona work. This research technique is also connected to **second-person action research**, where we have managed others as they reported on their online persona work, but also talked and developed and exchanged how they were shifting their approaches to restructure their online persona partly as a result of our own surveys and workshops. This approach we have privileged in our current and future studies of professional personas and is dealt with in greatest detail in Chapter 8.

The chapter outlines a method we call **prosopographic field studies** or PFS and it has been extended into visualizing the social networks that personas are imbricated in both developing and maintaining. PFS starts with building the data about the interrelations of a sample population and how they establish roles, positions, and power hierarchies through their forms of public displays. It is designed to adapt this historical research tool to the study of both persona in history, but also extended to close studies of collective persona constructions and relations in online cultures and communities. Our final method explored in Chapter 5 is **information visualization** of our networked selves. Applications are now available to provide ways to show relative interactions of particular online personas and thereby establish the way that networks shape and convey public identity.

Chapters 6–8 are our applications of our methods to provide some exciting new persona studies research. It is our efforts at bringing the concept, theories, methods, and approaches into clear case studies and applications. Our work is exploring persona construction that has developed online and in many ways we are seeing the negotiation and blending of online and offline identities in this work.

In Chapter 6, we explore the fringe artist persona and how they have constructed their online identity. Building from the contentious and powerful "artist persona" that has historically positioned a spectrum of artist practitioners, the chapter maps how artists engaged in activities such as tattooing, craftivism, and street art actually produce a persona in this public and publicity-centric world of online connection. The challenges of constructing registers of performance of persona are some of the most interesting elements of this work as the artists practice sharing and concealing aspects of their identities.

Chapter 7 tracks the long history of the affordances of games for experimenting with persona. It considers the tools that games have provided for circulating player personas in particular communities. The chapter then examines the impact of social media on the distribution of games across personal computers, dedicated consoles, and mobile experiences and the means by which these networked public platforms have allowed for the expression of a self as a player. It looks to the contested nature of the "gamer" and examines the dramatic transformation of contemporary games culture. The chapter charts the progression of the industry-related persona, emerging from the user-generated community of games modification and leading to the rise of "indie" games, not as a brand but a particular expression of a player experience outside of narrowly defined and heavily regulated genre boundaries. The indie game developer persona, is considered as part of a cultural expression of persona, as a "gameur," which is symbolically linked to combatting toxic gamer culture and the provision of non-normative game experiences by developers who are not constrained by the predictable demands of a mass media industry.

Chapter 8 provides a study of professional personas and how online culture presents challenges to the construction of an identity, the meaning of a particular position or job, and the way orbiting communities are also transforming what we think of as professions. It investigates the profession of lawyers, doctors, and academics predominantly and how they perform and navigate the perturbations of professional public identity in their online reconfigurations. A **VARP** analysis guides our professional persona analysis in the chapter and helps explain the shifting value and agency that are shifting our professions and their public presentations/performances of their positions.

This book represents a culmination of research into persona as well as a launching point for others to take these ideas and explore many other constructions of public identity. Although certainly not a requirement of reading this book, it makes sense to get the background fully in place by working through the concepts, new terminology, and ultimately the methods. This background is the material that will be nuanced as this field advances and we are encouraging all interested readers and researchers to engage and debate with our approaches on this strategic and now pandemic online identity we call persona. To further facilitate this exchange and research collaboration as well as recognize that we are building a field of study, the end of our book is not just the concluding chapter, but also a glossary of the terms we have generated as well as repurposed for our investigation of persona studies. You will also notice that words that are in the glossary are highlighted in their first usage in the text to help you navigate effectively through our work on persona and its contemporary transformations.

References

Arendt, H. (2013 [1958]). *The Human Condition: Second Edition*. Reprint. Chicago: University of Chicago Press.

Couldry, N. (2014). Mediatization and the future of field theory. In: *Mediatization of Communication* (ed. K. Lundby), 227–246. Berlin: De Gruyter Mouton.

Crawford, K. (2009). Following you: Disciplines of listening in social media. *Continuum* 23 (4): 525–535. https://doi.org/10.1080/10304310903003270.

Deleuze, G. (1992). Postscript on the societies of control. *October* 59 (Winter): 3–7.

Ess, C. (2014). Selfhood, moral agency and the good life in mediatized worlds? Perspective from medium theory and philosophy. In: *Mediatization of Communication* (ed. K. Lundby), 617–640. Berlin: De Gruyter Mouton.

Fiske, J. (1989). *Understanding Popular Culture*. Boston: Unwin Hyman.

Foucault, M. (1979). *Discipline and Punish: The Birth of the Prison* (trans. A. Sheridan). Harmondsworth: Penguin.

Goffman, E. (1959). *The Presentation of Self in Everyday Life*. New York: Anchor Books.

Gundle, S. (2008). *Glamour: A History*. Oxford: Oxford University Press.

Hearn, A. and Schoenhoff, S. (2015). From celebrity to influencer: Tracing the diffusion of celebrity value across the data stream. In: *A Companion to Celebrity* (ed. P.D. Marshall and S. Redmond). Malden, MA: Wiley Blackwell.

Latour, B. (2005). *Reassembling the Social: An Introduction to Actor-Network-Theory*. London: Oxford University Press.

Lundby, K. (2009). *Mediatization: Concept, Changes, Consequences*. New York: Peter Lang.

Lundby, K. (2014). Mediatization of communication. In: *Mediatization of Communication* (ed. K. Lundby), 3–36. Berlin: De Gruyter Mouton.

Mann, S. (2004). Intelligent image processing. *Proceedings of the 12th Annual ACM International Conference on Multimedia*, 620–627.

Marshall, P.D. (2006). New media – new self: The changing power of celebrity. In: *Celebrity Culture Reader* (ed. P.D. Marshall), 634–644. New York: Routledge.

Marshall, P.D. (2010). The promotion and presentation of the self: Celebrity as marker of presentational media. *Celebrity Studies* 1 (1): 35–48. https://doi.org/10.1080/19392390903519057.

Marshall, P.D., Moore, C., and Barbour, K. (2015). Persona as method: Exploring celebrity and the public self through persona studies. *Celebrity Studies* 6 (3): 288–305. https://doi.org/10.1080/19392397.2015.1062649.

Marwick, A.E. (2013). *Status Update: Celebrity, Publicity, and Branding in the Social Media Age*. New Haven, CT: Yale University Press.

McLuhan, M. (1989). *The Global Village: Transformations in World Life and Media in the 21st Century*. Oxford: Oxford University Press.

OED Online. (2018). Prosopography. Oxford University Press. https://en.oxforddictionaries.com/definition/prosopography (accessed March 7, 2018).

Smith, J.A., Flowers, P., and Larkin, M. (2009). *Interpretative Phenomenological Analysis: Theory, Method and Research*. SAGE.

Part I

Conceptualizing Persona

1

Persona and Its Uses

Persona as a term and as an analytical concept has emerged from the close study of the performance and assemblage of the individual public self. In this chapter, the exceptional value that is inherited from multiple academic domains and disciplines is unpacked. Here, we account for the work in establishing persona as a term with a broad range of historical, intellectual, and analytical precursors. More specifically, we begin to account for persona studies as a toolkit for exploring the production of the self in the era of self-presentation and presentational media. The key to this chapter is the exploration of what has altered over time, and what continues to change, in our cultures, communities, and interactions as a result of the digital technologies, networked media platforms, media services, and communication services that make specific requirements of us in the mediated assemblage of our public identities.

What propels the need for a detailed investigation of the movement from the personal to the public is clearly imbricated in the demands for an online presence in the contemporary period. Our online selves are deeply enmeshed within the economies of attention and the hierarchies of reputation that have acted to diminish the barriers between categories of the personal, the professional, the public, and the private. Involvement in any kind of public has always required a dimension of personal display, but now features a blending of interpersonal and presentational frameworks. The need for public identity management has simultaneously opened up access to complex and often intersecting online and offline publics, allowing for the creation of multiple "real" selves, each with their own roles, domains of participation, and fields of social interaction. We may be less formal with friends on Facebook than with peers on Twitter, or jovial and outgoing on Tumblr but guarded and careful on Reddit. Each instance differs from the others, or they may connect and be consistent across each platform, depending on the needs and practices of the individual.

Persona Studies: An Introduction, First Edition. P. David Marshall, Christopher Moore, and Kim Barbour.
© 2020 John Wiley & Sons, Inc. Published 2020 by John Wiley & Sons, Inc.

Persona Studies and the Public Self

One of the major principles in the analytical toolkit of persona studies is the recognition of change in the complexity of individual agency in the contemporary moment. The concept of agency has historically undergone enough change to challenge a complete and categorical definition. However, the dimensions of agency as it emerged from cultural studies are core to the efforts of understanding that structural inequalities and unequal power relations are replicated by new media and communication technologies and their everyday application under capitalism (Green and Singleton 2013, p. 34). Agency has been recognized as an important function of social media platforms and services, including Facebook, Twitter, and Snapchat, as a means for regaining control over the information and representation of the public self, especially by celebrities, politicians, and public figures. As will be discussed in this chapter, social media has enabled the detouring of the desire for closer access expressed in tabloid consumption and paparazzi-style images into a more immediate – if equally constructed – public performance that is grounded in the "official" status of the account user and its claims to the authenticity of the performance of the individual. This is a feature of social media with significant personal and political potential, recognized by postfeminist scholars as a form of agentic empowerment and a "call to authenticity" which also recognizes the surveillance properties of the social media platforms that are used to disclose constructed performance and self-representations as an essentially "real" public identity:

> The "call to authenticity" animates the idea that one participates successfully by disclosing on Twitter, so women are both lauded for being empowered through expressing themselves and criticized for the consequences of this display, enabling representations of women as enterprising individuals who willingly subject themselves to the gaze as a form of agency. (Dubrofsky and Wood 2014, p. 284)

This is not to suggest that all users are treated equally or that new degrees of emancipation and equality are present on social media. One of the contributions of cultural studies to the work of persona studies is the understanding of the value of individual agency that is deeply rooted in the inequalities of power, gender relations, race, education, and so on. The critical work of Tizania Terranova, Dimitry Kleiner, Christian Fuchs, Mark Andrejevic, Mark Hansen, and Nick Dyer-Witheford and others in political economy studies, including the integration of key thinkers such as Marx, Foucault, and Hardt and Negri, have detailed and expanded the analysis of social media beyond classical economics, particularly in the areas of surveillance, privacy, intangible labor and immaterial capitalism. One of the key trajectories we take for working with these concerns was recognized in John Fiske's *Understanding Popular Culture* as the "art of making do" (Fiske 2010 [1989], p. 28).

Preceding Fiske's work, in *The Practice of Everyday Life*, Michel de Certeau (1984 [1980], p. 30) perceives "making do" as a motif for an esthetic dimension to the work of those whose individual creativity is constrained and enlivened by spaces that are generated by languages and practices that are owned, consumed, and dominated by forces out of their control. Even in the algorithmically policed spaces of YouTube copyright controls, Facebook policy takedowns, Apple iStore regulations, and government-banned file sharing websites, the digital enables an unprecedented degree of boundary crossing between home and work, labor and play, personal and public. The elements of online circumstance therefore leave no choice but to exist in a mode of innovation and with a sense of plurality. This collective self-sufficiency has influenced the work on methods in persona studies (Marshall, Moore and Barbour 2015) with the attention to the sense of agency in the practices of persona formation. We take on de Certeau's notion of the individual tactics and collective strategic negotiations as a way through the world, despite, or perhaps because of, rapid technological, social, and political change. The use of available resources and their dynamic application in the purposes of assembling an identity online is concomitantly individual and social. To understand the growing importance, impact on, and meaning of public identity in our lives, persona studies investigates the practice and ecology in which it is negotiated.

Much of the attention of cultural studies has concerned the collective configuration of meaning, and this is particularly evident in the examination of subcultures, fandoms, and the recent "participatory" turn to understanding the acquisition, translation, and iteration of cultural, digital, and social skills and competencies needed for full engagement in the twenty-first century (Jenkins et al. 2009). Persona studies expands on the cultural studies inquiry to examine the movement of the individual into social spaces and the requirements on the public presentation of the self that this movement involves. The critical examination then becomes an investigation of how the individual gains and articulates agency within these spaces. Persona studies seeks to better understand to what degree and under what conditions must the individual negotiate, remix, strategize, and articulate identity formations in order to provide an account of the performances that both resist and stabilize the sociotechnical systems, platforms, and services that have contributed to the contemporary emphasis on public presentation. The reconfigured privileging of the individual in online culture as a participant (Jenkins 2006a) and gatewatching beyond the old media gatekeeping (Bruns 2005) makes this focus on agency central to understanding the complexity of the structures of power in the newly constituted era of networked personalization.

The work of producing an online persona involves the labor of identity management and the curation of a living archive of mediated information and ultimately "digital" objects. The conflation of the digital and the physical involves a series of moments and choices that we must reflect on, argues Stuart Hall (2001), and thus we need to look past the apparent randomness of personal collections to discern the crystallizing shapes and patterns of objects used for reflection and debate that require new tools for describing self-conscious and self-reflexive activity, whether it be the obfuscation of personal details in the Facebook profile or the contribution to a conversation via a Twitter hashtag. The living archive of an online persona is not "an inert museum of dead works" but an "on-going, never completed project" (Hall 2001, p. 89).

An online persona is an event in its continuous illumination of identity, and whose gaps involve information as much as the more recognizable patterns of dates, actions, locations, preferences, and other personal data that emerges from any analysis of the online self. The living archive of online persona helps us to identify what our online cultures, communities, and interactions achieve and represent. For Hall, who uses Foucault's distinctive concept of the "archive" as an organic and mutable artifact rather than a unified or unifiable collection, the living archive assists in answering questions about these kinds of operations, processes and relations. The living archive of persona maintains discursive formations via a heterogeneity of content, from topics and texts, to subjects, tastes, and themes, which resist superficial attempts of grouping and classification that render them "the same" (Hall 2001, p. 90). Each point on the network, each user profile and service account, from Netflix and Skype, to WhatsApp and Tinder create nodal points in the larger picture of activity that informs the network of our behaviors and collectively, and most often algorithmically, determines how we appear to others. Foucault drew attention to the apparently continuous forms and fields that are indicated by gaps, differences, interplay, distances, transformations, and unpredictable departures, and the "trick," suggests Hall, is not to allow the "oeuvre of a mythical collective subject" to dominate the description, but rather convey a sense of regularity and difference in accounting for its dispersion. It is a mistake to think then that we might tie down an account of persona, or a persona, that is immune to change.

From Personae to Persona

One of the changes that was often noted during the early subdisciplinary formation of persona studies was the shift in language, specifically the choice of the plural "personas," over the more familiar and perhaps believed-to-be proper term "personae." The latter is typically reserved by dictionaries, including the Oxford English Dictionary (2009), as the collective term for the members of a dramatic work. The term "dramatic personae" is historically used to denote the multiple characters of novel or serialized text, while "personas" is most often used to refer to the multiple aspects of an individual's character that are presented and understood by others at certain times and places and in certain roles. A politician, a mother, a celebrity, a sports fan, and an individual with a disability active in a Facebook community, are all personas. By contrast, the term "dramatis personae" is a Latin phrase referring to the characters of a dramatic work and given to the table of names introducing a performance. It is a simple but specially formatted text linking the performers and their roles, instruments, or characters. This simple spreadsheet conveys to an audience the idea that a performance is being conducted, one that is connected to the lives of the performers in various ways, but always at a distance from the content of the production. In other words, the *dramatis personae* is a paratext of the performance. Gerard Genette's (1997) term, which draws on the ambiguity of the prefix "para" in French, highlights the role of the paratext as that which enables the reader to better understand a text, performance, or practice as a threshold, a boundary to be traversed rather than a unique and wholly complete package. Similarly, the "cast lists" of cinematic and televisual works are paratexts serving an archival role as a means for an actor to record their contributions to a collaborative production. The term "dramatis personae" also works as reference to contemporary public performances that are not entirely staged but are clearly performed.

Persona is a more contemporary spelling of "personae" in the everyday lexicon, with the plural "personas." The meaning has shifted with this move but is still attached to the concept of a mask, a layer, or adornment used to obscure the underlying features of the performer, providing a new surface upon which to inscribe a public identity. Remaining in the term is a conceptual link to an identity that is somehow distinct from an "origin" or "real" source. This link is used to distinguish between the virtual, the digital, and the real, and it often leads to failure to see where they are indistinct and overlap. Persona continues to take on the dimension of the mask in the digital age, and as such is performed as a social role, one that is constructed through negotiation with a whole series of actors, networks, and institutions. Personas are frequently guided by informal rules in face-to-face interactions, but also through highly structured digital environments, like Skype, Tumblr, Reddit, or WordPress. The function of a persona is to convey the performance and, as such, it serves as a position from which to speak to an audience. A persona, however, cannot be located in a unique or a discrete object; a persona is formed by the relations of a series of performances and assembled objects, and is never a single act, object, profile, or account. Persona is accrued and curated. It is accumulated in carefully constructed assemblages as well as erratic, haphazard "living" collections. A persona is therefore an archive of processes, a description of network interfaces and interactions with other objects, systems, and personas, as will be explored further in later chapters. Personas are communicative acts of self-production, but the majority of freedoms in these processes only exist within the options provided by the builders and owners of the platform through which it is enacted.

Our intention is to deal with the different constitutions of agency that persona as a concept embodies and it is important that this agency be contextualized within the history of identity theory and within the economic and technological affordances of the various applications, platforms, and services employed for the expression of the public self. We will build on the approach that is mapped out in this chapter and identify, for example, how advertising, self-branding, and personal monetization of the public self are part of the developing exposure culture of presentational media embedded in the capitalized economic structure of online culture. The risks in creating public personas range from the mundane to the profound, but investment and trust in services and networks that are regularly monitored, break down, change their terms and conditions, monetize our data, and alter their interfaces, is undeniably part of the experience.

Personas are in the processes of interactions with other personas, systems, and objects, across all forms of media and communication. They are communicative acts of self-production, but freedoms in these processes only exist within the options provided by the designers, operators, and advertisers of the platform. A game world may appear free and open but is still limited to the constraints and affordances of the software and the hardware that the system operates on as much as the terms and service conditions of entry. All media are potentially social and any technologies that aid us in performing or fulfilling the social role of persona formation and management is a social media, but there have been more formal approaches to the terminology. The definition of social media by boyd and Ellison (2007) includes three key characteristics: (i) the ability to construct a public or semipublic profile within a bounded system, (ii) the capacity to articulate a list of connected users, and (iii) a system for traversing personal connections and others made within the system. The term "social media" is used in marketing to refer to Web-based and Internet-enabled technologies. As Christian Fuchs's work identifies, social media advanced as a term derived from "social networks" which has had a much longer history of use and meaning and contextualization in terms of the idea of the social (Fuchs 2017, pp. 36–51). Nonetheless, the majority of these relatively new, identifiable online social media all include in their processes functions that derive value from the user's construction and maintenance of persona, and their involvement in the act of communication. Social media users are not customers in a traditional sense, more often they are seen as the product for advertisers as their activity produces revenue streams via algorithmic analysis. There is a significant risk involved in the trust of these media forms, all usually owned by companies whose primary concern is an economic one, which understands privacy as a commodity and a currency that users trade for access.

Web-based platforms monetize the immaterial labor of our everyday interactions with imperceptible ease. Google takes our searches and sells our words,
and we pay this cost and sell ourselves at this price every time we use the
Google search, email, or document service. Facebook takes our preferences
and activities and packages us up as eyeballs and attention to advertisers looking to hone their targeted messaging to an unprecedented degree. We take
unknown risks with our identities providing our information in everyday interactions, risks that perhaps in some places would draw attention to the vulnerability of our lives, homes, and histories. We often assume online anonymity,
but find it impossible to avoid leaving digital traces and electronic trails wherever we go online. In the past such public traces were less ubiquitous and tied
to physical access to electoral rolls or the *White Pages* "phone book," which
functioned like a classical dramatis personae for a populous connected by geographical space and limited analog communications technologies (mail and
telephony). The phone book was a serious resource for the pre-Internet age.
Like the Web it extended the information available to us, and like the Web it
connected our public-facing identity and property to the wider world. The
degree of information is, of course, greater now, and the Web and its uses are
broader, but the literacies learned with the analog technology are often
reflected in the digital ones required for a public facing online self.

Online persona demands a range of digital media literacies in its production,
but there is a structural element to this kind of literacy – the distribution of
cognition across multiple technologies: followers and contact lists; cloud-based
spreadsheets; or even Wikipedia. These forms of social media extend our
knowledge and capacities in what Henry Jenkins (2006b) describes as "distributed cognition" that expands exponentially as users of networked media platforms and digital services increase in number. The shift to subscription-based
access to cloud storage, streaming media, and direct-from-provider models,
like the crowdfunding systems of Kickstarter and Patreon, has magnified this
trend. **Digital literacies** involve the distribution of cognition and interactions
that follow everchanging rules and demands, with technologies for recording,
searching, sorting, and representing information, making it easier for users to
identify, create, and produce digitally. Distributed cognition and the distribution of persona is formed in the use of hardware and software of technologies,
especially mobile ones: laptops, tablet devices, and mobile phones. Distribution
occurs as we increase our reliance on the machines and technologies that
expand the capacities of our brain and senses. The transformed distribution of
the social via distributed cognition as well as the use of media and communication tools enable us to build complex personas; but it is important to realize
that these kinds of distributions of the social can even be found in the most
basic of media when used to perform roles or duties: from the social simplicity
of the handwritten letter, to its articulation in SMS or even the private message
exchanges via the communication channels of an online role-playing game.

Unlike Facebook or Google services, which requires users to verify their "real" identities through various means, such as linking the user account to a particularly mobile phone number, Twitter is a social media Web-based platform with a user model that does not strictly require users to present themselves as offline selves, leading to novelty, humor, satirical, political, and other types of user accounts. Where Facebook and Google's terms of service agreements demand adherence to a singular account policy, Twitter is a less restrictive opt-in system, resulting in multiple satirical "parody" accounts and automated "bots." This openness forces powerful figures like the US president Donald Trump or actor Hugh Jackman to go through Twitter's verification service and prefix their profiles with "real," such as @realDonaldTrump and @RealHughJackman (see Hearn 2017). Twitter does not change its interface at the same pace as Facebook or Google, and its development has not outgrown its core practice that remains the simple enough "tweet"; at 280 characters, a tweet can be a powerful means for communication and conversation across a range of events and purposes. Arguably, tweets played a significant role in Trump's success as a presidential candidate in the 2016 election. Fan conventions and academic conferences come alive in reaction to a vibrant group of Twitter users equipped with a convenient hashtag that can be a source of discussion and debate, and, of course, heated exchange.

The Premodern to the Contemporary Self

The question of how we arrived at this point is examined in the following part of the chapter as we explore these claims about the contemporary self as they hearken back to premodern notions of the self that is much more about public comportment and visibility than the inner self. Identity theory is considered in this and later chapters. However, our emphasis is on the degree to which these approaches help to inform the analysis of producing a public self that includes being a citizen, a consumer, an audience member, and other categories of being public that are both qualitatively and quantitatively different to the understanding of interior selfhood. Central to this approach is to begin to understand how the techno-cultural shift described above has contributed to the production of new relationships and organizational practices of the self in terms of the public that often incorporate what would once have been deemed personal, private, and even intimate.

The etymology, or root, of the word persona, is the Etruscan and Latin word, derived from the Greek "prosopon." Persona meant the mask work by actors in classical Greek theater (see Figure 1.1). Sound was an important component of the masked performance, as the term suggests, persona is literally the sound (*sona*) passing through the wooden mask (*pers*) or the sound of the actor's voice through the wood of the mask. Persona is thus connected to the ideas of

Figure 1.1 A "prosopon" – Greek persona mask. *Source:* Photo: P. David Marshall.

the role, character, avatar, *personnage* (French), front (from Goffman), and facade. Persona indicates the projection of a character, or role, by an actor, through a mask out into an audience, an intentional projection outward to a public via the device of the mask. Persona identifies the work of the actor through their voice, but also an entirely embodied performance that includes sound, posture, movement, and other shaping effects of stance, projection, and circumstance. The value of persona as an analytical concept is to understand a self not as fixed, but as a constantly updated projection of identity presented and enacted for the benefit of communicating to, and maintaining relations with, others. Personas are a production/process of a visible performance, publicly accessible but still a masked presentation used to negotiate through the world.

Persona was also a term used in Ancient Rome to identify the mask of performance and it is clearly related to historically important ideas about acting and being in public. In addition, it is also a term used by Cicero as he tried to describe the four roles or personas that are essential to being human. Reiss's study of early European conceptions of the self found that in the ancient world there was no dominant concept of the private self, suggesting the inner psychological dimensions that we associate with the modern self provides little insight into how individuals thought of themselves in Ancient Rome or Greece (Reiss 2003). The "prosopon" or mask was primarily purposed toward symbolism and effective communication of character. Notably in use by 700 BCE, and perhaps most well known in the celebration of the festival of Dionysia, the trajectory of the mask's movement from fertility ritual to the theatrical comedies and tragedies is unclear and its exact use varied. Typically covering the head and face in helmet fashion, with eyes and mouth holes, the mask was often made from organic materials not meant for permanent or long-term use and were produced by the "skeuopoios" and the "maker of properties" (Brooke 1962). Brooke suggested that the role of a particular mask was not restricted to any single task or duty but represented multiple roles and purposes. The obfuscation and alteration of the visual features of the performer was a means to produce a new persona connected outwardly and physically to the body underneath; this is very much like a pre-cybernetic version of the connection between our physical bodies and the mediated ones that we present via social media. The mask served to distinguish and make an individual recognizable as a persona connected to a publicly performed role, much as the dramatis personae of an eighteenth century playbill. The mask also served to distinguish between characters for an audience, to help note the differences among and within a group of performers: the chorus, for example, has similar masks and is considered to be a singular figure. The contemporary notion of a costume is an embellishment of the prosopon, developing from the use of jewelry, adornments, and other pageantry to help separate different roles in a play or performance.

Applying Persona

Derived from performance and acting, Hannah Arendt's reading of the prosopon considered the construction of a public – and potentially political – persona as naturally removed from the private and domestic performances of home life and domesticity. The stage performance and the political persona are both deemed to have originated from a source that was separate to the domain of an everyday public life, and became part of it through the staged orchestration of an alternative identity, one in the service of a different script to the rhythms of the mundane. The classical division in ancient Greek culture between the public and private was anticipated and articulated, argues Arendt, through strategic public identity practices, which identified clearly separate but touching spheres of home – "oikos" or interior – and public – the "polis" or exterior – life. The popular portrayal of character or political identity by an individual was not considered to carry into the personal and private, as the constitution of the public identity occurred in the *polis*, the political realm, while private affairs occur under the umbrella of the *oikos* (Arendt 1958, p. 185). Arendt recognized the continuity in the historical need to construct clear and separate public and private identities, which continues today as an impulse but less clearly as a practice. The separation of the private and the public that was essential for the development of the political persona of a citizen has become a blending, merging, or overlapping of these spheres of identity in the contemporary era.

Persona in Psychology

Recent usage of the term persona gradually emerged in psychology and increases in frequency from the 1940s onwards, as seen in Figure 1.2. One particularly influential figure is Carl Jung, an important psychoanalyst and theorist whose work rivals Sigmund Freud for its impact on the way the public has come to understand psychology as a field that attempts to reveal the internal mechanisms of selfhood and subjective formation. For Jung, persona is "acting a role through which the collective psyche speaks" (Jung 1966, p. 157) and "adaptation to the social environment" (pp. 469–470) which is articulated through the desires, strategies, methods, and efforts to impress and conceal. Jung argued that an unregulated persona can lead to many problems for an individual, as if the self becomes unbalanced with the inner self of archetypes, or becomes too outer-world directed, a potential psychosis may arise. The key point here in terms of the history of the term persona and its relationship to the field of psychology, is that the persona is not simply the subject, the self or an identity, but instead is the interface, the connection, the medium between the individual and the social. Persona is the collective notion of identity by the individual.

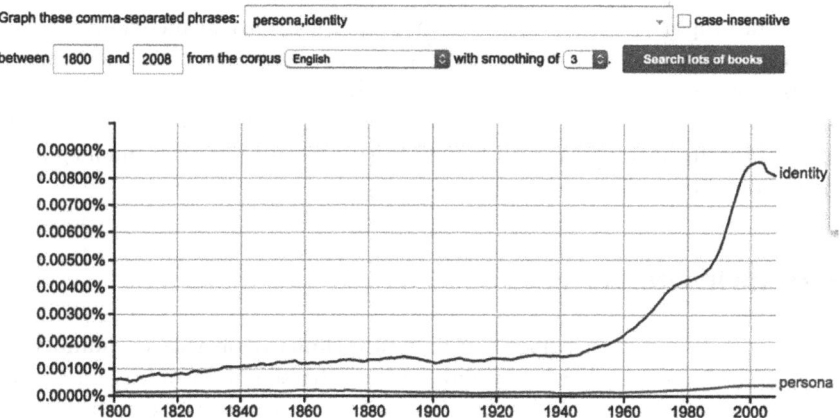

Figure 1.2 The Google ngram illustrates the comparative use of the term identity with the term persona in the Google books archive (https://trends.google.com.au/trends/explore?q=persona,Identity).

Psychology is a key site for the evolution of the term persona because, as noted by Marshall and Barbour (2015), Jung and Freud offer two different configurations of thinking about the relationship of the self to the social. Freud's account of the unconscious is underpinned by the expanded notion of self-consciousness, following the modernist obsession with the self in the twentieth-century literature of Joyce, Faulkner, and others. Jung's alternative path provided a different framework of archetypes and anima, and he used the word persona sparingly, but significantly in his work. Jung's concept of persona is "the arbitrary segment of the collective psyche" that the individual inhabits as "a mask that feigns individuality, making others and oneself believe that one is individual" (Jung 1966, p. 157) rather than a person playing a particular collectively defined role. Thus Freud and Jung maintained entirely different ways of understanding the unconscious; while Freud's approach was individualized Jung appealed to a universalized humanized unconsciousness which dismantles the presentation of the "outer personality" or persona, but not the "inner-personality" or anima (Jung 1991, pp. 466–467). Persona in Jung's model is influenced by "adaptation to the [social] environment" (Jung 1991, pp. 469–470) and a concerted effort to make oneself understood and recognized, which Jung explains as the persona's function "to impress and conceal" (cited in Fawkes 2010, p. 4). Jung's brief account of persona captures central components explaining why persona is an important and significant means for analyzing and describing the contemporary condition. The mask of the individual in Jung's model is the persona derived from the social environment. This version of persona is performed as a means of interaction between the individual and society, standing in for the individual in a socially acceptable format. Marshall and Barbour (2015) take from Jung an understanding of persona as representing a potential threat, a potential to reveal an unbalanced self that needs to be overcome. Important in this recognition is that the externally mediated identity can be mistaken for the whole of a being. Jung's approach enables us to understand persona as a strategic public identity, one that is not always in tension with the "inner" or "real" self (Jung 1966, p. 303), and a means to imagine and account for the past, present, and emerging dimensions of a life and its public formation of the self.

Persona in Literature

The history of the term persona in literature similarly provokes a number of competing accounts and ideas about the author, characters, narrators, and works as a whole. One key example is *The Cantos* by Ezra Pound (1996), which is an incomplete poem composed between 1915 and 1962 that includes themes of culture, history, government, and economics, and features cross-cultural characters, moral tales, and a speculative, if fragmentary, reflection of human existence. The poem begins with Odysseus's voyage into Hades, but later the poem presents a series of different identities from poets to warriors and explorers. Right from the outset, argues Richard Whitaker (1990), and right through to the conclusion, though intermittently, Pound assumes the persona of Odysseus:

> No doubt it was precisely the hero's versatility and many-sidedness that recommended him to Pound. For, as the compositions of the Cantos progressed and as his circumstances and the concept of his poem radically altered, so Pound was able to dwell on new and different aspects of his persona's varied experience. (Whitaker 1990, p. 37)

The loose and seemingly structureless style of the Cantos builds a presence, a layering of themes, scenes, and events which produced a persona to the work itself. The poem, although disjointed, constructs an edifice and an appeal for the value of art and literature over war, economics, and politics. Pound's own persona evolved over his career and lifetime and he himself became a literary persona: a luminary and enigmatic figure recognized for his ambitions as a poet and editor. Pound demonstrated an ability to strategically leverage his public persona in order to assist in publishing the works of T.S. Eliot, another major literary persona of the twentieth century.

The new literary traditions (see Marshall and Barbour 2015) appearing at the outset of the twentieth century, saw persona emerge as a term that poets, including Ezra Pound, labeled part of a movement called Imagism. The Imagists deployed persona as a description of the subsumption of identity into an objective, observable reality transformed by the new subject–object relationship they were describing. Everyday settings, items, tools, or people were expressed in a poetic language that produced a persona or character that was beyond the authorial identity. Pound stands in contrast to the affective romantic expression of the self with his use of a persona to separate the poet's identity from the poet's work. T.S. Eliot, James Joyce, Faulkner, and others helped Pound to define a relationship to the self in modern literature divergent from the understanding of self as consciousness. Baddick summarizes this use of persona in literary criticism as "the assumed identity or fictional 'I' … assumed by a writer in a literary work; thus the speaker in a literary poem, or the narrator in a fictional narrative" (cited in Fowler and Burchfield 2004, p. 588).

Persona in Performing Arts

Another term in the arts that involves the strategic construction of a persona is "method acting," which covers a broad range of performance training techniques orchestrated to allow for the performance of sincerity to register emotionally with an audience. There have been a number of important contributors to method acting, which has influenced the preparation of actors "getting into character" and greatly influenced Hollywood through the delivery of affective and deeply expressive performances. The method acting system was developed by Konstantin Stanislavski, Lee Strasberg, Sand Meisner, Stella Adler, and others and is part of the contemporary mode of screen acting (Vineberg 1991). Ingmar Bergman, the Swedish film writer and director, took the notion of screen affect into new psychological realms with his black and white film, *Persona*, in 1966, which was heavily censored by cuts to reduce its impact. *Persona* stars Bibi Andersson as Alma. Liv Ullmann plays a stage actress, Elizabeth, who has lost the ability to speak. The title of course implies the constitution of a fabricated identity but refers to the masks worn by actors on stage. The *mise en scène*, acting, editing, and general film language of *Persona* makes it narratively confusing, as the onscreen performances have a layering in its pictorial minimalism that adds up to an unmistakable identity of the film itself as bleak; there is an emphasis on emotions and condition of "the unwell," focusing on mental instability and mortality.

Method acting strategies continue to be popular among Hollywood stars and celebrities to mixed success. For every Cate Blanchett, whose performances are described as "actor's acting" "because it plays with the veils of identity and is a study on how those fabrications can become more real" (Marshall 2014) there is a dozen less-than-successful actors whose character performances fail to connect with audiences. Method acting has become part of the malady of Hollywood, suggests Richard Brody, describing the modern devotees of Strasberg's method as an inclination "toward deformations of character" (Brody 2014). Reports of Jared Leto's preparation for the role of the Batman comic book villain, the Joker, for the 2016 film *Suicide Squad*, include consumption of streaming media of brutal crimes and refusing to break character between takes. This is only one example among many such "heroic" lengths actors pursue which are used as part of the marketing strategies used to promote the movie. Ledger, De Niro, Hoffman, Bale, and DiCaprio have all publicly aligned themselves with "the Method," but Anjelica Jade Bastién (2016) criticized the performance martyrdom of the trend in *The Atlantic* suggesting that:

> The underpinning of this strategy is the belief that to create great art one must suffer. But method acting has also become wrapped up in a brand of identity politics that tries to make the art form resemble more traditional forms of male labour, and by extension limiting the kinds of actors who receive praise.

Persona as Performance

The persona of performance, embodied by method acting, was extended as a ubiquitous experience in the dramaturgical analogy presented by notable twentieth-century sociologist Erving Goffman in *The Presentation of Self in*

Everyday Life (1959). Goffman has regained attention as his dramaturgical analysis has proven to be highly fruitful in making sense of the increasingly everyday experience of social interaction online and the performed elements of persona. Goffman's account of the "front" and "back" stage elements of human behavior can be understood in terms of identity that is foregrounded or backgrounded by the individual. Goffman's contributions to the field of Symbolic Interactionism help to reveal the performed elements of identity and the connection between the self and a frontstage public or audience. His insights into the degree to which the self is partially a construction of its interaction with others take on new dimensions of importance when we start to consider the massive techno-social infrastructure of the hardware and software of the Internet age and its role on the individual's sense of self and their performed identities online.

According to Goffman, when an individual enters a social situation the conception of that person's self – their identity – is continually reassembled and performed as a composition of information about the individual, informed by the parameters defining the situation and any prior or advanced knowledge of the individuals, locations, and the relations between them. Individual expression in these instances is a sign system that conveys streams of information, which along with our judgments and assumptions about the given social setting, such as who is likely to be present and their relation to us, enable a degree of anticipated and understandable behavior. Walking into a high school classroom, for example, students can immediately understand their social identity roles as they are scripted by experience, and can judge the entry of other persons based on their relationship to them individually as well as how these roles are socially defined by the physical location itself. In Goffman's model, we understand that facts about individuals always exist beyond the time and space of any interaction. Other facts are deliberately concealed by individuals within the interaction with others, such as health conditions, beliefs, attitudes, or emotions: some of these conditions can be ascertained indirectly by others and circumvent the individual's efforts at concealment. As Goffman suggests, social signs, even overt or direct ones, do not always correlate with the senses. This noncorrelation with cognate senses can be magnified in the online environments of Facebook chats, SMS exchanges, virtual worlds, email, and Web forums.

Goffman (1959) divided such expression into two categories: *"given"* and *"given off"* (or projected). Given expression includes the verbal symbols of speech we interpret as conventional communication, which can be performed for reasons other than the apparent, including misinformation and direct deception. *Given off* expressions are involuntary, and since, as Goffman suggests, we live by inference and not by statistics or science, both types of expression will have a promissory character whose true value is known after their absence. The conduct of others toward the performed self, notwithstanding individual objectives, is central to Goffman's inquiry. The desired responses of others are influenced by the expressions of individuals and the definition of the situation which others formulate enables the individual to influence others to act voluntarily and in accordance with their own plan without conveying impressions of invested interest. Goffman uses the example of the telephone call to demonstrate the socialization of public telephone use which can assist the receiver to impress their popularity on others involved in the situation (in his example roommates who are overhearing the phone call). An online equivalent might be Instagram, where a shared image is hashtagged with multiple and not-always-relevant hashtags in order to attract more views and likes and thereby give an impression to a social circle of being more popular and successful.

Persona Through Personalization

While software studies and political economy theory identify the potentially harmful influence of the algorithm at work in software platforms and social media, there is still an important degree of agency in the individualization and personalization that is afforded to users typically in the post-Web 2.0 digital environment. Devices that are worn, or are quite personal, such as the Apple Watch or the iPhone, are the same as everyone else's; yet each one, once observed, can demonstrate a massive range of personalization and are examples of the ways we all recreate ourselves in and with these media devices. This personalization also points to how central the devices are for many in accessing the Internet and producing themselves online. The Apple iPhoto roll is an example of this everyday phenomenon, and an example of the way and degree to which we recreate and mediatize our lives in all sorts of ways. We also share these images so that more of our lives become visible to our audiences and networks. What is new in the current situation is the degree to which **presentational media** has been made a cultural regime thanks to the ubiquity with which we all produce personalized content and the means by which we share such personal content with others. Everyone everywhere is making versions of themselves, in public, in private, at play, at work, and at rest, through ubiquitously connected devices and the result is a persona which represents the strategic public identity, purposefully and directed.

As introduced above, Goffman uses theatrical metaphors to highlight the contextual nature of expressions. His insights map directly onto the concept of persona as an analytical tool to explore the contemporary production of the self in an era of presentational media. The presentation of performance, not just the act of performance, is an extraordinarily important part of public life and the identity of a public figure. It has long been the case for politicians that popularity and the perception of their public performance of self has been a factor in how policies are accepted or rejected. Celebrity performance is not limited to the text, but also includes the paratextual industries, creative industries, and the niche domains of fandom, through interviews, advertising, and commercial sponsorship. The private lives of celebrities too have become part of the panoptic gaze of their public consumption, reducing the boundaries of performance described by Goffman's sociological account. Goffman understood performance of the self as a conscious staging and managing of norms and expectations, defining a difference between the backstage and frontstage of self-characterization that has proven more historically liminal for celebrities. The ritual of self-performance in celebrity culture has revealed a more nuanced collaboration between the public and private; as Marshall (2010) notes, the actor Vin Diesel has used social media platforms Facebook, Instagram, and Twitter to carefully reveal aspects of his private self that he has used to connect to fans and promote his public and professional self, which is expressed through a range of interests from extreme sports to the role-playing game Dungeons and Dragons. The personal is interspersed with more traditional elements of publicity such as behind-the-scenes images, production meeting lunches, and studio-sanctioned interviews. The notion of authenticity is reorganized to be understood as a public construction of the private, presenting an accessible but equally constructed "performance of the actor's everyday life" (Marshall 2010) as a series of strategies that can be replicated as a marker of success by his fans.

Today, more than ever, writes Glenn D'Cruz (2015), we find ourselves performing our personal selves in public as much as our professional ones – parent, worker, lover, friend, hobbyist. He argues that these multiple and conflicting identities have become more difficult to make distinctions in and between. Even in the home, he argues, there is a great deal of compulsion to adopt persona in order to make emotional connections, quell animosity and provide pedagogical guidance for those closest to ourselves, reducing those sites of "back stage" performance where we are not under the critical gaze of an audience.

The modernist, argues Gergen (1991, p. 272) understands the self as one who "should" possess a unified identity, and modernist discourse considered the self fully knowable and coherent. The challenge of technological innovation and its popular adoption gave way to the postmodernist inversion of the unified notion of the self, where "there is little lament, anxiety, or dread at aimless fragmentation, which simply becomes a way of life without strongly negative connotations." The postmodern sense of identity is a crowded population of multiple selves. The modernist concept of a "core" identity gave way to the postmodern realization of identity as forms of social construction of roles, costumes, and settings, simultaneously encouraging the development of the identity industries, where the personal is assembled according to the material outcomes of professionalism: the resumé, reference, or curriculum vitae. These artifacts and practices all work to construct the individual and construct the reality of the actor. Klapp's (1964) contribution to the conception of a persona is derived from a social psychological perspective. Klapp identifies a type of influence that circulated between the performance and audience, as it circulated within and outside the entertainment industries, particularly Hollywood and television, but also radio and print. The imagined, constructed, and expressed desires of the target audience become symbolically significant in the representation of the professional performer.

Our inquiry into the dimensions of the public self and the formation of personality for popular consumption and derived from what might be called celebrity culture now sets the scene for the development of wide scale public individualism. For example, the subversive politics of hip-hop culture as its staged resistance through play and its adoption of the mask as a form of subversion, enables rap artists to confuse, divest, overplay, and undermine the music industry's unequal standards of authenticity and the requirements of advertising and marketing (Hess 2005). Hip-hop music, as Mark Fisher (2009) remind us, is entirely a spectacle of individualism that cannot escape capitalism. Its generic performance identity as producing the "real" or "uncompromising" self has enabled hip-hop's easy absorption into a "real" narrative of economic instability that permits the production and performance of "authenticity" in a highly marketable way.

Social media and social network sites are fundamentally organized symbolically and economically around the individual's presentation of the self and that presentation's relations to others in ways that have created a new hybridity of personal, private, interpersonal, and mediated information and messages that are distributed by what Marshall (2010) calls "presentational media." The celebrity discourse of the self foreshadows and provides pedagogical tools for the expanding domain of presentational media, which is not a shift away from representational media but rather its inculcation as an element in the DNA of new media culture.

Celebrity culture is an important tool for making sense of the new middle of self-expression that is part performance, part assemblage of objects, part mediation and part interpersonal communication. Stars, politicians, and public figures have been navigating this terrain intensely for the better part of a century and now find themselves often at the center of social media networks, Internet cultures, and mobile media consumption whose audience and participants reflect their activities. Despite ongoing criticism of the value of celebrity culture, its composition of famous individuals and their audiences continues to grow at the increasing cost of the personal. Prior to the Internet's domestication through home computers and its ubiquitous presence via smart phones and wireless devices, the transgression of famous figures' personal lives for public consumption was framed as tabloid consumption, at its best, and an illegal invasion of privacy constituting criminal harassment, at its worst (Roberts 1997). We have now moved into a wider and more pervasive expression of public identity and looking at it through the lens of persona helps us understand its expression of individuality in a collective and mediated environment.

References

Arendt, H. (1958). *The Human Condition*. Charles R. Walgreen Foundation Lectures. Chicago: University of Chicago Press.

Bastién, A.J. (2016). Hollywood has ruined method acting. *The Atlantic* (August 11). https://www.theatlantic.com/entertainment/archive/2016/08/hollywood-has-ruined-method-acting/494777 (accessed October 29, 2018).

Bergman, I. (1966). *Persona* [Film] Svensk Filmindustri.

boyd, d. and Ellison, N.B. (2007). Social network sites: Definition, history, and scholarship. *Journal of Computer-Mediated Communication* 13 (1): 210–230.

Brody, R. (2014). Is method acting destroying actors? *The New Yorker* (February 21). http://www.newyorker.com/culture/richard-brody/is-method-acting-destroying-actors (accessed October 29, 2018).

Brooke, I. (1962). *Costume in Greek Classical Drama*. London: Methuen.

Bruns, A. (2005). *Gatewatching: Collaborative Online News Production*. New York: Peter Lang.

D'Cruz, G. (2015). Section introduction: When are you most like your self? *Persona Studies* 1 (1): 1–2. https://ojs.deakin.edu.au/index.php/ps/article/view/461/477 (accessed October 29, 2018.

de Certeau, M. (1984 [1980]). *The Practice of Everyday Life* (trans. S. Rendell). Berkeley: University of California Press.

Dubrofsky, R.E. and Wood, M.M. (2014). Posting racism and sexism: Authenticity, agency and self-reflexivity in social media. *Communication and Critical/Cultural Studies* 11 (3): 282–287.

Fawkes, J. (2010). Cultural complexes in professional ethics. *Journal of Jungian Scholarly Studies* 6 (8): 1–13.

Fisher, M. (2009). *Capitalist Realism: Is There No Alternative?* Winchester: John Hunt Publishing.

Fiske, J. (2010 [1989]). *Understanding Popular Culture*, 2e Reprint. New York: Routledge.

Fowler, H.W. and Burchfield, R.W. (2004). *Fowler's Modern English Usage*, 3e. Oxford: Oxford University Press.

Fuchs, C. (2017). *Social Media: A Critical Introduction*. London: SAGE.

Genette, G. (1997). *Paratexts: Thresholds of Interpretation*. Cambridge: Cambridge University Press.

Gergen, K.J. (1991). *The Saturated Self: Dilemmas of Identity in Contemporary Life*. New York: Basic Books.

Goffman, E. (1959). *The Presentation of Self in Everyday Life*. New York: Anchor Books.

Green, E. and Singleton, C. (2013). "Gendering the digital": The impact of gender and technology perspectives on the sociological imagination. In: *Digital Sociology: Critical Perspectives* (ed. K. Orton-Johnson and N. Prior), 34–50. Houndmills: Palgrave Macmillan.

Hall, S. (2001). Constituting an archive. *Third Text* 15 (54): 89–92.

Hearn, A. (2017). Verified: Self-presentation, identity management, and selfhood in the age of big data. *Popular Communication* 15 (2): 62–77.

Hess, M. (2005). Metal faces, rap masks: Identity and resistance in hip hop's persona artist. *Popular Music and Society* 28 (3): 297–311.

Jenkins, H. (2006a). *Fans, Bloggers, and Gamers: Exploring Participatory Culture*. New York: New York University Press.

Jenkins, H. (2006b). *White Paper Confronting the Challenges of Participatory Culture: Media Education for the 21st Century*. Berkeley: MacArthur Foundation.

Jenkins, H., Purushotma, R., Weigel, M. et al. (2009). *Confronting the Challenges of Participatory Culture: Media Education for the 21st Century*. Cambridge, MA: MIT Press.

Jung, C.G. (1966). *Two Essays on Analytical Psychology*, 2e (trans. Gerhard Adler and R.F.C. Hull). Princeton: Princeton University Press.

Jung, C.G. (1991). *The Collected Works of C.G. Jung. Volume 6: Psychological Types*. London: Routledge.

Klapp, O.E. (1964). *Symbolic Leaders: Public Dramas and Public Men*. Chicago: Aldine.

Marshall, P.D. (2010). The promotion and presentation of the self: Celebrity as marker of presentational media. *Celebrity Studies* 1 (1): 35–48.

Marshall, P.D. (2014). Seriality and persona. *M/C Journal* 17 (3): http://journal.media-culture.org.au/index.php/mcjournal/article/view/802 (accessed October 29, 2018.

Marshall, P.D. and Barbour, K. (2015). Making intellectual room for persona studies: A new consciousness and a shifted perspective. *Persona Studies* 1 (1): 1–12. https://ojs.deakin.edu.au/index.php/ps/issue/view/82 (accessed October 29, 2018.

Marshall, P.D., Moore, C., and Barbour, K. (2015). Persona as method: Exploring celebrity and the public self through persona studies. *Celebrity Studies* 6 (3): 288–305.

Oxford English Dictionary. (2009). s.v. personae. Oxford: Oxford University Press.

Pound, E. (1996). *The Cantos of Ezra Pound*. New York: New Directions Publishing (Pound 1996).

Reiss, T.J. (2003). *Mirages of the Selfe: Patterns of Personhood in Ancient and Early Modern Europe.* Stanford: Stanford University Press.

Roberts, R. (1997). The princess and the press: A dance ending in death. *Washington Post* (September 4), p. D1.

Vineberg, S. (1991). *Method Actors: Three Generations of an American Acting Style.* New York: Macmillan Reference USA.

Whitaker, R. (1990). The figure of Odysseus in Ezra Pound's "Cantos". *English Studies in Africa* 33 (1): 37–48.

2

The Contemporary Significance of Persona

Introduction

In this chapter, we build on the historical framework introduced in Chapter 1 and connect to some of the theoretical frameworks that inform our understanding of persona studies. Beginning with the concept of **intercommunication**, we consider how the relationship between communication and mediatization works to focus our attention on persona. This incorporates discussion on specific **presentational media** and its role as panopticon or oligopticon. We consider the role of *celebrity as a pedagogical tool in relation to the media technologies of surveillance*. The chapter explores how celebrities demonstrate persona work for the wider public, teaching us how to create, use, and monetize our public presentations of self, redrawing what is understood as "privacy" or the "private life" in the process. Through this discussion, we utilize the theories of Erving Goffman, Alison Hearn, Michel Foucault, Bruno Latour, Sylvan Tomkins, and Lawrence Grossberg in locating our theorization of the contemporary moment of the persona as the locus of meaning in contemporary **mediatized** society.

Intercommunication: The Human–Machine Interface

The concept of intercommunication is a means to examine the blending of previously independent domains of communication through networked technologies and digital media practices. Where there was once a clear division between what was considered media and what was described as communication, a new hybridity has occurred. Distinct from convergence (Jenkins 2006), intercommunication focuses on the practices of use that converged media allows, rather than on media technologies or industries, social structures, or embedded cultural ideologies. This crossover between mediatization and

Persona Studies: An Introduction, First Edition. P. David Marshall, Christopher Moore, and Kim Barbour.

communication has been accelerated by the production of interpersonal cultural content diffused across networks of connections, and algorithmically influenced behaviors of views, likes, shares, and other exchanges. Intercommunication as a term points toward the increased remediation of interpersonal communication through social media platforms and cultural practices, exemplified by the popularity of selfies, **memes**, and other user-generated content that is distributed independently from the previously dominant legacy media forms of television, radio, cinema, and print. The new hybridized structures of communication and processes of media practice have transformed the conception of the public sphere, elevating the presentation of personal identity as a requirement for a participant in a range of organized publics. This transformation demands that the individual develop new strategies for the presentation of the public self and acquire new literacies to understand the tactical deployment of identity by others.

For hundreds of thousands of years, humans have been imagining and producing technologies that have fundamentally altered what it means to be human. The wheel, the printing press, the telegraph, the railroad, radio, X-rays, nuclear power, computers, and the Internet, among many others, have all provided new communicative futures for humanity, whether understood in utopian or dystopian terms. A range of different authors have described ways in which these relationships between technologies, people, and communication have opened up new vistas of opportunity and oppression. One very important voice is Pierre Teilhard de Chardin, a French philosopher and priest with training in paleontology and geology, who formed the concept of the Omega Point, a spiritual belief of spiraling fate: an inevitability of divine unification that is relatable to the idea of the technological singularity in which a hypothetically created artificial intelligence is capable of reprogramming itself eventually leading to self-consciousness and universal level intelligence. This imaginary scenario is often played out in cyberpunk fiction, especially William Gibson's *Neuromancer* (1984), and the manga series *The Ghost in the Shell* (first serialized in 1989), its 1995 anime, and 2016 live action remake. Teilhard de Chardin is also famous for expanding on the concept of the noosphere, a term variously attributed to Édouard Le Roy (1913) and the work of Vladimir Vernadsky (1945) that describes the third domain of the Earth, beyond the geosphere and the biosphere, created by humankind's power over the elements and the atom. Both the Omega Point and the noosphere represent the relationship between humanity and technology as the power of networks giving rise to an autonomous organism that is at a distance to humanity, a gap that is bridged only by communication (Steinhart 2008).

In 1949, Norbert Weiner's *New York Times* article imagined the future of computers, warning that automation would lead to a cruel future in which the factory worker would be too expensive to hire when a machine could do the same task. Weiner's dystopian imagination has haunted generations as automation has increased exponentially. With current innovations in robotics, this vision may yet come to pass (Ford 2015, p. 88). Another idea which has accounted for the changing conditions brought on by human and machine synthesis is "collective intelligence," popularized by Pierre Lévy (1997) who understood distributed networks as enabling new forms of collaboration between individuals communicating via contribution of knowledge from discrete nodes. Collective intelligence accounts for the way consensus is achieved, and new knowledge is constructed by groups acting in synergy via the new networks of open information communication technologies. Open Source software, social media, and fandoms are examples of both cultural products and systems of organization made possible by the methods of distribution, replication, and redundancy of information structures like the Internet. Langdon Winner's term "autonomous technology" highlights the fears and paranoia over the types of dystopia that may result in our increasing reliance on information and media technologies, which are automatic, described by "technics out of control" (Winner 1997). Alvin Toffler's *Future Shock* (1971) captured the zeitgeist of concerns about the types of societies and cultures that would result from the rapid technological change. Dystopian imaginaries are a dominant part of the cyberpunk and science fiction worlds of writers like William Gibson, Bruce Sterling, Neal Stephenson, and Cory Doctorow, who are the techno-prophets of the digital age, exploring the fears and hopes of new generations growing up in a networked and hyper-mediated age.

The Internet has been the defining locus for speculation regarding the future of human and machine relations since it began to colonize the domestic sphere in the early 1990s, introducing networked communication via the World Wide Web into the home. Emerging out of the military-industrial complex and universities more than forty years ago in the late twentieth century (Winston 1998), the Internet brings together information networks, social organization, and cultural production in ways that have revived attention to the ideas and predictions of Marshall McLuhan (1994). McLuhan's conceptualization of "the **global village**" worked to describe the contraction of the geographical barriers to communication enabled by the age of satellites and cable television, which McLuhan saw as having a significant impact on social spheres, macroeconomics, and political change. The phrase has an optimistic sound, but also holds a core of concern about what happens to culture when it is globalized and when human consciousness extends on a planetary scale. McLuhan was quite disturbed by changes to communication that would allow everybody to see and comment on everyone else's private domain. Dystopian critiques of the Internet are not at all uncommon, most often expressed as moral panics over new technologies which deteriorate the gatekeeping functions of institutions like banking, education, health and medicine, journalism, and politics.

Many observers (see Bucher 2012; Elmer 2013; Waycott et al. 2017) have drawn dystopian comparisons to Facebook and the **panopticon**, a model of the "ideal" prison proposed by English social theorist and philosopher Jeremy Bentham (1791). A panopticon is a type of prison that allows the guard to observe the inmate at all times, without their knowledge or being able to determine if, in fact, anyone is watching. Bentham thought of the panopticon as a metaphor for effective, utilitarian institutions and equally applicable to hospitals, schools, and lecture halls, as the subject is forced to modify their physical behavior in responding to the prison's ability to control the mind through the fear of continuous **surveillance**. Michel Foucault drew on this metaphor in the book *Discipline and Punish: The Birth of the Prison* (1975) in an interrogation of the social and theoretical mechanisms driving the development of prisons in the West in the modern age. Foucault developed a critical account of the concepts of surveillance, discipline, biopower, governmentality, and discourse, arguing that the panopticon served as both historical mechanism and philosophical metaphor. Foucault's approach is useful for thinking about Facebook as a modern disciplinary system, enforcing conformist behavior and punishing deviant ways as aberrant, determined by its corporate controls and executed algorithmically: such as Facebook's notorious ban on breastfeeding images (Sweney 2008). Facebook, however, fails as a digital panopticon. It may be successful in its imposition and normalization of a highly pervasive force in our society, but its content-sifting algorithms are not the only guards in the system. Facebook's guards are also its users, who are surveilling each other in a constant circulation of personally mediated images, thoughts, shares, likes, and tags. Facebook is what Bruno Latour calls an oligopticon (2005, p. 181), which functions in an opposite mode to the panopticon. Rather than being the all-seeing-eye like a digital version of Sauron in *The Lord of The Rings*, Facebook is more like a super-bright torch or streetlight, throwing a cone of surveillance over a very personal domain of life through the networked communication activity of social media. The oligopticon functions like the light in the dark of Plato's cave in its revealing of much about what is merely the surface reflection of the reality of everyday life. Facebook is a power surveillance technology in that it sees everything, but only if "everything" constitutes what exists within a slight, narrowly defined and constructed area of life and living.

Celebrity and Surveillance

The techniques of surveillance involve the active monitoring of a subject and the desire to effect control at a distance; while digital media and communication technologies have dramatically extended the former, the Snowden, Wikileaks, and Cambridge Analytica revelations, among others, have documented the extent of the state and corporate apparatus of the latter. These include XKeyscore, PRISM (US), UPSTREAM (UK), the collaboration of the Five Eyes network (Canada, UK, Australia, New Zealand, and the US) and the knowledge that the National Security Agency (NSA) is capable of intruding most of the world's communication systems (see Greenwald 2014; Gurnow 2014; Harding 2014). Technologies with the capacities for surveillance, that is to say all modern consumer hardware and software, have become enmeshed in the competing concerns over issues of privacy and property and are dematerialized by the regulatory responses to both. In the following section, we take a closer look at the celebrity as a key figure in the pedagogy of presentational media strategies replicated by millions of social media users every day, empowered by technologies of surveillance.

The experiences of celebrities adapting to the new publics of social media have involved a renegotiation of the channels of production and participation. The industrial methods of mediatized celebrification (Schudson 1992) remain intact, but the broadcast industries have been repositioned in the chain of celebrity content production, aggregation, and curation. Celebrity culture has helped ensure the rise of Facebook, Twitter, YouTube, and other social media platforms by repositioning the audience as public contributors to formerly private insider networks. Twitter's early successes can in part be attributed to users such as actor Ashton Kutcher (@aplusk), who was the first to reach the then-impressive one million follower mark. The platform entered a new era with constant attention as a result of providing unfiltered access to the president of the United States, Donald Trump. In a similar vein, the Indian prime minister, Narendra Modi, invoking what has been described as the fifth estate has used social media to circumvent mainstream media and control the news media agenda in his efforts to speak directly to key constituents and citizens. Equally, the role of pop stars Selena Gomez and Ariana Grande, along with reality TV star Kim Kardashian, in the rise of Instagram is clear, as is the role of Kardashian's younger sisters Kendall and Kylie Jenner in SnapChat. No longer do studios, agencies, paparazzi, editors, PR agents, and handlers have a clear hierarchy in the self-production queue of celebrities, politicians, and other public figures. The individual choices of self-mediation are now among the primary forces in the presentational media strategies of online persona performance.

One of the key pedagogical contributions of celebrity in the twentieth century was to instruct consecutive generations in how to incorporate consumer culture in the assembly of one's public self (Marshall 2014b). This continues in the twenty-first century, particularly with the rise of **microcelebrities** (Marwick 2015; Senft 2013) and the success of the creative, niche, and **paratextual** industries (Consalvo 2007; Genette 1997; Grey 2010), from which has emerged a new generation of media performers from YouTubers and Instagrammers, to cosplayers and eSports stars. These participatory content producers have continued to reimagine the combined practices of consumption and production in their capacity to embody individual experimentation with the "transformative power of consumer culture" (Marshall 2010, p. 37).

Celebrification, advertising, **branding**, and publicity all provide a continuity of discourse around the representation of the self for public consumption. The more affective dimensions of these modes of communication are absorbed within the presentational media processes of individuals whose patterns of sharing on and between social networks has redefined audiences and the economies of reputation:

> self-production is the very core of celebrity activity and it now serves as a rubric and template for the organisation and production of the online self which has become at the very least an important component of presentation of yourself to the world. (Marshall 2010, p. 39)

The saturation and convergence of digital cameras, mobile phones, and high bandwidth Internet services has been embraced by a globalized celebrity culture, whose practices are endlessly replicated and remixed by their fans and followers. This is typified by the genres of self-mediated participation, including the meme, the selfie, the hashtag, and other types of publicly directed but personally generated content categories of media production.

Celebrity culture has intensified its long contribution to issues of privacy, property, and surveillance, but despite massive intrusions into phone call records, social media profiles, text messages, and image repositories, celebrities have been reluctant to criticize the curtailment of intellectual property and privacy rights involved in the expanding attention economy. Rogers (2014) revises Hardt's (1999) critique of the attention economy as the exploitation of immaterial and affective labor under "cognitive" capitalism, framing the individual as involved in a negotiation with techniques of attention management at the intersection of pragmatic "crowd control, human capital, and neurocognitive resource management that have together opened a transactional reality" (Rogers 2014, p. 200). This transactional reality includes the unauthorized distribution of an extensive number of stolen celebrity nude images in 2014, which characterized the cost to privacy as "stolen property" and was identified by the Twitter hashtag "#thefappening" (Marwick 2017; Massanari 2017). The number and degree of privacy and copyright infringing channels of distribution was unlike any previously manufactured "celebrity nude scandals" or Kim Kardashian-style career-making sex-tapes. The massive intrusion into the private domains of female celebrities took advantage of the voluntary creation of content intended for a very intimate audience – in some cases the images were only for the creator of the images herself. The subsequent distribution of the images was made possible by the fact that digital content cannot be entirely controlled by its creators or the operators of the platforms and services across which they are stored and circulated. The spreading of private female celebrity photos also reveals the deep divide of Internet culture which has absorbed both the extensive sexualizing gaze of the traditional broadcast media industries and the objectification of women through both narrative fiction and paparazzi-style invasion and remediated these to an unprecedented degree in the networked era.

The invasive potential of the leaked personal photos in the lives of celebrities also reminds social media users of their own precarious practices. This was brought home through the 2015 security failure of the online "extra-marital affair" site AshleyMadison, which resulted in the hacker group, The Impact Team, releasing hundreds of gigabytes of data containing the personal details and credit card information of 37 million users of the website (Temperton 2015). Both cases illustrate the unrelenting nature of personal data, which can be described as digital objects involved in intimate relations. The ubiquitous nature of personal digital objects also directs our attention to the degree to which the surveilling functions of new media technologies are used by others to constitute our identities, including the capacity to make connections on our behalf, without our permission, and without our knowledge. The repeat intrusions into the systems of Sony, Google, Microsoft, and the US Department of Justice (Kessler 2013) works to reveal the precarity of digital objects that are curated in the presentation of the online persona. These objects range from credit card details to phone records, instant messages, likes, shares, browser cookies, to other metadata including geophysical location information. Further, they reveal our online personas simply as nodes in an elongated series of obfuscated relations; each is a link in the chain of what Bruno Latour calls "black box" interactions which serves as a personal archive of the digital past. This archive is as unforgiving as it is unlikely to forget, resulting in the role of digital objects in the fundamentally unpredictable firmament of the "digital ecology of memory" (Schwarz 2014, p. 7). We return to examine the role of digital objects further in Chapter 4.

Making sense and extracting value from the aggregation of nodal points of individual information through algorithmic analysis has become a multi-billion-dollar industry. Both Facebook's and Google's operational procedures and business models are dependent on the extraction of intellectual property from user's data, made possible by the surveillance of the user's activities. Details of the massive breach of Facebook user information, by companies like Cambridge Analytica, resulted in the summoning of Facebook CEO, Mark Zuckerberg, to testify in front of the US Senate in 2018. The scale of social media surveillance is matched only by the massive global consortium of intelligence agencies and government-sponsored programs of spying that similarly makes use of these services. The wider public's response has been a mixture of grudging acceptance and casual concern, and despite Snowden's whistleblowing account of secret global surveillance programs, there are no signs of the reversal of government or corporate surveillance, or of users shying away from social media or mobile communication devices. Despite the #DeleteFacebook hashtag which trended following the Cambridge

Analytica scandal, the public share value of Facebook increased 4.5% following Zuckerberg's Senate appearance, the largest gain in 2 years, earning the company an increase of 21.3 billion in market value (Shen 2018). It is not that we have become complacent, but rather we have begun to share in the collaborative experimentation with the surveillance techniques of digital objects and their role in our personal communication networks. This play is not without risk and potential harm but is nonetheless a necessary collective evaluation of relevant digital media literacies, as well as a public interrogation of surveillance techniques that includes an active participation, creative mediation, and a significant investment in the acts of persona management.

The rise of the surveillance state has its prior cultural expression in the reality television franchise *Big Brother*, which popularized the close proximity of normally restricted televisual coverage as entertainment. As a genre defining "reality" series, *Big Brother* closed the gap between the technologies and audiences of mobile telephony, broadcast media, and pervasive domestic monitoring. The success of *Big Brother* was in part the inversion of the once mass public concern over the state surveillance system, which was perfected during the Cold War, argues Clissold (2004), by incorporating the average citizen as nodes in the intelligence network. The development of electronic and digital technologies made surveillance more discreet, as well as more effective at enfolding public institutions and corporate entities. Television domesticated surveillance anxiety and the panoptic gaze (Holmes 2004) with the program *Candid Camera*, launched in 1948 and continuing to the 1970s, which functioned as an outlet for the fear and anxiety over the surveillance society emerging from the Cold War (Clissold 2004, p. 38). The humor in the surveillance revealed at the close of the *Candid Camera* skit is used to pacify concerns over personal and intimate behaviors being under watchful view and being shared with mass media audiences (Clissold 2004, pp. 30–42).

The panoptic gaze continues to be reformatted in the new media technologies at our disposal and users have redefined traditional broadcast industries with experiments in streaming media apps, like Meerkat, Live.ly, and Periscope, turning every Internet-enabled smartphone into a user-operated, location enabled video recording and content broadcasting surveillance device. This type of technology is now included in social media sites such as Facebook and Instagram, meaning users do not even have to download and learn a new app to participate. Surveillance has become a common form of entertainment as millions of viewers follow the daily personal and often intimate lives of video bloggers (vloggers) and tune into the live streaming shows of gamers and artists via Twitch.TV. Comedy has also changed under the dome of networked surveillance, as illustrated by the work of pranksters like Australian Jamie Zhu in 2015, who convinced some in the international media of the authenticity of one of his "Awkward Uni Situations" YouTube video series. Zhu, in his student persona, is filmed "accidentally" broadcasting the sound of pornography from his laptop in a university lecture hall by another student's mobile phone camera. In appropriating the representation of the individual caught in the panoptic gaze of *Candid Camera* and *Big Brother*, the technical features of surveillance are put to the work of an individualized form of participatory and presentational media entertainment. The techniques of surveillance are appropriated to produce and frame the entertainment of the experience, taking less pleasure in the revelation of being watched and putting more stock in the affect of embarrassment as an expression of public life.

The differences between *Big Brother*, *Candid Camera*, and the streaming media of mobile apps, such as Periscope and Meerkat, webcam sites, and vlogging micro-celebrities arise from the strategies of media production involved in the remediation (Bolter and Grusin 1999) of the representational screen language of the broadcast industries. Branding, editing, staging, framing, lighting, narrative, pacing, nondiegetic cues, including music and text, and so on are all fixtures of representational media that have been remixed within the presentational processes of persona assembly. Similarly, the structures of the web and the surveillance features of digital objects formed in the practices of online activity are incorporated in the distribution of this presentational content via multiple channels of intercommunication (Marshall 2015a) between social media sites, between new media and legacy media industries, and by the flows and connections of the networks that are obscured by the demands of commerce and security. Social media is made immensely useful and powerful by the techniques of surveillance, which have been incorporated within the user's presentation of the public self, particularly those in the niche, creative, and paratextual industries of blogging, podcasting, and video streaming. While it is necessary to draw attention to the potential for surveillance to enact harm via extensions of the command and control operations of the cybernetic interactions of the web – directing, controlling and channeling user behaviors – the dystopian narrative is not one that has gained significant attention from users who are in the processes of negotiating a set of parameters and practices for dealing with digital objects in ways that successfully manage their appearance to others. This was also the observations of danah boyd (2014) in her study of young people's social media behaviors, where content creation is performed with explicit provisions for those who are known to be watching and those unknown but suspected, usually authority figures, teachers, parents, police, but also potential peers and rivals.

Intercommunication

Central to the argument that follows is the desire to look closely at the technocultural shifts described above that have constituted different relationships to, and organizations of, the self in terms of the public, the personal, the private, and the intimate. This will lead us to recognizing different strategies involved in the production of online persona that are newly fundamental to the contribution of community, culture, politics, and institutions as tactically aware and strategically engaged individuals in the new territories and grounds that have demanded of us new constitutions of the self. Conceptually, we argue, the public world is undergoing a distinct transformation, resulting in a new configuration that can be described as intercommunication: a complex and detailed layering of types and forms of communication that are individually directed, systematically filtered, automatically tracked and recorded, and engaged with by individuals, organizations, and machines in multiple ways. Celebrities are a cultural category of individualization that is useful in identifying and examining intercommunication because they have been at the forefront of interpersonal and highly mediated contemporary online culture. We have an enduring fascination with the role of celebrity because of the way it points indexically to terms that are long-term in their development. The power of celebrity has been to transform journalism, generating an intensive amount of news media coverage and journalistic materials that are consumed by hundreds of millions of consumers whose interests sit outside what is typically considered the domain of the fourth estate. The power of celebrity is not bound up with notions of investigative journalism, but rather the values of sentiment and emotion within the narratives that have characterized the "press" in the late twentieth century. We can understand the power of celebrity as an ur-text, as kind of a script for the critical interplay that exists as an articulation of the private self that is expressed through a public individual. The term intercommunication is a way to describe how the representative system of celebrity has transformed. The representational power of celebrity, so carefully built up by cinema, television print, music, and advertising industries over the past century has now become part of a new model and explanatory mechanism for understanding the movement between public, private, and intimate that characterizes contemporary celebrity discourse. Particularly evidenced by social media, our technologically enhanced cultures are quite conclusively bound up in systems of presentational media.

Presentational media is media that is performed, produced, and exhibited by the individual, which does not replace the structures of representational media, but does shift the degree of influence that previously dominant media corporations have in producing materials relevant for the expression of the self to others. Presentational media involves the sociocultural transformation of social networks, which includes the redirection of traditional media content – toward the layering of the online self – which means that our persona emerges as an expression of the self across networks over time through the digital objects that we produce and share.

Representational media is an all-encompassing term for dominant media forms that are still with us, including print, film, radio, and television and involve images and narratives that have been used to personify their audience. The stories of representational media quite literally represent the cultures they are generated within and sold to and have been closely partnered with the political systems and other cultures also represented and delivered as part of a sense of collective polity. Celebrities, politicians, and other high-profile public figures are part of the elaborate system of personalities, enabled through the representational media paradigm to speak to and on behalf of audiences, voters, consumers, and the populace at large: they embody collective configurations through their representative – and public – individuality. This media paradigm is far from being replaced, but it is being eroded through hybridity and traditional media images, advertising, photographs, or quotes, that are now blended with interpersonal chats, memes, links, and the panoply of digital objects that serves as the content of that media platform distributed by the individual to audiences of friends and followers. Presentational media is media that is performed and produced by the individual and exhibited to a personal audience of friends and followers, distributed on platforms and by collectives that sit alongside the organizations of representational media, which are mostly large media corporations. Online tools, mobile applications (apps), Web 2.0 protocols, and social media platforms support the ability of individuals to make content that is expressive of the self and is publicly available to others without the kinds of barriers to entry for which the representational media paradigm is famous.

Presentational media involves mediatized digital objects that have subjective-forming properties. This could include activities such as the sharing of a link to a music video that marks us as a fan, or expressing personal attitudes or opinions via the sharing of a meme, or documenting and broadcasting the self in a YouTube video that gains attention via Facebook, Snapchat, or Twitter, which serve as the intercommunication technologies. The term presentational media locates the self at the center of contemporary media activity and transactions that still involve representational elements but address and spread through audiences according to entirely new structures and practices.

It is the intercommunicative properties of digital objects that makes them such useful elements for persona performance and online surveillance: "Intercommunication is an elaborate layering of types and forms of communication that are filtered and directed and engaged with by particular individuals in interpersonal ways" (Marshall 2010, p. 41). The practice of adding to our online persona in the everyday, involves the labor of monitoring and editing ourselves, connecting with strategic purpose to other individuals and objects, and building public reputations (Marshall 2015b). This labor, and indeed the emphasis on the relation between salaried work and persona work, has only intensified in the last decade, which is connected to the change in how we collectively imagine the relationship of the self to earnings. The increased casualization of traditionally stable domains of labor in the service, administration, education, and other knowledge economies has produced a situation in which individuals are contracting themselves for specific times and projects. The result has been a shift in the way that large organizations represent workers and the increase in portfolio culture, signaled by the dominance of labor-related sites such as LinkedIn, and the emphasis on the presentation of the self online. Actors, for example, have long required tokens of themselves – images, summaries of roles, performances, and awards – in order to secure further work. An entire management industry of agencies and agents emerged as this portfolio culture encompasses actors, writers, directors, and producers and this culture quickly spread to managerialism itself. Facebook is very much an extension of contract and portfolio culture, a summation of a publicly imagined center of identity, which like the curriculum vitae stands in for the individual as a publicizing of the self. Today students are advised early in high school quite explicitly how to carefully and strategically manage their social media profiles with the anticipation of future employers, organizations, and institutions as audiences. This "work persona" has been hyper-attenuated into a practice of individual branding, which Hearn (2008) identified as becoming part of a wider phenomenon of contemporary consumer capitalism.

In the age of casualization, portfolio culture demands that individuals create work personas, which depend on significant public knowledge of what is considered important within the industry. The video game industry, which will be discussed further in Chapter 7, is a clear example of this phenomenon, as very few games companies hire permanently, preferring instead to increase and decrease employees depending on certain times of development and intensities of project progression. Potential employees must signal their capacity to work and be agile, delivering on short-term and project-based contracts. Membership in professional Facebook groups and having particular skills recognized by others in LinkedIn is important, as is demonstrating they are part of the public conversations on game development via Twitter and being active in online communities. As Gill (2010) notes, when a game is finished and delivered to a publisher, only a small staff is retained to manage updates and bug fixes. The project teams are disbanded and, if lucky, move on to the next project and, if not so fortuitous, they rejoin the large lines of individuals cueing for the next job. The rise of "indie" and independent games has, in part, been a result of the dismantling of the studio system in games production with the exception of larger companies. In addition, self-publishing through services like Steam and the Android and iOS game stores has risen in prominence, dramatically reducing the overheads of game production and returning the industry to its halcyon days of garage programmers and bedroom designers. However, the persona labor in these instances has not diminished but intensified, as the success of an "indie" game often relies on the public presentation of the self by developers, making one's self available to a massive public of potential consumers and fostering community support.

With its integration and interplay of both mediatization and communication, intercommunication is a useful term in understanding the two dimensions of the constitution of a contemporary public self: it is both

- a produced form of culture and
- a public form of exchange.

The celebrity is a model for considering the strategies of self-dissemination, and the tactics of linking to other media that are constitutive of an organic, ongoing version of the self. The core of celebrity activity is devoted to the production of the self. This can be observed in the practice of new celebrities and social media entertainers like JennaMarbles, Michelle Phan, GiGi Gorgeous, and the VlogBrothers who have become important for understanding how the latest generations of online content consumers are presenting themselves to the world. In essence, new generations are taking cues and direction in terms of how to perform themselves in public from those who have already successfully garnered (and monetized) visibility. The development of what are called "influencers" connected to fashion, DIY advice, games, and humor has helped generalize the objective of making a public version of the self through the intercommunication industries as a pathway to monetizing the self into a career. Online persona as self-branding, however, is fraught as individuals work to build their networks large enough to generate the interests of corporate sponsors derived from their platform's advertising structure or their own personal endorsements (see Abidin 2015; Duffy and Wissinger 2017).

A public persona is a mediatized identity and presentational self that shares the common and critical component of performance. Donald Trump, the 45th president of the United States, understands that performance and, its contemporary consort, attention are more important than knowledge, truth, facts, or even the policies promulgated. Trump's 2016 campaign and early presidency was marked by an attack on journalists and the media, not because of their ability to debunk his team's use of "alternative facts" but because of their ability to critique his performance in public. Trump's repeated animosity toward Alec Baldwin's *Saturday Night Live* Trump portrayal, expressed via Twitter, is similarly not because the performance undermines Trump's claim, but that it undermines his brand of public performance. Celebrity actors like Baldwin – along with musicians, athletes, and politicians – have come to understand the performative dimension of public appearances as *paratextual* (Genette 1997). The paratextual dimensions of being a celebrity actor involve a public performance of the self both in social media and traditional media in interviews, advertisements, endorsements, award nights, and other "staged" events. Celebrities are under pressure to perform themselves as cultural commodities in order to maintain their status, endlessly producing their professional selves in public. This performance has a pedagogical function through the normalization of elements that have now become second nature for millions if not billions in the contemporary moment even though they are most obviously presented by our most celebrated and visible individuals. The celebrity performance encourages audiences to understand that having a public persona means to be under perpetual and ubiquitous surveillance, from both the traditional representational media paradigm and the presentational media dimension of fans and followers, who are just as likely to seek out mobile phone selfies with stars as the paparazzi are to follow them about with telephoto lenses.

As we identified in Chapter 1, and through our integration and adaptation of Goffman's work (1959), we have collectively and individually come to an understanding that the performance of the self is a conscious act of the individual. We comprehend that careful stage-managing of the maintenance of the self through deliberate composure and navigation of norms has been internalized as a contemporary model of celebrity *and* applicable to all individuals operating in digital networked environments. In this chapter, we have considered the degree to which surveillance has been normalized, labor has been liquidized, and the degree to which the celebrity functions pedagogically in navigating the demands of the online persona.

One other key framework that also emerged from the study of celebrity has migrated from the representational media paradigm to the presentational one and that is "affective power." The primary function of celebrity, as described by Marshall (2014a, pp. 54–55) is the capacity to embody and perform the emotional investment of their audiences and fans. Sean Redmond's (2011) account of the role of emotion in the public "confessions" of personalities captures the importance of the public's relationship to the performance of affect and Henry Jenkins's work on fan culture describes the intensity of emotional connections between groups and the objects of their fandoms (2013 [1992]).

Intercommunication and Affect Theory

The blended experience of communication and mediatization that is described by our account of intercommunication results in unusual and unexpected experiences, which can be thought of in terms of their affective potential. The response to the use of the Pepe the Frog meme by legacy media organizations and the Anti-Defamation League (Andrews 2016), for example, was not responding to any particular or individual "meaning" of the meme, but rather the impression of its use by the "Alt-Right" posters on social media appropriating the frog from its comedic use on 4chan. **Affect** is an important component of the framework for understanding the increased role of public identity in the contemporary moment, and we are able to draw on multiple traditions that intersect in compelling and useful ways for revealing the significance of emotional investment in persona. One key contribution to the "turn to affect" in cultural studies derives from psychology and the work of Sylvan Tomkins, whose account of affect has underpinned the examination of the flows of emotion and investment in contemporary culture (see Sedgwick and Frank 1995; Tomkins 1991). The second convention for thinking about affect is Brian Massumi's (2002) take on Deleuzian thought, which suggested that affect is a useful means for reintegrating the humanities with perceptions of biology and the body. Massumi provides a challenge by drawing on scientific metaphors to reconsider affect as a prerational element in the presentation and organization of the self in relation to others. The Deleuzian approach to investigating the role of affect in making sense of popular music was a crucial contribution to cultural studies by Lawrence Grossberg, who saw affect as an organizing element in the strategic management of emotion in American politics that dominated both the right and the left, from the moderates to the extreme fringe. Grossberg identified this concept as the "affective economy" (1987) in which emotion is clearly ascribed and extenuated. He saw this economy working as a congealing of attention and support for the ways that public individuals, from rock stars to presidents, not only gained approval but distinct clustering of followers in large networks that became communities, not unlike the way Facebook and other social media sites are organized around lists of "friends" and other categories of audience.

Persona studies draws productively from these various readings of affect to analyze the new cultural connections that are not always derived from purposeful, targeted, or rational trajectories. The notion of "**virality**," for example, can be understood in Tomkins's model as not simply a vectoral or infectious metaphor, but a biologically embedded one. The ALS Ice Bucket Challenge, which raised more than US$100 million (ALS Association 2014) to combat amyotrophic lateral sclerosis (also called motor neuron disease and Lou Gehrig's disease), went viral across Facebook in part due to celebrity participation, including former US President George W. Bush, Tom Cruise, Chris Pratt, Taylor Swift, David Beckham, and Gwyneth Paltrow and the act of nominating others to participate or donate. It also captured the public's attention for the way that the deeply physical response to the bucket of icy water poured over the head affectively produced emotional memories of similar bodily encounters that are unconscious, unexplored, potentially complicated as pleasurable and physically unsettling. The Ice Bucket Challenge is an example of the intercommunicative way that affect can be transmitted across networks as a mediated experience and attach itself to emotional memories and contribute to the network's ability to produce patterns of contagion and amplification. Anna Gibbs (2002, p. 337) summarized the value of affect and mapped its importance as a concept in the humanities as organizing both intra- and inter-corporeality, suggesting that affect is integral to "social responsiveness."

By synthesizing affect theory with our attempts at understanding the role of social media and online networking in the reorganization of the media industry, from a representationally dominated paradigm to a more entangled version of presentational media, we have begun to see the rise of the intercommunication industries, made up of companies including Facebook, Google, YouTube, Twitter, and Apple. Together these corporations have produced a new media environment for social interaction that operates through new networks of connection that permeate self-generated media forms blended with interpersonal communication as affect clusters. These clusters are important to online advertising as it operates via Instagram marketing systems and Google's Adwords, and affect is a useful explanatory tool for unpacking the flows of connections and the patterns of organization that have come to power in contemporary culture, and a starting method to locate the role of agency in this new conglomeration. The individual, in their intensively invested construction of the visible and mediatized self, builds power through connections to affect clusters in the intercommunication industries. Through interpersonal forms of communication, strategic management of the performance of the self, and regular exchange of mediated forms and networked activity of likes and followers, agency takes on new dimensions. These dimensions have inherited the problems of the representational media paradigm, most especially privilege, gaze, stereotype, normalized behavior, and other inequalities. However, the agency, reach, and capacity to impact public discourse enabled by presentational media and intercommunication has also led to an open public renegotiation of those problems. Perhaps most publicly, this is being achieved by movements like Black Lives Matter, Marriage Equality, #metoo, and #TimesUp, as evidenced by global changes in attitudes toward race, sexuality, and gender; although racism, homophobia, sexism, and misogyny still persist, these discourses are increasingly, publicly questioned and challenged.

Conclusion

In this chapter, we have identified the role of technologies, celebrities, surveillance, labor, performance, and affect in the transformation of the communication and media ecology and have begun to locate the qualitatively different experience of intercommunication. A term that assists in making sense of the new presentational media environment, intercommunication is part of the analytical toolkit for examining those aspects of our everyday lives that are a blended public and personal experience. In summary there are three core elements to the concept and theory of intercommunication that can be usefully restated here before we move on to examining other important domains and concepts involved in persona studies. The first is that intercommunication implies a hybridized interpretation of the flow between representational and presentational media. The second is that intercommunication implies that the interpersonal has now moved into a central and pivotal part of networked communication infrastructure. Finally, intercommunication is not only a blend of representation and presentation but equally and most significantly it identifies the simultaneity in the form of online public identity and the increasingly mundane movement between media and communication.

References

Abidin, C. (2015). Communicative intimacies: Influencers and perceived interconnectedness. *Ada: A Journal of Gender, New Media & Technology* 8: https://adanewmedia.org/2015/11/issue8-abidin (accessed October 22, 2018).

ALS Association. (2014). The ALS Association expresses sincere gratitude to over three million donors (August 29, 2014). http://www.alsa.org/news/media/press-releases/ice-bucket-challenge-082914.html (accessed March 16, 2018).

Andrews, T.M. (2016). Once-comic Pepe the Frog has been declared a hate symbol. *The Washington Post* (September 28). https://www.washingtonpost.com/news/morning-mix/wp/2016/09/28/once-comic-pepe-the-frog-has-been-declared-a-hate-symbol (accessed October 29, 2018).

Bentham, J. (1791). *Panopticon or the Inspection House*. London: T. Payne.

Bolter, J.D. and Grusin, R. (1999). *Remediation: Understanding New Media*. Cambridge, MA: MIT Press.

boyd, d. (2014). *It's Complicated: The Social Lives of Networked Teens*. New Haven, CT: Yale University Press.

Bucher, T. (2012). Want to be on the top? Algorithmic power and the threat of invisibility on Facebook. *New Media & Society* 14 (7): 1164–1180.

Clissold, B.D. (2004). Candid camera and the origins of reality TV: Contextualising a historical precedent. In: *Understanding Reality Television* (ed. S. Holmes and D. Jermyn), 33–53. London: Routledge.

Consalvo, M. (2007). *Cheating: Gaining Advantage in Videogames*. Cambridge, MA: MIT Press.

Duffy, B.E. and Wissinger, E. (2017). Mythologies of creative work in the social media age: Fun, free, and "just being me." *International Journal of Communication* 11: 4652–4671.

Elmer, G. (2013). IPO 2.0: The Panopticon goes public. *MediaTropes* 4 (1): 1–16.

Ford, M. (2015). *Rise of the Robots: Technology and the Threat of a Jobless Future*. New York: Basic Books.

Foucault, M. (1975). *Discipline and Punish: The Birth of the Prison*. London: Penguin Books.

Genette, G. (1997). *Paratexts: Thresholds of Interpretation*, vol. 20. Cambridge: Cambridge University Press.

Gibbs, A. (2002). Disaffected. *Continuum: Journal of Media & Cultural Studies* 16 (3): 335–341.

Gibson, W. (1984). *Neuromancer*. New York: Ace Books.

Gill, R. (2010). "Life is a pitch": Managing the self in new media work. In: *Managing Media Work* (ed. M. Deuze), 249–262. London: SAGE.

Goffman, E. (1959). *The Presentation of Self in Everyday Life*. New York: Anchor Books.

Greenwald, G. (2014). *No Place to Hide: Edward Snowden, the NSA, and the US Surveillance State*, 1e. New York: Metropolitan Books.

Grey, J. (2010). *Show Sold Separately: Promos, Spoilers, and Other Media Paratexts*. New York: New York University Press.

Grossberg, L. (1987). Rock and roll in search of an audience. In: *Popular Music and Communication* (ed. J. Lull), 175–197. Newbury Park, CA: SAGE.

Gurnow, M. (2014). *The Edward Snowden Affair: Exposing the Politics and Media Behind the NSA Scandal*. Indianapolis: Blue River Press.

Harding, L. (2014). Writing The Snowden Files: "The paragraph began to self-delete". *The Guardian* (February 21). https://www.theguardian.com/books/2014/feb/20/edward-snowden-files-nsa-gchq-luke-harding (accessed October 29, 2018).

Hardt, M. (1999). Affective labor. *Boundary 2* 26 (2): 89–100.

Hearn, A. (2008). "Meat, mask, burden": Probing the contours of the branded self. *Journal of Consumer Culture* 8 (2): 197–218.

Holmes, S. (2004). "All you've got to worry about is the task, having a cup of tea, and doing a bit of sunbathing": Approaching celebrity in *Big Brother*. In: *Understanding Reality Television* (ed. S. Holmes and D. Jermyn), 111–135. New York: Routledge.

Jenkins, H. (2006). *Convergence Culture Where Old and New Media Collide*. New York: New York University Press.

Jenkins, H. (2013 [1992]). *Textual Poachers: Television Fans and Participatory Culture*. New York: Routledge.

Kessler, R. (2013). Anonymous hacks Department of Justice website, threatens to launch "multiple warheads." Gawker (January 26). http://gawker.com/5979203/anonymous-hacks-department-of-justice-website-threatens-to-launch-multiple-warheads (accessed October 29, 2018).

Latour, B. (2005). *Reassembling the Social: An Introduction to Actor-Network-Theory*. Oxford: Oxford University Press.

Le Roy, E. (1913). *The New Philosophy of Henri Bergson*. London: Williams & Norgate.

Lévy, P. (1997). *Collective Intelligence*. New York: Plenum/Harper Collins.

Marshall, P.D. (2010). The promotion and presentation of the self: Celebrity as marker of presentational media. *Celebrity Studies* 1 (1): 35–48.

Marshall, P.D. (2014a). *Celebrity and Power: Fame in Contemporary Culture*. Minneapolis: University of Minnesota Press.

Marshall, P.D. (2014b). Persona studies: Mapping the proliferation of the public self. *Journalism* 15 (2): 153–170.

Marshall, P.D. (2015a). Intercommunication and persona: The intercommunicative public self. *The International Journal of Interdisciplinary Studies in Communication* 10 (1): 23–31.

Marshall, P.D. (2015b). Monitoring persona: Mediatized identity and the edited public self. *Frame: Journal of Literary Studies* 28 (1): 115–133.

Marwick, A.E. (2015). Instafame: Luxury selfies in the attention age. *Public Culture* 27 (1): 137–160.

Marwick, A.E. (2017). Scandal or sex crime? Ethical implications of the celebrity nude photo leaks. *AoIR Selected Papers of Internet Research* 6: https://spir.aoir. org/index.php/spir/article/view/1324 (accessed March 16, 2018).

Massanari, A. (2017). #Gamergate and The Fappening: How Reddit's algorithm, governance, and culture support toxic technocultures. *New Media & Society* 19 (3): 329–346. https://doi.org/10.1177/1461444815608807.

Massumi, B. (2002). *Parables for the Virtual: Movement, Affect, Sensation.* Durham, NC: Duke University Press.

McLuhan, M. (1994). *Understanding Media: The Extensions of Man.* Cambridge, MA: MIT Press.

Redmond, S. (2011). Celebrity. In: *The Encyclopedia of Literary and Cultural Theory* (ed. M. Ryan). Blackwell Reference Online https://onlinelibrary.wiley. com/doi/10.1002/9781444337839.wbelctv3c001 (accessed October 29, 2018).

Rogers, K. (2014). *The Attention Complex: Media, Archeology, Method.* New York: Springer.

Schudson, M. (1992). Watergate: A study in mythology. *Columbia Journalism Review* 31 (1): 28–31.

Schwarz, O. (2014). The past next door: Neighbourly relations with digital memory-artefacts. *Memory Studies* 7 (1): 7–21.

Sedgwick, E.K. and Frank, A. (1995). Shame in the cybernetic fold: Reading Silvan Tomkins. *Critical Inquiry* 21 (2): 496–522.

Senft, T.M. (2013). Microcelebrity and the branded self. In: *A Companion to New Media Dynamics* (ed. J. Hartley, J. Burgess and A. Bruns), 346–354. Oxford: Wiley Blackwell.

Shen, L. (2018). Here's why Facebook just gained $21 billion in value. *Fortune* (April 10). http://fortune.com/2018/04/10/heres-why-facebook-just-gained-21-billion-in-value (accessed October 29, 2018).

Steinhart, E. (2008). Teilhard de Chardin and transhumanism. *Journal of Evolution & Technology* 20 (1): 1–22.

Sweney, M. (2008). Mums furious as Facebook removes breastfeeding photos. *The Guardian* (December 30). http://www.theguardian.com/media/2008/dec/30/facebook-breastfeeding-ban (accessed March 16, 2018).

Temperton, J. (2015). Ashley Madison data published – and it's worse than anyone thought. Wired (August 19). www.wired.co.uk/article/ashley-madison-hack-data-leaked-online (accessed October 29, 2018).

Toffler, A. (1971). *Future Shock.* London: Pan Books.

Tomkins, S.S. (1991). *Affect Imagery Consciousness. Volume III: The Negative Affects: Anger and Fear*. New York: Springer.

Vernadsky, V. (1945). The biosphere and the noösphere. *American Scientist* 33 (1): 1–12.

Waycott, J., Thompson, C., Sheard, J. et al. (2017). A virtual panopticon in the community of practice: Students' experiences of being visible on social media. *The Internet and Higher Education* 35 (October): 12–20. https://doi.org/10.1016/j.iheduc.2017.07.001.

Winner, L. (1997). *Autonomous Technology: Technics-Out-of-Control as a Theme in Political Thought*. Cambridge, MA: MIT Press.

Winston, B. (1998). *Media Technology and Society: A History: From the Telegraphy to the Internet*. London: Routledge.

3

Intercommunication and the Dimensions and Registers of Persona

Introduction

In this chapter, we seek to expand the analytical toolkit of persona studies in several important directions. First, we build on the understanding of intercommunication, its critical components, and its further implications. Second, we provide an analysis of the "registers of persona" as ways of understanding how a single persona can work to negotiate the collapsed contexts of online spaces. And third, we provide a detailed breakdown of the five dimensions of persona that are relevant to further analysis.

Contemporary culture has undergone profound changes and therefore we can gain insights into understanding effective and fruitful online persona management by drawing on examples from everyday life – from politics, law and business, marketing, sports, celebrities, and so on. As outlined in the previous chapter, intercommunication is a result of the distinctive transformation of public engagement, which identifies the transposition of media use and the intersectional forms of personal and mediated interpersonal communication. The interpersonal operation of online activity acts as a highly sophisticated filter, one that can result in the fine-grained control over the flow of messages that move within and between a variety of platforms. This personal form of gatekeeping and fine-tuned customization has been widely criticized, suggesting that it can result in what Van Alstyne and Brynjolffson (2005) call the "cyberbalkanization" of personal interests. Dimitri Williams's (2007, p. 403) study of Internet users' interests noted, however, that the cyberbalkanization hypothesis was not supported. Williams (2007) concluded that while Internet use promoted diverse online interactions and fewer offline ones, the entrance and exit costs to different online communities meant that individuals were highly engaged in disseminating and discriminating between interests, which subsequently indicated a higher likelihood of finding new ones.

Persona Studies: An Introduction, First Edition. P. David Marshall, Christopher Moore, and Kim Barbour.

Social media is comprised of a variety of interpersonal communication systems and a highly mediated form of communication; from Facebook which mixes personal updates with externally sourced media, to YouTube with its mediation of the self as televisual producer and remixer of content. Sites like Tumblr and Reddit see the endless self-distributed circulation of mediated expressions that knit and connect the individual to different groups and previously unconnected worlds of interest. The categorical elements of intercommunication have several fundamental components that are individualized, interpersonal, indexical, and internetworked as will be further unpacked below. It is also important to consider how these elements of intercommunication have multiple registers and involve multiple dimensions of persona formation which will be considered in the last half of this chapter.

Persona as Individualized

Most, but not all, services of the contemporary generation of online activity are organized in some way around the individual. From hyper-personal social media sites to deeply personalized layouts of mobile technologies such as the smartphone (Moore and Barbour 2016), the individual self is the nexus for the economics of online activity. Popular sites and social media platforms such as Instagram, Twitter, WeChat, and Reddit are populated by individual subscriptions. The structure of the user's experience of these sites is dependent on the individual registration of preferences that transforms the experience based on the user's designated interests and varies widely from person to person. Even the most ubiquitous of online correspondence services, email, which often involves some form of corporate, institutional, or organizational branding, may still be personalized with an individual signature.

It is the individualized composition of online culture that facilitates the relationship to personal security and has led to the prevalent discourse of protection and privacy that circulates around concerns over the security of personal information. The constant surveillance of the devices to which we are connected leads them to act and inform on our every move. The rise of end-user license agreements and terms of service contracts, which reserve the rights of organizations and corporations to monetize and market our personal information, ties into larger concerns about the rise of the surveillance state in the digital era.

Arguably, it is this individualization as a form of online affordance that has contributed to the success of the online economy, not only as a means for supporting widespread adoption and integration of Internet banking, but also highly individualized payment and account structures across sites like eBay and Amazon. A significant degree of online global retail is enabled by PayPal, which facilitates multiple individualized payment methods. The crowdfunding economy of sites like Kickstarter and Pozible and the rise of cryptocurrencies like Bitcoins, mined by individuals and individual computational devices working away at complex blockchain algorithms, all contribute to the individualization of the online economy.

The success of application-based economies is intimately tied into the individualized economy of online culture. The rise of apps and new app-based business structures within the Apple iPhone and Google Android smartphone ecologies has largely been based on individuals seeking to expand the functionality of their devices through downloading the software or online platform onto their mobile phones (Goggin 2011). Although initially free of charge for many apps, the embedded in-app economies of games and services have added new dimensions to the online economy as it has demanded an individualized structure of registration that has emphasized financial identity and activity. Software and hardware personalization drives a huge range of paratextual industries of personalization from the eBay and Etsy markets of personalized mobile phone cases to the personalization of games like Pokemon GO, which enables users to augment their in-game avatars through cosmetic items bought through the exchange of real money for in-game currency.

Persona as Interpersonal

From its earliest origins, the World Wide Web has been about making connections. Much of the attention given to the move from the Web's first iteration to its Web 2.0 versions has been about the power of users to make connections to each other and about the capacity to make and maintain networks. Similarly, there appears to be a move to what Tim Berners-Lee (cited in Shadbolt, Berners-Lee, and Hall 2006) calls the Semantic Web in process, which indicates the embedded facility of the power of the Web to sense and relate information, and to produce data for those in control based on algorithmically discovered connections. The language of the current generation of social media sites and services is based around interpersonal networks: Facebook and Snapchat privileges the presumption of "friends" by connection; Twitter's relations between users are determined by the terminology of the prophet-like "followers." As with SMS instant messaging, these social media platforms have reduced the more formal elements of communication present in "snail mail" letter writing and even its digital counterpart, email. Studies of the effects of SMS and "txting" have revealed that despite fears and moral panics over deteriorating standards of formal written expression in secondary and higher education there exists little to no evidence of this (Aziz et al. 2013). Instead what has been found is that users adapt to situational formats for appropriate language and expression, what Gibbs et al. (2015) term platform vernaculars, switching between interpersonal language and the more formal requirements of register and style depending on the context.

The original 140-character limitation of Twitter's microblogging platform was an imposed replication of the SMS text messages, which in Latin-derived languages, including English and French, is limited to 160 characters. This SMS limitation is due to the maximum encoding of 1,120 bits of information in the Global System for Mobile communication (GSM) that provides 7 bits of information per character. Despite doubling the character limit to 280 for users in 2017, Twitter's artificial limitation continues to privilege short aphoristic forms of communication that imply a highly interpersonal understanding between followers and "followees."

The rise of threaded communication on Facebook, Twitter, Reddit, and Instagram brings together the chains of interaction seen via email, and the comfortable shorthand of SMS, resulting in half-sentences and caption-like and emoji-filled interactions. This value of the interpersonal is privileged in the use of social media, and very few platforms and online services restrict or omit the heavily image-based direction that online communication is taking. Online communication has also gained a recognizable degree of ranking and rating that equates to a measure of interpersonal prestige (discussed further below), which is bestowed by the numbers of "friends" and "followers" that one has in the system. It is the interpersonal connections that define the valuation of social media over other forms of media, especially traditional broadcast media, which become the content that is "shared" and "liked." Further, the related actions of liking, retweeting, starring, and "favoriting" are the measures that the interpersonal prestige wealth is determined by and function as the engine of entire online economies of sites like YouTube and Facebook. The movements of shared information define the relative interest and create the locus around which individuals are interpersonally aggregated. The attraction of the user and the content they share draws others to them. This attraction, and sharing, by users is the epicenter of the monetizing and surveillance activities and the economic engine that drives social network platforms and their associated companies.

Persona as Indexical

Intercommunication is in part defined by the qualities of sharing and exchanging, and these have become the core experiential elements of the social media format. They also underscore the value of what can be described as indexical forms of communication. Chandler (2007, pp. 37, 42–44) defines the semiotics of the indexical sign as one that points to or implies a relationship to another sign. The indexical quality of intercommunication via social media identifies the way in which the various forms of advertising and cultural industries work to insinuate themselves into the personal construction of value that social media produces. The indexical dimensions further highlight the way in which communication is extended and augmented in online cultures.

One of the most significant examples of the power of online indexical communication is the website Reddit, self-described as the "the front page of the internet." Reddit resembles an old-style pre-Internet bulletin board system (BBS), with content divided into user-defined "subreddits." Unlike standard social media sites, Reddit, like the website DIGG before it, allows users to both "like" and "dislike" content shared on the site using the "Upvote" and "Downvote" mechanic. Reddit's algorithm then sorts the number of votes and aggregates all the content on the "r/All" showing the most "popular" content. The indexical dimensions of Reddit contributions and activity are fascinating as the calculations are based on the open-sourced "hot ranking" algorithm (Salihefendic 2015). This means that the timing of submission and voting has an impact on the ranking of the content, newer stories are indexed higher on the page, and the first 10 upvotes are ranked as high as the following 50. This also means that "controversial" content, which attracts equal number of upvotes and downvotes, drops in the rankings, while shared material that gets constantly high upvotes and low downvotes will be ranked higher and vice versa. These relations are far from democratic, as online spaces are intensely "demotic" in the sense that Graeme Turner (2010) uses to suggest that contingent media forms depending on audience participation are never fully predetermined by organizational categories of content, but nonetheless are unlikely to radically alter the daily political, social, or cultural agenda of the time. Turner reminds us that the demotic conventions that sites like Facebook, Twitter, and Reddit give us to indicate a favorite, a like, or an upvote, are not democratizing conventions at all, but structural shifts in the conventions of participation that are susceptible to the downward pull of standardization and commercialization. This is particularly evident on Reddit, which has been infiltrated by armies of automated bots (these number in the tens of thousands) and legions of marketeers who are hired to promote brands and sabotage rivals (Edwards 2013).

Persona as Internetworked

The final categorical element of intercommunication is internetworking, which comes from the way that online culture is individualized and yet continuously aggregated. This category is related to the element of the interpersonal as users of social media are directed toward connecting and making connections. Internetworking extends from relations between individuals to networks of connections between platforms, for example, the movement of mediated communication between 4Chan and Reddit. It also involves the movement and connectivity between groups of interest and communities of practice. Gamers are an important example here as players of games across a multitude of formats are encouraged and rewarded for their abilities to develop networks in different online settings. Players of Massively Multiplayer Online (MMO) games must form "guilds" to beat high-level content, managing the schedules of up to 50 players to coordinate their activities. The rise of Multiplayer Online Battle Arena (MOBA) style games, such as *League of Legends* (LoL) and *Dawn of the Ancients 2* (DOTA2), is entirely dependent on the internetworking of players who use online social media to organize teams and establish followers. The recent popularity of MOBAs is intimately connected to massive audiences via YouTube and the live streaming website Twitch TV. Even mobile games are internetworked as players on the iOS operating system can communicate and compete with friends and family across multiple titles all connected via the Apple Game Center. The "voice over Internet protocol" (VoIP) application, Discord, has found an immense audience of 100 million users following its launch in 2015, as a means for supporting gaming communities spread across different platforms and hardware systems (Alexander 2017). The Discord application is a social media service that enables users to communicate with each other, and move between communities of players, outside of any one particular game software. The success of this kind of paratextual industry, alongside the increased number of games review sites, niche sales of collectibles and merchandize and the persona-driven markets of cosplay, are all made possible by the internetworking of social media services like Discord, Reddit, Etsy, and Instagram.

The significance of internetworking for the individual, is the ability to define a different iteration of the self across multiple instances. Twitch streamers and YouTubers, for example, may indicate their professional aspirations via a live performance of their eSports skills. The same players might, however, demonstrate a more jovial or intimate self via a private Discord community. The industrial significance of internetworking occurs where the users are en masse assembling connections and producing networks that clearly establish economic value, from marketing and advertising revenue to more imbricated layers of intellectual property through data analytics.

The inter-related quality of online identity has been a vibrant medium for the growth of different kinds of information to be generated and has been fertile ground for exponential development of the exchange of user-generated content. The informational content of shared media and personal expression further works to define our online persona and these materials become the economic fuel for the Semantic Web. While it is clear that personal information and communication has helped to define the online social world and the reputational dimensions of the user, it also regularly shapes the ways that identity intersects with commodities and services. For example, if our interpersonal communication consistently addresses topics like health, personal fitness, and exercise, then it is highly probable that the persona generated as a result will have an impact on the intercommunication environment. The user will both be a target of marketing bots and algorithmic advertising; it will also result in a personally generated network of links, images, and connections to fitness applications, exercise advice, and products. The internetworked movement of information of the self generates personalized content that in its direct address plays with older media's more removed form of register of advertising address.

Registers of Performance

As the presentation of a digital self has become increasingly ubiquitous with the widespread use of social and professional networking and media platforms, the ways that individuals engage with these platforms and negotiate their performance of self for different audiences of friends, family, fans, and followers drives new ways of theorizing identity and self-presentation. Drawing on Barbour (2015), the following section conceptualizes three registers of performance – the professional, personal, and intimate – by focusing on the instance of the creative artist working in the contemporary era of public personas. The conceptualization of registers of performance makes a metaphor of vocal registers, defined as "a series or range of consecutive frequencies that can be produced with nearly identical voice quality" (Hollien 1972, p. 1). Just as a single human voice can move between different vocal registers, so can a single online persona move between different performance registers. Equally, Hollien (1972, p. 3) notes that many people can produce sounds at frequencies which seem to "lie between" vocal registers, and there are elements of persona performance which appear to sit between the professional and personal, or personal and intimate performance registers.

These three registers of performance engage with different elements of the social and cultural construction of the artist's role. For example, in the professional register we see independence and preoccupation with work, displays of genius or skill, the search for novelty or innovation; in the personal register we see a performance of rebellion against established norms and systems; in the intimate register we see the performance of emotional sensitivity and intensity. However, the negotiation of a range of different types of experience has resonance outside of the performance of "artistness." Through these experiences, we can see how these artists engage with digitally networked spaces to create an online persona, and from here consider how the professional, personal, and intimate registers of performance operate for other persona types.

Professional

In choosing the term "professional" to describe the first of the three registers of performance it is important to recognize the contested nature of what counts as professional in an unlicensed, unregulated work environment such as the arts. Indeed, as Smeby et al. (2011, pp. 1–2) outline, and as discussed in Chapter 8, even outside of the arts, the definition and use of the term is disputed: in everyday terms professional can be a synonym for occupation, as with a "professional hairdresser" or "professional chef"; it can be used descriptively to indicate people who use expert knowledge in their work, such as doctors or lawyers; or "professional" can indicate the adoption of normative models of quality and ethics, such as in journalism or public relations. Codell's (2003) professional category in her typology of Victorian artists judges professionalism on the basis of membership to specific clubs or societies, or inclusion in shows and events. More recent creative industries' discourse of artist identification as professional includes these Victorian elements, along with a requirement for income generation for the artist, self-identification as an artist, and art-making as the individual's primary role.

Personal

The term "personal" as a title for the second register of performance needs to be understood in comparison to the professional and the intimate. Where the professional register describes the relationship between the artist and their art practice, and the intimate describes sharing the very private (see below), performance in the personal register accounts for those aspects of an individual's life occurring between the two. Rather than being personal in the sense of not being publicly accessible, the personal register accounts for the performance of hobbies, interests, events, or activities outside of the arts: the artist at leisure. The artists' performances in the personal register, "the participation in public culture and in publicly visible popular culture" (Driscoll and Gregg 2010, p. 16), gives a rounded view of the person behind the persona and behind the art. Additionally, the nature of many of the digitally networked platforms used in online persona creation privileges and rewards sharing of personal moments. Facebook in particular, designed from the outset as a social rather than professional network, encourages a focus on the personal, and what Melissa Gregg (2011, p. 89) describes as "a certain comfort with sharing relatively personal information in a comparatively public space that may be subject to outside manipulation." Making connections to other profiles and pages, sharing and commenting on posts made by others, and having posts, profiles, and pages connect to the persona, all give depth and a holistic view of the persona and add to the experience of persona creation by the participant.

Intimate

The information, stories, and performances seen in the intimate register could be interpreted in relation to the increasing comfort with which Western society at large discloses personal information through new technologies, which

Lambert (2013) explores in depth in relation to Facebook. In introducing the increasing publicity of personal information, Lambert comments that although we now have the capacity to connect regularly with a much wider range of people through Facebook, leading to what he terms "zones of gregarious intimacy," the lack of control over how these disclosures are then circulated means that the unintended distribution of the intimate can be felt as "a kind of loss of self" (2013, p. 2). A number of writers and scholars have traced the way that the experience of intimacy has changed over time (Clough, Frank, and Seidman 2013; Giddens 1992; Illouz 2007; Lambert 2013), while others, particularly journalists writing for popular press, connect increasingly intimate sharing and self-disclosure in digitally networked spaces with a perceived loss of privacy and security (AAP 2013; Farrer 2010; Wroe 2013). The *Oxford Online Dictionary* (2018) defines the adjective "intimate" as "closely acquainted" or "familiar," or "private and personal." Drawing these threads together, and by labeling the third register of performance the intimate register, we address a level of sharing of the personal that could previously be seen only among the very closely acquainted, that is, immediate family, very close friends, or lovers.

Five Dimensions of Persona

Multiple researchers have considered how technologies work to produce functional digital identities. Digital sociologists Harrison Rainie and Barry Wellman have developed the idea of "networked individualism" (2012) which works to account for the connections between online activity and the formation of subjectivity. They argue that no technologies remain isolated, that they are being incorporated into individuals' lives and into each other as part of the "operating system" of the way people and technologies connect, communicate, and exchange information. Zizi Papacharissi (2010) offers a media and communication perspective, with the term the "networked self," a vastly personal ideology which is performed across multiple and simultaneous streams of acute social awareness that increases autonomy, potentially reduces agency, and requires constant self-surveillance and monitoring. Other key researchers in this field, such as Nancy Baym, have demonstrated how mediated interpersonal forms of communication accelerate novel constitutions of "personal connection" (Baym 2010). She further developed the idea of the digital identity, drawing on Donath's (2007) notion of signaling that locates social position within an information saturated society. Anna Poletti and Julie Rak, oriented within biographical and autobiographical studies, offer a perspective of "identity technologies" that sees them as an undeniable and fundamental part of the online world in the contemporary era (2014).

These writers, among others, have proposed ways of understanding the new constructions of identity and the individual that include online culture, digital connections to social institutions, and the networked organization of everyday life, that is fundamentally different to what has come before. In the following section of this chapter we consider five dimensions of online persona that occur as a pattern in the connections between the individual, collectives, communities, and other social groups. We argue that the concept of persona through these dimensions is key to understanding the configuration of online identity in the contemporary era, although we accept that there may be other dimensions not accounted for here. We identify and explicate five dimensions of persona as: publicness, mediatization, performativity, collective construction, and intentional value.

Public Dimension of Persona

The first dimension is that online persona is public. This first dimension has a wide range of publicness and a potential to go from a very small shared public to a massive and global public through viral sharing. This potentiality parallels the historical notion of the production of the public self, and the ideas of celebrities and stars that start out performing to small publics, but later attain a larger audience. This trajectory gives us insights into fully understanding the dynamics of online persona creation that always anticipates this shift from small to larger scale publics and can also be understood in terms of political figures, sport stars, and infamous figures of notoriety, such as criminals, freedom fighters, or even fictional personalities. In the industrial model of the individual, the public self is the "official" version that the celebrity offers up to the world, a highly polished, scheduled, and controlled self that includes the release dates of launches, premieres, and appearances. The public self of the celebrity involves the promotion of special events and performances, promoting pathways to ticket sales, or directing donations to worthy causes. High profile celebrities and public figures have teams of publicity assistants and staff that work to maintain a consistency in the public persona which is valued globally as a cultural commodity. Organizations, brands, institutions, and commercial entities similarly have this public facing dimension of their online persona with teams of social management operatives conducting official online persona management; but they also have a range of employees with quasi-official public selves connected to these identities. Celebrities, brands, and organizations are all especially important public figures because of their pedagogical functions, as they help us to identify new aspects of agency and risk. In the past the media gatekeeping of celebrity would have relegated figures like Kim Kardashian to tabloid notoriety, but the degree of agency provided by control over the public presentation of the online self has meant a new interconnected global celebrity built on careful management of that initial public notice into a remarkably enduring fashion, music, marketing, and promotional career.

Mediatized Dimension of Persona

The second significant dimension of persona is that an online persona is a mediatized identity. This mediatization, following the first dimension, is a public expression of the self that utilizes and often combines multiple technologies and formats operating under various conditions. Mediatized persona works under quite heavily regulated commercial imperatives and structures in order to be visible and constitute an online persona. An Instagram selfie is framed by a mobile phone while a Facebook livestream is produced with a webcam, but both are constrained by the terms of service conditions and user policies which ban the presence of a female nipple. What is new in this scenario is the naturalization of this framing of user agency and platform censorship. Any mediatized identity is therefore both a material and informational source and is something therefore that can be characterized as data (see Lundby 2014). The mediatized identity is often a remixed appropriation of materials for the purpose of the presentation of the public self, often annotated and layered with photographic filters, emoji, and augmented reality layers of photo manipulation. Mediatized identity draws on memes and popular culture and is constantly undergoing transformation, revision, remediation, and recirculation in blogs, v-logs, podcasts, tweets, and endless "posting." Because the mediatized dimension of online persona is almost always connected to corporate entities it also has to be seen as representing a commercial asset. The value and function of intellectual property in the knowledge economy is easily exchanged. It is becoming impossible for users to stop giving away data, and increasingly clear that governments and businesses want access to metadata to serve economic, commercial, and surveillance ends – whether you are using an Apple phone, uploading to Instagram (which is owned by Facebook), or uploading to YouTube (which is owned by Google). As will be discussed in the following chapter, mediatized identity is comprised of digital objects that at some level have a materiality that means they simultaneously exist locally on the user's phone, across Internet service provider records, and across the global digital networks of cloud storage such as the servers and clusters of machines in giant warehouses owned by Facebook, Google, or Amazon.

Performative Dimension of Persona

The third dimension of an online persona is its role as a performative identity. We perform our profession online, our gender, our tastes, and our interests from the way we comment on posts to the way we frame a selfie. It is important not to confuse the notion of an online persona as a performative identity with the understanding of a "real" identity as something that is underlying. The performance through assembly and intercommunication of an online persona expresses a public version of the self that is neither entirely "real" nor "fictional."

The construction of a performative identity means that a persona, as a term, captures a sense of the liminal dimensions between all three of the registers of persona. Each one is a performance that connects the personal, the intimate, and the public in a mesh with the primary identifiable characteristics that are intended to interact with the public in some quotidian fashion. The dimension of performance connects to the work of Judith Butler (1999) whose approach to the performativity of gender understands the idea of a presented quality that is constructed and negotiated as opposed to something inherited or innate. The presentational quality of persona is both enabled and constrained by the technologies, networks, and cultures in which the public identity is assembled and performed.

Goffman (1959) chronicled the cyclical patterns of self-presentation in accounting for the methods of impression formation, which considers the multiple platforms or stages that individuals perform on daily. He understood that we have many "faces" that emerge depending on the situation and its requirements. These faces are identifiable roles that provide a basis for interaction with others, and none are less real or more fictional than the others. As Papacharissi (2010) notes, these interactions quickly become patterns of action that unfold during the performance of the self. Patterns that can be thought of as "routines" reflecting the normalized and expected narratives about dominant modes of behavior considered appropriate to the situation. The performance of the self online becomes patterned through our interactions with the members of our networks and the interfaces to the systems themselves. Generations of users of social media and mobile technologies have developed approaches to the performativity of online persona routines that are not static, and they continue to evolve to meet the demands of perceived publics (see boyd 2014). The Habermasian notion of the "Lifeworld" (Habermas 1987) is useful here as a way to understand the performance of the public self online. The lifeworld of persona online, particularly for young users, is full of technical communication devices, channels, platforms, and modes of behavior that force a hybridization which results in culture and technology practices that inform one another continually. It is not simply that we are online all the time (Middleton 2007; Perrin and Jiang 2018) but that we are more easily pointed to by our relationships to devices and systems, regardless of our current connection to the Internet. Ken Hillis (2009, p. 29) invites us to consider the naturalized ideology of the "pull-down menu" and the "taxonometric" logic that has become normalized in the choices made available to users attempting to present themselves as avatars in virtual worlds or as social media users. He argues that the performance of gender, height, age, profession, location, attitude, and relationship to others is ritualized as a result of the limited options available to users in the system (Hillis 2009, p. 29).

Collective Dimension of Persona

Building on the ritualized relationships developed through the mediatized dimension of persona, the fourth dimension describes the ways an online persona works to produce some collective or public activity. This aspect of online identity is understood in the way that all forms of social media have some degree of friending and following (boyd and Ellison 2007). The collective dimension of persona is reflected in the connections and networks that users form directly by using services and platforms like YouTube, Facebook, WeChat, Twitter, Tumblr, and Instagram. Participation in these online networks results in multiple publics that are significantly different from the public associated with traditional broadcast media or political association. No longer is the individual "part" of a collective, but rather the individual is connected to multiple collective publics. In each one, the individual is a node, but they simultaneous orbit nodes in other networks. The complex overlapping of networks, however, can still be thought of as having a central point; the user's persona and the melange of activity from friends and followers across all these intercommunicating networks can be described as a "micro-public" (Marshall 2014), to be discussed further in the next chapter. Similar to the notion of a "personal public" (Schmidt 2013), the concept of a micro-public is one that considers the practices of social media such as sharing, tagging, and mediated expression in the forms of personal images, memes, likes, and dislikes. This intercommunication activity occurs as part of the interpersonal communication of the self, where self-mediations are linked to self-promotional activity across multiple platforms, sites, and services (Marshall 2015). Take, for example, the eponymous selfie, which is framed using an Internet-connected device and distributed via multiple platforms each with their own, possibly overlapping audience. Instagram is designed with this purpose in mind, offering the user to send the image to Facebook, Twitter, Flickr, and other services at the point of self-publication (see Albury 2015; Katz and Crocker 2015; Roberts and Koliska 2017). Micro-publics have a tremendous porousness, connecting to other networks effortlessly and with often unpredictable and unforeseen consequences.

The concept of micro-public is crucial to persona studies as a core means for describing the collective dimensions of online persona and the ways that groups, associations, and networks have become central to contemporary cultures. Micro-public formations are explored in various other interactions by researchers, including Senft (2008), Marwick (2013), and Marwick and boyd (2011), but the term serves as a means to highlight a new duality. Personas are comprised of a potentially massive audience and can feature tens, hundreds, thousands, and even millions of individual followers, who are all nodes in a personal network. Micro-publics are micro, not concerning scale, but with regards to a network that is regularly and privately updated by a single central identity. A micro-public is attached to a unique persona, personally producing, responding, and broadcasting in the tradition of previously dominant media institutions which make it also a quasi-public network. To fully grapple with the emergence of the online persona, we look closely at the strong connections between individuals and the multiple overlapping micro-publics to which they are central. Twitter is an important platform for micro-public formation: it is heavily relied upon by journalists developing followings and building affective connections to listeners, viewers, and readers that may never visit or consume their home publications. Similarly, the public personas of such journalists are not like the standardized cut-outs of representational culture but are living and breathing presentational figures who have direct and often unfiltered connections to their audiences. The dynamic of the audience is complicated by the friending and following relationship that amplifies the affective bond between celebrity and fan, politician and voter, author and audience, that has contributed new interpersonal dimensions to cultural expression, governance, and consumption. We can see this emerge in what Marshall (2014) describes as the intercommunication industries which service micro-publics, both massively large ones achieved by popular artists and those smaller but equally successful achieved by more independent operators who are still central to their own networks and maintain modest, vibrant, and active followings. Professional social media sites, such as LinkedIn and Academia.edu, are examples of platforms which service the operation of micro-public formation and management related to specific skills, interests, and themes. Public personas emerge from and across these presentational media forms and their micro-public intercommunicatively forcing a renewed focus on the management of reputation (Barbour and Marshall 2012). The very complex construction of publics as micro-publics intersects with larger and well-established media and communication systems that produce powerful cultural tropes; these in turn contribute to a new orientation of value and agency which can be observed in the last dimension of online persona.

The Fifth Dimension of Persona: Value, Agency, Reputation, Prestige (VARP)

Finally, our fifth dimension of an online persona is a series of overlapping facets of personal investment or value that includes agency, reputation, and prestige, not as subdimensions but equally important examples of what represents intentional speculation and investment in the public self (Marshall 2016; Moore, Barbour, and Lee 2017). Producing and curating a social media site is not just a construction of public identity, it is an investment through personal activity that involves engaging and making connections with others. The work of this investment is to determine the varying levels of commitment that regulate what is significant and monitoring what connections are valuable to an individual's persona. Various types of online activity are also ways of expanding influence; the choices that people make about what they show, what they connect with and to, what they "like" or "favorite" are all signs of building the value of a persona. Value is the connective term to examples of agency, reputation, and prestige that we will contend with in the final part of this chapter. Value, agency, reputation, and prestige are thought of as complex assemblages in online spaces because they are also linked to the forms of connections and investments that other people are making simultaneously. It is through the engagement with others that we determine the various levels of investment and activity that will produce the worth of an online persona to ourselves and others. We negotiate our individual sense of worth through the activities that appear valuable to others indicated by the markets of the attention economy (Davenport and Beck 2001): the competing economies of likes, favorites, shares, follows, and other measures of spreadable online content.

There are many forms of activity that are means and measures of expanding and evaluating online influence; the options that individuals take about what they show, with who they connect, and what they like are all examples of self-signification of value and investment. Value, agency, reputation, and prestige (simply summarized as VARP) are all complex value constructions in the online space, linked by the number of connections and the degree of activity with which people engage with and invest in a variety of ways. The concept of being professional and the adoption of a professionality in the expression of an online persona, for example, is judged by the status and reputation of the performances of those personas through which individuals network and the degree of perceived authenticity with which those presentational media forms are viewed (Marshall 2010). The strategies for negotiating between audiences and institutions that shape public life are simultaneously local and global, and there are consistent structural similarities across all professions (further explored in Chapter 8) regarding the value of public performance that are complicated by the movement of the self between professional, personal, and intimate registers.

There are important questions of engagement, authenticity, and reputational legitimacy which are directed at emerging types of public professionals adopting new online persona formations. These are extensions of the types of questions of validity that have been applied to traditional domains of professionalism as they move online: lawyers and doctors face the same types of interrogation over the value of their personas as eSports stars and YouTubers. This is because professionals are required to operationalize themselves via the same presentational platforms that have come to service new domains of professionalization through the mediatization of the self, bringing new types of public spaces to light via digital networks. To be professional, and to have a professional persona, is to recognize the real monetary as well as the reputational value of online persona. It means investing in monitoring the flow of relevant and popular social media practices, such as having a carefully curated Facebook profile or personal Web domain and moderated blog comments. Professionals, as their public identities migrate into social media spaces, are expected to manage the value of the online self expertly and to incorporate media flow into their micro-publics with strategic competence.

Value

Social media contributes to the discourse of value by privileging the interpersonal and organizing social life around the public presentation of the self. As a result, individuals have become pragmatic and strategic in the incorporation of an "intercommunication ethos" (Marshall 2016, p. 77), and thereby making the personal and the private the engine and fuel of online culture. The shift toward a highly managed public persona is one which Hannah Arendt (1958) forecast as democracy's lost division, where we no longer valorize the separation of public and private, but rather service their enfolding. The aspiration for visibility is the new center of online activity that once cherished anonymity above all else as the liberating democratic potential of the Web (Barlow 1996). Memes, virality, and spreadable media are now esteemed in the processes of circulation and repetition that have come to define the undertaking of an online identity. Through replication and recirculation, personas form out of serialization that is not merely predicated on humorous, political, or esthetic conditions, but active connections and the labor of appropriation, remix, and constancy. The cultural condition of the intensified focus on the construction and management of a public self as an employee (or potential hire), as a student, a patient, a fan, a peer, or a colleague, recognizes that the value of persona is precarious and conditional on forces often outside of the individual's control.

Celebrity helps to reveal the real potential economic and monetary aggregate of persona value, which Currid-Halkett (2010, pp. 23–45) identifies as "celebrity-residual": the idea that public individuals can possess value in their appearance, sentiments, and statements. The celebrity residual is not possessed by all celebrities, and some are more charged than others. Politicians, musicians, socialites, and movie stars, for example, attract extra attention to details of their personal lives than science commentators or business magnates. The personal lives of Kanye West, Taylor Swift, and Justin Bieber draw more attention and have a greater extra-personal dimension, according to Currid-Halkett, than tech-entrepreneurs like Elon Musk, Larry Page, or Mark Zuckerberg.

The notion of celebrity capital (Driessens 2013) is another important way of understanding the methods that celebrities deploy to accrue value via the movement across different media. Kim Kardashian West is one of the most followed celebrities on Instagram and is able to leverage her audience on that site to earn up to half a million dollars per endorsement campaign. Activities that can be found in her Instagram and other social media platforms are replicated in her mobile app game "Kim Kardashian: Hollywood," which generated

$1.6 million in revenue in the five days following its launch and stayed the fifth highest-grossing game on Apple's App Store for 2014 (Wortham 2014). The interconnections between the game, social media activity, and physical public presence have taken on a new prominence, but their strengths, consistency, and relative value are still at the experimental stage for most of us who are not celebrities. Twitch.TV is one platform investigating the connections between the qualitative and the quantitative accumulations of value in the production of online cultural activity. Purchased by Amazon in 2014 for USD970 million, Twitch.TV is a live streaming site (Weinberger 2016). Originally designed for gamers, Twitch has branched out into the live streaming of cooking, chat shows, and the creative arts, from painting and sculpting, to digital music creation and glass blowing. Twitch streamers are experimenting with individual structures of labor, patterns of work, and replicating older media forms, establishing novel social media habits, and developing new fields of activity and influence. In the process, Twitch streamers are generating new areas of cultural intermediation that produce real monetary value that has been able to support individuals in forming full-time media careers. Twitch also reveals new phenomena of social media, such as the resurgence of interest in the career and media products of painter Bob Ross who died in 1995. In launching Twitch Creative, Twitch.tv streamed a marathon of Bob Ross's "The Joy of Painting" over nine days which attracted 5.6 million viewers and led Netflix to add Ross's series *Beauty Is Everywhere* to their ongoing lineup (Porter 2015).

Agency

The notion that a persona is a mask, enacted by individuals, construed by media, and constructed across communications systems, is a means for understanding the role and value of intention and agency. Personas are mutable public masks worn, not to obscure our features, but to present them to the world. For many, the deployment of a persona is deemed to be superficial, a frontage that is as flimsy as appearance. And yet personas have the ability to move us, to convey great affect, and embody deeply held personal values. Agency is an important concept for understanding the way that personas express, incorporate, resist, and embody power (Marshall 2013).

That power can be seen in the totemic caricature, such as Starbucks investing in Free Trade Coffee or Bono's Red campaign which provides funding for AIDS education and treatment in Africa through the consumer-driven activities of corporate branding. The pedagogical power of celebrities is undeniably important as stars like Scarlett Johansson and Sandra Bullock actively campaign to combat AIDS in Africa, or Angelina Jolie, whose preemptive mastectomy derived from genetic knowledge, promoted breast cancer awareness is powerful evidence of agency. These are private individuals whose power and degree of agency can affect change in the world (see Marshall and Barbour 2015).

At a small scale, but no less devoid of agency, is the individual who campaigns for indigenous rights on Instagram, campaigns against council corruption via Facebook, or who uses Twitter to speak back to politicians criticizing refugees. These "channels" or platforms are often occupied and filled with less politically charged interests; nonetheless this does not reduce their potential to act as platforms from which to actively engage in the world. This level of political engagement and agency is evident through the use of online platforms by teenagers following the Parkland school shooting in Florida in February 2018. Their online agency allowed the politics of gun control to move well beyond the usual dead-end political divides that have left the issue unresolvable.

The origins of the agency involved in persona production can be traced to the development of consumer cultures where products are used to perform and produce identity and what Giddens (1992) has described as a postmodern identity, but which existed well before the turn to postmodernism. Online personas are the deliberately produced public displays of the self through which we connect with others, and the agency – or "will-to agency" (Marshall 2016) – enacted in their production demonstrates a desire to connect, to perform the self in particular ways for particular networks of others involved in work, leisure, or both. In addition to considering the agency of those who produce personas in networked online spaces, we can also consider the *persona as agent*. Bruno Latour's use of agency in his actor-network theory (ANT) and its reformation of what defines the social is also useful to understand how persona is an agent (Latour 2005, pp. 53–62). For Latour, agents and their ability to act as some form of intermediary in our world is relational and they can include objects as much as human-related intermediaries (pp. 63–86): persona – as a strategic and constructed formation – builds its power and influence in relation to other online agents which include other personas as well as the intercommunication industry that services the construction of these entities. The online persona operates to produce value in a variety of relational ways, including connecting and organizing networked micro-publics, sharing and publicizing interactions with other personas, and collecting and storing a massive quantity of data about how the person or people creating the persona travel around the Web.

It is necessary to always consider the limits of agency in relation to persona creation. The affordances and constraints of the platforms on which the personas are produced will necessarily limit the types of presentation of self that are enacted, while wider ideological structures are similarly constraining. The choices offered through drop-down lists of identifiers for gender, sexuality, employment, education, and so forth all variously encourage particular types of personas to be produced. Other constraints, such as image orientation or aspect ratio preferences (as with Snapchat and Instagram), or character limits (as with Twitter), also quite directly influence the type of personas that can be produced on different platforms. Social norms of particular spaces also impact on the types of personas being produced, down to what levels of aggression are acceptable to display: Rösner and Krämer (2016) found that social group norms had a larger impact on the aggressive nature of a space than whether a space was anonymous or identifiable. These affordances and constraints, both technological and social, could be perceived to be undermining users' agency in the types of personas they produce online. However, "our capacity to reflect actively on our own subjectivity becomes a part of the way we understand ourselves" (Barbour 2015, p. 59), and so it is possible that the activity of producing online persona actively contributes to a sense of agency in the production and performance of self in both corporeal and digital settings.

Studies of celebrity imply a kind of individual agency as much as a social and industrial construct (Marshall 2013) and have helped to challenge existing conventions around subjectivity stemming from the work of poststructuralists. In particular, celebrity studies speaks back to Foucault's (1991 [1974]) concept of the "author function," which describes a systematic process connected to ideas of power, authenticity, and legality rather than an attempt to engage with the agency of those who produce ("author") texts. Rather, celebrity is described in relation to versions of the self that are used by the entertainment industry to support commercial and creative goods, or to provide a nodal point in a network of fans and followers: the celebrity's audience or micro-public was produced through and by their deliberately created public self in ways that preempted (and served as a model for) the production of self online by a diversity of social media users. Celebrities who contravene the rules, performing versions of the self which broke down existing expectations of appropriate behavior, were in effect opening up the possibilities in terms of what we can expect to know, or share, about ourselves and others.

Reputation
How we understand the value of the personas we produce can influence how we understand the significance of the reputation that those personas maintain. Specific characteristics may be emphasized in online spaces to produce a particular type of reputation and research conducted into the aspirational nature of online identity performances (Wittkower 2014; Yurchison, Watchravesringkan, and McCabe 2005; Zhao, Grasmuck, and Martin 2008) appears to support the idea that aspirational characteristics often are eventually subsumed into an offline persona, even if they were initially exaggerated in their online form. Although we do not see online personas as necessarily "fake," this could be understood through the adage of "fake it 'til you make it." Personas are both the cause and effect of reputation, and can be created with a sense that the desired reputation *already exists* prior to its actual development. This projecting concept of what persona entails intersects comfortably with the idea that persona is a form of "hoped-for possible" self (Yurchison, Watchravesringkan, and McCabe 2005), where the persona operates as a part of a "hoped-for, possible reputation."

Along with the idea that personas are performed or enacted for the purpose of producing a reputation sits an expectation that we are actively managing the production of an online reputation. This can be translated into an expectation that we will all engage in the labor of managing our personas, thereby seeking and continually reinforcing a public identity that operates within the predominant capitalist culture that, as explored by De Botton (2004) and even more comprehensively investigated by Origgi (2018), has been developing over the past two centuries. It may be that the interconnected networks of friends and followers that are central to the intercommunicative online reputation are important not solely in terms of quantity and numbers (and therefore reach) but also quality; networks (and individuals within those networks) differ in their power and influence. Convincing others of one's own power and influence may also be central – this may even be essential to the development of a positive reputation, as illustrated by Alice Marwick (2013) in her study of Silicon Valley culture. Persona's reputation migrates and morphs into a brand in this highly economically charged environments and becomes a pathway for commodifying elements of the self that ultimately may prove one's value to others.

Prestige

The final component of our VARP approach to reading persona is "prestige"; that is, the capacity for an individual to gain widespread respect and admiration through the development and use of a persona. Whereas reputations can be good or bad, prestige is by definition a positive affirmation of someone's value. As noted in Moore, Barbour, and Lee (2017), the significance of a persona's prestige is that it draws together value, agency, and reputation, and is in fact reliant on those dimensions in its production. We can also consider prestige as scaled. For example, a persona with a smaller micro-public may garner a lower level of prestige than a persona with a wider reach; however the positive affirmation is received, whether from a larger or smaller group, may be understood as having greater personal value for the person who created it particularly if those bestowing the prestige have greater value for the one producing the persona: "producing an active, engaging persona for an admiring extended family group may be felt as prestigious for one person, while another may be dissatisfied with an enthusiastic Twitter following numbering in the hundreds of thousands" (Moore, Barbour, and Lee 2017, p. 7).

The processes involved in the production of prestige itself are also worth considering. As mentioned above, scale can have an impact, as the number of friends and followers one has will help to both indicate and drive the value that a persona has within a system. However, more than this scale is the vital role that interpersonal connections holds. "Liking," "sharing," and/or "favoriting" all demonstrate the respect and admiration other users have for the content and substance of a persona. It is through these practices of connecting processes that one's prestige becomes visible. And, importantly, these visible indications of value *must* be produced by others. For many users, this makes the development of a persona's prestige dependent on one's micro-public and suggests a real need to produce useful, interesting, and shareable content for an audience. For others, including the personas of many politicians, celebrities, brands, and other possible social media influencers, those markers of value might be produced en masse through purchasable likes, shares, retweets, and so forth, or by engaging with bots. In a sense, outsourcing the production of prestige markers in this latter way works to undermine the process of building prestige at all, as users and micro-publics become increasingly suspicious of high levels of engagement with banal or otherwise questionable content.

Conclusion

In this chapter, we have explored how intercommunication and the industries associated with it have shaped the way that we can think about registers of online persona. We have developed a working lexicon for understanding how the online structures of the interpersonal and highly mediated dimensions of intercommunication have led to a formation of contemporary persona. To conclude our explanation of the registers and the *"per-formations"* (Biddle and Jarman-Ivens 2007, p. 5) of persona, it is important to highlight the political-economic dimension which runs through the constitution of online persona. As Axel Bruns's research has illustrated (see Bruns 2013), there is a quality of "produsage" in the current online economy – a blending of production and consumption that allows the participant – or "user" to employ an older term that described an individual's Internet and Web activity – to have the dual sense of augmenting, transforming, and/or simply sharing online content and information. We have explored this activity in this chapter and have identified the qualities of that work that have an economic dimension. Indeed, it is difficult to think of any of the major platforms that produce our intercommunication environment – for example, Facebook, Twitter, Instagram, Weibo, Wechat, YouTube – and not see that some other economic formation of the public self is emerging. Alice Marwick's pioneering work on the tech scene in Silicon Valley specifically charted this emerging "new economy" individualism (Marwick 2013). Social media has produced a culture of economic aspiration and is expressed through the burgeoning culture of what are usually called "influencers" which has been effectively explored by Alison Hearn and Stephanie Schoenhoff (2016), Florencia García-Rapp (2017), and Crystal Abidin (2015). The persona we have identified with all its complexities is linked very closely to the possibilities and potentials that have often been attached to a neoliberal ethos and identity. This privileging of the individual to make themselves visible for some form of economic value is creating new work and labor economies that push these individuals into imagining themselves as both self-employed and entrepreneurs. Followers and friends in these social media environments are thus not just a sign of influence, but an extended indexical sign of potential promotion and sponsorship of the self by other commercial entities. In the new world of intercommunication, our interpersonal connections are doubly valuable. First, this equally new reconfigured capitalism provides a possible but nonetheless rare model of persona construction that leads to advertising revenue through the platform for the most successful "influencers" with their hundreds of thousands of followers. Second, the exploitation of our activities, relations, connections, words, and emotive communication choices are data property of the platform itself that are combined, reconfigured, sold, and exchanged across and through the intercommunication industry.

Our online personas with their registers of performance of individuality, with their varied and elaborate interplay of public, professional, private, and intimate registers are a dueling game of massive interpersonal connections and communication twinned with the ethics of a neoliberal sensibility of value and political economy. What we produce online, what we share and build into micro-publics is never simply a utopian reconstruction of a public self; these activities are at the core of value for this new political economy and a new naturalized culture of being in contemporary culture.

As a 2018 *New York Times* exposé revealed, thousands of people have been drawn to construct and validate their online Twitter identities with literally thousands and, in some cases, hundreds of thousands of fake followers to build, but also maintain and sustain, their economic and cultural value. The fake identities allowed celebrities to claim greater numbers of followers; but equally, corporate influencers, politicians, and many others paid a company named Devumi to produce these fake followers. Along with the industry of social media influencers, we now have a parallel industry of producing (fake) follower numbers for social media influencers (Confessore et al. 2018).

Perhaps we are in the early stages of learning – and exploiting – these extensions of the self into online personas. Our new world of intercommunication, industrialized through platforms, individualized through our activities and investments of time and communication, and endlessly monetized by ourselves, by platforms, and by the movement of now personalized, linked, and resold data is complex. The strategic building of our masks – our personas – lets us negotiate this newly massively mediated, internetworked, individualized, and differently collectivized world.

References

AAP. (2013). Social media sites erode privacy: Study. *The Age* (February, 5). www.theage.com.au/digital-life/consumer-security/social-media-sites-erode-privacy-study-20130204-2dujq.html (accessed October 29, 2018).

Abidin, C. (2015). Communicative ♥ intimacies: Influencers and perceived interconnectedness. *Ada: Gender, New Media, & Technology* 8: 1–16.

Albury, K. (2015). Selfies| selfies, sexts and sneaky hats: Young people's understandings of gendered practices of self-representation. *International Journal of Communication* 9: 1734–1745.

Alexander, J. (2017). As Discord nears 100 million users, safety concerns are heard. *Polygon* (December 7). https://www.polygon.com/2017/12/7/16739644/discord-100-million-users-safety (accessed October 29, 2018).

Arendt, H. (1958). *The Human Condition*. Chicago: University of Chicago Press.

Aziz, S., Shamim, M., Aziz, M.F., et al. (2013). The impact of texting/SMS language on academic writing of students – what do we need to panic about? *Linguistics and Translation* 55: 12884–12890.

Barbour, K. (2015). Registers of performance: Negotiating the professional, personal and intimate in online persona creation. In: *Media, Margins and Popular Culture* (ed. E. Thorsen, H. Savigny, J. Alexander, et al.), 57–69. Basingstoke: Palgrave MacMillan.

Barbour, K. and Marshall, P.D. (2012). The academic online: Constructing persona through the World Wide Web. *First Monday* 17 (9). http://firstmonday.org/ojs/index.php/fm/article/view/3969 (accessed October 29, 2018).

Barlow, J.P. (1996). A declaration of the independence of cyberspace. Electronic Frontiers Foundation. https://www.eff.org/cyberspace-independence (accessed March 5, 2017).

Baym, N.K. (2010). *Personal Connections in the Digital Age*. Cambridge: Polity Press.

Biddle, I. and Jarman-Ivens, F. (2007). Introduction: Making masculinity in popular music. In: *Oh Boy! Masculinities and Popular Music* (ed. F. Jarman-Ivens), 1–17. New York: Routledge.

boyd, d.m. (2014). *It's Complicated: The Social Lives of Networked Teens*. New Haven, CT: Yale University Press.

boyd, d.m. and Ellison, N.B. (2007). Social network sites: Definition, history, and scholarship. *Journal of Computer-Mediated Communication* 13 (1): 210–230. https://doi.org/10.1111/j.1083-6101.2007.00393.x.

Bruns, A. (2013). Exploring the pro-am interface between production and produsage. In: *Frontiers in New Media Research* (ed. F.L.F. Lee, L. Leung, J.L. Qiu and D.S.C. Chu), 241–258. Hoboken: Taylor & Francis.

Butler, J. (1999). *Gender Trouble Tenth Anniversary Edition*, 2e. New York: Taylor & Francis.

Chandler, D. (2007). *Semiotics: The Basics*. New York: Taylor & Francis.

Clough, P.T., Frank, A., and Seidman, S. (eds.) (2013). *Intimacies: A New World of Relational Life*. Abingdon: Routledge.

Codell, J.F. (2003). *The Victorian Artist: Artists' Lifewritings in Britain, ca. 1870–1910*. New York: Cambridge University Press.

Confessore, N., Dance, G.J.X., Harris, R., et al. (2018). The follower factory. *The New York Times* (January 27) Online edition. https://www.nytimes.com/interactive/2018/01/27/technology/social-media-bots.html (accessed October 29, 2018).

Currid-Halkett, E. (2010). *Starstruck: The Business of Celebrity*. New York: Farrar, Straus and Giroux.

Davenport, T.H. and Beck, J.C. (2001). *The Attention Economy: Understanding the New Currency of Business*. Boston, MA: Harvard Business School Press.

De Botton, A. (2004). *Status Anxiety*. New York: Vintage Books.

Donath, J. (2007). Signals in social supernets. *Journal of Computer-Mediated Communication* 13 (1): 231–251. https://doi.org/10.1111/j.1083-6101. 2007.00394.x.

Driessens, O. (2013). Celebrity capital: Redefining celebrity using field theory. *Theory and Society* 42 (5): 543–560. https://doi.org/10.1007/s11186-013-9202-3.

Driscoll, C. and Gregg, M. (2010). My profile: The ethics of virtual ethnography. *Emotion, Space and Society* 3 (1): 15–20.

Edwards, J. (2013). Advertisers are sabotaging competitors' brands to get them banned from Reddit. *Business Insiders* (July 30). http://www.businessinsider. com/advertisers-cheating-on-reddit-with-fake-spam-upvotes-2013-7/?r= AU&IR=T (accessed October 29, 2018).

Farrer, G. (2010). When it comes to online privacy, Facebook is not the only problem. *The Sydney Morning Herald* (June 3). www.smh.com.au/technology/ blogs/untangling-the-web/when-it-comes-to-online-privacy-facebook-is-not-the-only-problem-20100603-x2cr.html (accessed October 29, 2018).

Foucault, M. (1991 [1974]). *The Foucault Reader* (ed. P. Rabinow). London: Penguin Books.

García-Rapp, F. (2017). Popularity markers on YouTube's attention economy: The case of Bubzbeauty. *Celebrity Studies* 8 (2): 228–245. https://doi.org/10.1080/19 392397.2016.1242430.

Gibbs, M., Meese, J., and Arnold, M., et al. (2015). #Funeral and Instagram: Death, social media, and platform vernacular. *Information, Communication & Society* 18 (3): 255–268. https://doi.org/10.1080/1369118X.2014.987152.

Giddens, A. (1992). *The Transformations of Intimacy*. Cambridge: Polity Press.

Goffman, E. (1959). *The Presentation of Self in Everyday Life*. New York: Anchor Books.

Goggin, G. (2011). Ubiquitous apps: Politics of openness in global mobile cultures. *Digital Creativity* 22 (3): 148–159.

Gregg, M. (2011). *Work's Intimacy*. New York: Wiley.

Habermas, J. (1987). *The Theory of Communicative Action: Lifeworld and System: A Critique of Functionalist Reason*, vol. 2. Boston: Beacon Press.

Hearn, A. and Schoenhoff, S. (2016). From celebrity to influencer: Tracing the diffusion of celebrity value across the data stream. In: *A Companion to Celebrity* (ed. P.D. Marshall and S. Redmond), 194–212. Malden, MA: Wiley Blackwell.

Hillis, K. (2009). *Online a Lot of the Time: Ritual, Fetish, Sign*. Durham, NC: Duke University Press.

Hollien, H. (1972). On vocal registers. *Communication Sciences Lab Quarterly Progress Report 10.1.* University of Florida, Communication Sciences Laboratory.

Illouz, E. (2007). *Cold Intimacies: The Making of Emotional Capitalism.* Cambridge: Polity Press.

Katz, J.E. and Crocker, E.T. (2015). Selfies| selfies and photo messaging as visual conversation: Reports from the United States, United Kingdom and China. *International Journal of Communication* 9: 1861–1872.

Lambert, A. (2013). *Intimacy and Friendship on Facebook.* Basingstoke: Springer.

Latour, B. (2005). *Reassembling the Social.* Oxford: Oxford University Press.

Lundby, K. (ed.) (2014). *Mediatization of Communication.* Berlin: De Gruyter Mouton.

Marshall, P.D. (2010). The promotion and presentation of the self: Celebrity as marker of presentational media. *Celebrity Studies* 1 (1): 35–48. https://doi.org/10.1080/19392390903519057.

Marshall, P.D. (2013). Personifying agency: The public–persona–place–issue continuum. *Celebrity Studies* 4 (3): 369–371. https://doi.org/10.1080/19392397.2013.831629.

Marshall, P.D. (2014). Seriality and persona. *M/C Journal* 17 (3): http://journal.media-culture.org.au/index.php/mcjournal/article/view/802 (accessed October 29, 2018.

Marshall, P.D. (2015). Intercommunication and persona: The intercommunicative public self. *The International Journal of Interdisciplinary Studies in Communication* 10 (1): 23–31.

Marshall, P.D. (2016). *The Celebrity Persona Pandemic.* Minneapolis: University of Minnesota Press.

Marshall, P.D. and Barbour, K. (2015). Making intellectual room for persona studies: A new consciousness and a shifted perspective. *Persona Studies* 1 (1): 1–12.

Marwick, A.E. (2013). *Status Update: Celebrity, Publicity, and Branding in the Social Media Age.* New Haven, CT: Yale University Press.

Marwick, A. and boyd, d. (2011). To see and be seen: Celebrity practice on Twitter. *Convergence: The International Journal of Research into New Media Technologies* 17 (2): 139–158. https://doi.org/10.1177/1354856510394539.

Middleton, C.A. (2007). Illusions of balance and control in an always-on environment: A case study of BlackBerry users. *Continuum* 21 (2): 165–178. https://doi.org/10.1080/10304310701268695.

Moore, C. and Barbour, K. (2016). Performing the networks of domestic and public persona. *Persona Studies* 2 (1): 1–11.

Moore, C., Barbour, K., and Lee, K. (2017). Five dimensions of online persona. *Persona Studies* 3 (1): 1–11. https://doi.org/10.21153/ps2017vol3no1art658.

Origgi, G. (2018). *Reputation: What It Is and Why It Matters* (trans. S. Holmes and N. Arikha). Princeton: Princeton University Press.

Oxford Online Dictionary. (2018). s.v. intimate. https://en.oxforddictionaries.com/definition/intimate (accessed November 12, 2018).

Papacharissi, Z. (2010). *A Networked Self: Identity, Community and Culture on Social Network Sites*. New York: Routledge.

Perrin, A. and Jiang, J. (2018). A quarter of Americans are online almost constantly. *Fact Tank. Pew Research Centre*. http://www.pewresearch.org/fact-tank/2018/03/14/about-a-quarter-of-americans-report-going-online-almost-constantly (accessed October 29, 2018).

Poletti, A. and Rak, J.(eds. (2014). *Identity Technologies Constructing the Self Online*. Madison: University of Wisconsin Press.

Porter, M. (2015). 5.6 million people watched Bob Ross's Twitch marathon. *IGN* (November 9). http://au.ign.com/articles/2015/11/09/56-million-people-watched-bob-ross-twitch-marathon (accessed October 29, 2018).

Rainie, L. and Wellman, B. (2012). *Networked: The New Social Operating System*. Cambridge, MA: MIT Press.

Roberts, J. and Koliska, M. (2017). Comparing the use of space in selfies on Chinese Weibo and Twitter. *Global Media and China* 2 (2): 153–168.

Rösner, L. and Krämer, N.C. (2016). Verbal venting in the social web: Effects of anonymity and group norms on aggressive language use in online comments. *Social Media + Society* 2 (3): https://doi.org/10.1177/2056305116664220.

Salihefendic, A. (2015). How Reddit ranking algorithms work. *Medium*. https://medium.com/hacking-and-gonzo/how-reddit-ranking-algorithms-work-ef111e33d0d9#.19p2m5ag2 (accessed March 6, 2017).

Schmidt, J.-H. (2013). Practices of networked identity. In: *A Companion to New Media Dynamics* (ed. J. Hartley, J. Burgess and A. Bruns), 365–374. Chichester: Wiley.

Senft, T.M. (2008). *Camgirls: Celebrity and Community in the Age of Social Networks*. New York: Peter Lang.

Shadbolt, N., Berners-Lee, T., and Hall, W. (2006). The semantic web revisited. *IEEE Intelligent Systems* 21 (3): 96–101.

Smeby, J.-C., Johnsson, E., Nerland, M., et al. (2011). Editorial. *Professions and Professionalism* 1 (1): 1–3. https://doi.org/10.7577/pp.v1i1.140.

Turner, G. (2010). *Ordinary People and the Media: The Demotic Turn*. London: SAGE.

Van Alstyne, M. and Brynjolffson, E. (2005). Global village or cyber-balkans? Modeling and measuring the integration of electronic communities. *Management Science* 51: 851–868.

Weinberger, M. (2016). Amazon's $970 million purchase of Twitch makes so much sense now – it's all about the cloud. *Business Insider Australia* (March 17). www.businessinsider.com.au/amazons-970-million-purchase-of-twitch-makes-so-much-sense-now-its-all-about-the-cloud-2016-3?r=US&IR=T (accessed October 29, 2018).

Williams, D. (2007). The impact of time online: Social capital and cyberbalkanization. *Cyberpsychology and Behaviour* 103: 398–406.

Wittkower, D.E. (2014). Facebook and dramauthentic identity: A post-Goffmanian theory of identity performance on SNS. *First Monday* 19 (4): http://www.ojphi. org/ojs/index.php/fm/article/view/4858 (accessed October 29, 2018).

Wortham, J. (2014). Kim Kardashian, an unlikely mobile video game hit. *The New York Times* (July 30) Online edition, sec. Bits – Business, Innovation, Technology, Society. https://bits.blogs.nytimes.com/2014/07/30/kim-kardashian-an-unlikely-mobile-video-game-hit/?_r=0 (accessed October 29, 2018).

Wroe, D. 2013. Cyber criminals target mobile users, social media. *The Sydney Morning Herald* (February 8). www.smh.com.au/digital-life/consumer-security/cyber-criminals-target-mobile-users-social-media-20130208-2e2nv.html (accessed October 29, 2018).

Yurchisin, J., Watchravesringkan, K., and Brown McCabe, D. (2005). An exploration of identity re-creation in the context of Internet dating. *Social Behavior and Personality: An International Journal* 33 (8): 735–750.

Zhao, S., Grasmuck, S., and Martin, J. (2008). Identity construction on Facebook: Digital empowerment in anchored relationships. *Computers in Human Behavior* 24 (5): 1816–1836. https://doi.org/10.1016/j.chb.2008.02.012.

4

The Collective Constitution of Public Persona

This chapter is designed to pick up on three key concepts central to the collective constitution of public persona – micro-publics, digital objects, and surveillance – and further expand on their contribution to the everyday presentation of the public self online. As introduced in the previous chapter, a "micro-public" results from the collective constitution of public persona. This chapter will begin with micro-publics as an example of the way digital networks have transformed the relations between individuals and audiences into collectives. The chapter then turns to the rise of microcelebrities and draws on the work on Senft (2008, 2013) and Marwick (2015a, 2015b) to explore the relationship between micro-publics and acts of contemporary celebrification, seen in the powerful expression of agency by the social media influencers documented by Abidin (2015). The chapter then turns to examine the rise of surveillance capitalism and the activities of "persuasive" technologies, drawing on the work of Tufekci (2014) and Zuboff (2015). The chapter theorizes the underlying power of surveillance technologies as belonging to the qualities of digital objects, which we extrapolate using Morton's (2010, 2013) notion of the hyperobject and Serres' (1982, 1995) understanding of quasi-objects. We build on Gehl's (2011) description of "autosurveillance" to propose a qualification of quantified self data, not as an act of liberation, but a reclaiming of agency through the work of persona formation.

Micro-publics

Geographer Ash Amin (2002) deployed the term "micropublics" to describe the experience of the negotiations of difference such as the structural effects of national rules of citizenship on ethnicity in urban environments. John Keane used the term "micro-public spheres" in 1995 to differentiate between micro-, meso- and macro-public spheres in his updating of the Habermasian definition

Persona Studies: An Introduction, First Edition. P. David Marshall, Christopher Moore, and Kim Barbour.

of public life. Keane's account sees the "micro" as operating at the subnation-state level, compared to the "meso-public" sphere of the nation-state framework and the global dimension of the supranational "macro-public" life. Keane considers micro-public spheres to be a vital part of any social movement which utilizes public means of communication to challenge and transform the dominant codes of everyday life. The book club, the church, the clinic or the quiet chat over a drink between friends are examples of micro-public spheres where individuals come together to "question the pseudo-imperatives of reality and counter them with alternative experiences of time, space and interpersonal relations" (Keane 1995, p. 10). Contained within the formation of each micro-public sphere is the potential for mediatization and coalescence as a political event, such as a protest for LGBTQI rights or disputing local "fracking" for coal seam gas. Paradoxically, suggests Keane, micro-public spheres draw strength from their latency:

> Although they appear to be "private" acting at a distance from official public life, party politics, and the glare of media publicity, they in fact display all the characteristics of small group public efforts, whose challenging of the existing distributions of power can be effective exactly because they operate unhindered in the unnewsworthy nooks and crannys of civil society. (Keane 1995, p. 10)

Keane gives the example of young video game audiences as a developing micro-public sphere, who were very much in their nascent state in the mid-1990s, which shows the degree to which the Internet has collapsed the distinction between the micro and the macro by enabling micro-dimensionality and agency of video game audiences on a global scale, as can be seen by the large number of views and fans that *Minecrafters* or *Fortnite* fans, for example, currently command on YouTube.

It is clear from both these preceding exemplars that the term "micro-public" is no longer feasible as a means to consider the individual as part of a singular public or mass audience, if it ever was. Instead, we conceptualize persona as a multiplicity of nodes in a distributed network, where each node connects to a different micro-public comprised of members who frequently overlap via media platforms or communication services. An individual's public persona is not the sum of the nodes, but it does involve a collection of multiple micro-publics. A persona is not Facebook, Instagram, *plus* Twitter, but rather Facebook, Instagram, *as well as* Twitter; each instance of the user's persona has a micro-public of its own, comprised of groups of members which may overlap. A public persona is therefore communal; it connects to the micro-publics of others, forming clusters, and has multiple micro-publics of its own, which complicates its shape and presentation.

The increased importance of micro-publics is a result of the phenomenon of self-publicity that has followed the implicit and explicit reportage of the public self in news media and journalistic formats. Where self-publicity was previously the near-exclusive tool of celebrities and public figures, it has expanded into a normalized activity for a significantly increased percentage of the population. This has been made possible by "technologies of the social," the term Marshall (2013c) uses to describe the social networking applications associated with Internet, computers, and mobile connections that resemble previous apparatuses such as television, print, and radio, but enable more people to draw together their own audiences and collective experiences. Social mediation has repositioned the individual, privileging them in the chain of communication, enabling elaborate intercommunication and adding a mundane dimension to self-publicity as a requirement of the contemporary configuration of the public self.

Marshall (2014) understands that micro-publics identify a new duality: that followers and friends are often connected to a range of content that is produced by an individual in a "private" network, which is simultaneously updated and regularly responded to in the tradition of broadcast and print media forms of address that is typical of a traditional "public" audience. The relationship between new and old media paradigms is not simply of one replacing the other, but a growing system of mutual interdependence and support. Legacy media outlets can provide substantial boosts to an individual's micro-public, in terms of followers who are fans *and* potential detractors. Social media microcelebrities can inversely direct their micro-publics toward legacy media broadcasts and reciprocally boost audience numbers and traditional ratings figures. As mentioned in the previous chapter, micro-publics are not "micro" because of their scale, but because they do away with the larger requirements of self-publicity, such as the accouterments of the studio system. Although politicians and celebrities still rely on a staff to support their self-publicity, the individual can replicate the activities of self-promotion without the attendant need for specialized photographers, managers, representatives, aides, and so on. This has the added effect of reducing gatekeepers and returning a serious degree of agency to individual self-publicity. Blogs, YouTube channels, Twitter, Instagram feeds, and Facebook pages do not require millions or billions of audience members to be considered "successful," although they have the inbuilt capacity to scale and reach such numbers. YouTube content creators of all sizes rely on their micro-publics across multiple social media platforms to drive attention to their videos, which compensates for the lack of traditional media advertising models. The growing importance of micro-publics has increased the value of sites like Patreon, which offer crowdfunding management services permitting micro-publics to directly determine the funding of individual projects and therefore shape the direction that content production takes. Successful

YouTubers, such as Philip DeFranco, the SciShow, and Australian travel video producers, LaVagabonde, have taken to Patreon to directly involve fans and followers in the production of new content, as changes to the YouTube advertising model has negatively impacted on their established business and content-generating practices.

Microcelebrity

The concept of micro-publics helps us to describe how public persona is configured differently in the twenty-first century. The highly developed use of presentational media forms such as social media relies on the appropriation, remix, remediation, and recirculation of already established representational elements. As such, a significantly different cultural politics is emerging from that supported by purely representational media forms, which produced the essence of celebrity culture in the twentieth century. Theresa Senft (2008) used the term "microcelebrity" in her book *Camgirls*, which documented the strategies employed by individuals seeking to increase their micro-publics and expand attention to their online activities across video streaming platforms, blogs, and other social media. In Senft's view, microcelebrities replicate the conditions of celebrification through narratives of self-publicity without requiring the overt manipulation of previously privileged representational media forms. The celebrities' embrace of the selfie, the blog or vlog, and the self-presentation without the "perfect hair" (Senft 2008, p. 16) or other representational fixtures of celebrity, meant that microcelebrities also gained new degrees of recognition and audiences of followers than was previously possible. Alice Marwick (2015a) describes the difference between celebrity and microcelebrity as the difference between being and doing; in the broadcast era celebrity was something people *were*, while in the Internet era microcelebrity is something that people *do*. Social media enables microcelebrity as a highly successful self-presentational technique directed toward multiple micro-publics, each with its own set of fans and followers consuming the strategic intimacy of the microcelebrity practitioner (Marwick 2015a; Marwick and boyd 2011; Senft 2013).

The rise of microcelebrities and the success of the creative, niche, and paratextual industries (Consalvo 2007; Gray 2010; Genette 1997) includes a new generation of social media "influencers" and media performers from YouTubers, Twitch.TV streamers, and Instagrammers to cosplayers and eSports stars, and this field is still emerging. These participatory content producers have continued to reimagine the combined practices of consumption and production in their capacity to embody individual experimentation with the "transformative power of consumer culture" (Marshall 2010, p. 37). Celebrification, advertising, branding, and publicity all provide a continuity of discourse around the representation of the self for public consumption as presentational media. The more affective dimensions of these modes of communication are absorbed within the presentational media processes of individuals whose patterns of sharing on and between social networks have redefined audiences and the economies of reputation:

> self-production is the very core of celebrity activity and it now serves as a rubric and template for the organisation and production of the online self which has become at the very least an important component of presentation of yourself to the world. (Marshall 2010, p. 39)

Marwick (2015b, p. 334) suggests that even when microcelebrities have small numbers of followers, they are able to "inhabit the celebrity subject position" by the very same social techniques of politicians, actors, musicians, models, and athletes. The "micro" nature of microcelebrity practice also means a hyper-attenuation to audience, which depends on the social context of the practitioner's performance, such as the eSports YouTube star or the fitness and fashion guru on Instagram. Microcelebrities are able to attract hundreds of thousands, even millions, of fans and followers via their specific niche, and be entirely successful and self-sustaining without ever gaining attention from the mainstream (Marwick 2015b). Often when microcelebrities, like YouTube star PewDiePie, for example, enter into the mainstream it is as the source of criticism and derision (Dredge 2015).

Some microcelebrities are so entirely successful in their chosen niche, they become digital "Influencers," a term Crystal Abidin (2015) uses, inspired by Katz and Lazarsfeld's (2009) notion of "personal influence," to describe social media users who attain a following through the "textual and visual narration of their personal lives and lifestyles" (Abidin 2015). Influencers are microcelebrities who monetize their fan-base through highly personalized promotional product and service placement. Social media influencers, argues Abidin (2016, pp. 2–3), are microcelebrities who use selfies to gain both monetarily and through self-actualization by endorsing products and services to their micro-publics, comprised of followers whom they engage with through ritual strategies of interpersonal communication. Abidin draws on Goffman's concept of the backstage of identity performance, suggesting that influencers deliberately reveal a highly constructed and strategic view of their "private" life in order to give their micro-public audience an authentic sense of access to the personal and otherwise inaccessible areas of their lives, revealing that which traditional celebrities have typically considered as "off limits" to the press and public.

Surveillance Capitalism and Persuasive Technologies

The earliest intimation of an Internet-based society, in which anonymity provided the basis for a society of freedom, expression and collective participation ended with the rise of social media and the "real name" policies of sites like

Facebook. We are now part of an interconnected society unlike any before it, but with this ubiquitous connectivity, we observe similar patterns of fragmentation and the influential steering toward monopolization that comes with all varieties of capitalism. It is not paranoia to be concerned with the role that social media is playing as a potentially powerful fulcrum around which new methods of persuasion and authoritarian control are being leveraged. The fear that social media is enabling a new kind of "surveillance capitalism" recognizes the power of persuasive technologies, particularly algorithmically determined advertising, and the social media business model that works to capture attention and convince us to click on advertising, sign up to micro-publics, and ultimately make political choices and economic decisions. Social media are persuasive technologies because they function to persuade us to act in particular ways and to replicate commercially desirable behaviors. This is not a new phenomenon as persuasion has always been the long-term goal of advertising, but it is now occurring through new media technologies and new social media platforms that are different to the communication technologies of the past. Broadcast media technologies look like wood-block printing compared to the speed and effectiveness of the industrial printer when placed alongside powerful algorithmically driven applications like machine learning. Facebook and Instagram advertising uses vast reserves of data coupled with machine learning to produce extremely efficient results. This new business model is entirely dependent on surveillance techniques and the use of data generated by the billions of users of social media, mobile media, and Internet-based media. Unlike previous generations where broadcast media figures were shared with the public in terms of ratings and audience numbers, social media data is more asymmetrical, because while users are being surveilled, the only result that is observable is the advertising being targeted back at them. Even hits, views, favorites, and liking information cannot be considered transparent due to the large numbers of bots and other methods targeting these tallies in order to "game" the system.

Social media data is more powerful than traditional audience data because it contains many more markers of identity. This data can be used to infer information about users that they do not disclose directly, through computational inference and psychological profiling. Critics, such as Sam Harris (2017), Zeynep Tufekci (2014), and Shoshana Zuboff (2015), fear that this is the perfect setup for authoritarianism because it allows for corporations and governments to survey populations and to shape their opinions both at scale and individually. Unlike traditional media programs of persuasion, social media targeting is hyper-individualized, going unnoticed because users do not see the messages being targeted to them as being different to other users. By contrast, media campaigns in newsprint, radio, and television can be seen by audiences outside of the targeted group. The infrastructure of authoritarianism is being constructed by social media platforms that are popular digital technologies.

Digital media co-opts our attention and directs the labor of investment, argues Tristan Harris, author of the app and website Time Well Spent, where he claims that social media is a medium where every element is organized around delivering user attention to advertisers. This would not be overly problematic for well-adapted and savvy users, but the majority of users have not yet developed sophisticated means for retaining autonomy and agency in the face of these designs and the decisions that they require us to make. These platforms have been used to make positive changes in people's lives: Twitter, Facebook, and Reddit, for example, have all been used productively as platforms for social change, from improving the lives of refugees to increasing the visibility of animal welfare groups, organizing fundraising, or advocating for legal representation for the homeless. However, to be active in the civic world, argues Tufekci (2014), means using these platforms that are not designed with social justice in mind and engaging with the world on their terms. Similarly, those in power are looking to utilize these platforms to effect control through persuasion. Governments and corporations benefit from the negative consequences of these platforms, specifically the formation of "filter bubbles" (Pariser 2011) in which users are less likely to access information which challenges their worldview and established personal philosophies.

One of the problems emerging in and from our digitally mediated lives is that culturally we have shifted to a world where we are endlessly reinforcing our own worldview based on our captured attention and what confirms that worldview. Another problem is the degree of control, or at least persuasion, that these new forms of advertising enable. Social media are a form of surveillance technology, because they provide a means for collecting information that can be partnered with command and control functions in order to enact persuasion from a distance. For example, Cambridge Analytica, is a British strategic communication company, whose services include data mining and analysis, which claimed to be able to apply behavior science methodologies to identify and target users with highly focused media messages (Osborne 2018). The firm employed data from 50 million Facebook users to deliver pro-Trump campaign material during the 2016 US elections. The company specifically targeted individuals based on "psychographic" reading of their personalities, identified using machine-learning techniques, which the company claimed were more effective than traditional advertising (Ingram 2018):

> With this model, Cambridge Analytica could say that it was identifying people with low openness to experience and high neuroticism. But the same model, with the exact same predictions for every user, could just as accurately claim to be identifying less educated older Republican men. (Hindman 2018)

Although the techniques employed by such firms are simply demographic analysis and personality tests, the advanced machine-learning algorithms being used have access to an unprecedented amount of information, offer a tremendous speed of calculation, and present a higher degree of accuracy than has been previously feasible.

Mobile media, such as smart phone cameras, are also a partnering between surveillance technologies and command and control techniques, because they are ideally suited for inferring details about users from information that is not intentionally shared, such as metadata, which includes geolocative information. Images, shared via social media, are also convenient for determining a user's psychological profile, through algorithmic analysis. Wang and Kosinski (2018) claim that "deep neural networks," a form of machine learning, can be used to determine information about sexual orientation from a single image, using an analysis of facial structure in a repository of images, such as selfies shared via Facebook. However, Agüera y Arcas, Todorov, and Mitchell (2018) argue that the current generation of facial recognition is flawed due to sensitivities to head position and facial expression: "Therefore – at least at this point – it's hard to credit the notion that this AI is in some way superhuman at 'outing' us based on subtle but unalterable details of our facial structure."

Although the technology might not be perfect at this stage, it is clear that research is being conducted on the use of social media data to algorithmically determine a user's sexual orientation, their political preferences, or religious affiliation and other psychological and behavior preferences not directly shared by the user. What is unique to this situation is that these unannounced user qualities can then be silently targeted by advertisers, political groups, and government agencies in ways that are manipulative at a level previously unknown to media advertising. Problems arise when asymmetric surveillance capitalism meets authoritarianism and high-order capitalist manipulation, which results in laser-like precision of effective targeting, without being public and drawing attention to itself. Tristan Harris (2016) asks what happens when billions of people are subject to the steering influence of social media, an influence based on the algorithmic analysis of the surveillance of the largest repository of user information ever created.

Persona as Digital Objects

In order to provide a response to the rise of surveillance capitalism and to support the diversity of strategies for engagement with persuasive technologies, we draw on the concept of embodied virtuality and the posthuman as described by N. Katherine Hayles (2008) and take a critical approach inspired by Latour's (2005) view of the nonhuman actor as a mediator. Under surveillance capitalism then, a persona can be understood as a sociotechnical assemblage of publicly presented digital objects and their networks of connections. This means that digital objects connected to the public profiles of users have micro-public constellations all of their own. A persona is therefore the visible summary of the user's relations with the digital objects that lend their subjective properties to create an identifiable figure. Online personas are built up from the networks of digital objects: from profile images, links, tags and likes, to passwords, IP addresses, and the other digital detritus of everyday networked activity. All digital objects are comprised of multiple other objects even if they are only entries in a database (see Harman 2011). A persona "operator" is not always the same as the persona "referent"; organizations and institutions often require multiple operators to manage their social media activity and information flow. Individuals may manage elements of a corporate persona, but rarely are they its owner: this structure of ownership is more likely determined and regulated by intellectual property laws, terms of service contracts, and end user license agreements attached to the conditions of the platform's use. The extent of the state and corporate surveillance apparatus embedded inside these techno-legal systems means that we should be more attentive to considering the multiple ways in which we are always within constant negotiation with digital objects, and yet many of these objects come unbidden and unknowingly to us.

Individuals, even when empowered with freedom of information (FOI) rights, can only access and add meaning to a very small percentage of the digital objects that make up their public persona and are typically distanced from the value extraction mechanisms generated by their ubiquity and scale. Despite these limitations, these users are still capable of enacting qualitatively different relationships and organization of the self in terms of the public, private, and intimate registers of persona (Marshall 2010). Take, for example, the change of the relationship between the celebrity and the "candid" or unrehearsed image. Once the exclusive domain of the professional studio photographer or the paparazzo, a captured photo of the celebrity is now only as far as the nearest smart phone. The formerly rigid boundaries of celebrities, carefully constructed screen selves, became permeable on contact with the networks of everyday users whose devices may be required for their surveillance functions at any moment. This content may then be incorporated within the "official" modes of persona performance through the intercommunicative channels of fans and followers.

Due to the proximity of content flow enabled by the platforms of the web and the density of available mobile phone cameras in metropolitan and urban locations, the role of the paparazzo has diminished. The success of fan-produced images has contributed to new conversational celebrity spaces, such as Reddit, which helped to popularize the impromptu celebrity photo and the celebrity selfie. The identity politics are not equal, however, as Emily van der Nagel and Jordan Frith observed: women are more likely to be subject to inequitable dimensions of power and social pressure, even when intimate content is publicly volunteered (Van der Nagel 2013; Van der Nagel and Frith 2015).

Digital Objects, Micro-publics, and Hyperobjects

Meme culture, made possible by ubiquitous image editing software and Internet connections, is part of new media activity organized around repurposing and remediating content to create new digital objects. Memes are highly intercommunicative digital objects that mediate and move between the types of interpersonal communication integrated within persona presentations (Marshall 2015). Shifman (2014, p. 18) views memes as digital objects that:

> Although they spread on a micro basis, their impact is on the macro level: memes shape the mindsets, forms of behavior, and actions of social groups.

Building on the work of Richard Dawkins in *The Selfish Gene*, Shifman argues that memes have three attributes that make them central to the participatory culture of the Internet:

> (1) a graduation propagation from individuals to society, (2) reproduction via copying and imitation, and (3) diffusion through competition and selection. (Shifman 2014, p. 18)

The participatory media cultures (see Jenkins 2006; Raessens 2005) of transmedia texts, such as *Star Wars, My Little Pony, Pokémon*, and the Marvel universe, similarly rely on the provision of intercommunication processes and the participatory remediation and sharing of content to actively make new micro connections and create alternative pathways into the macro layers of experience of blockbuster movies, televisual series, and video games. The concept of intercommunication recognizes a transposed public sphere where the interpersonal is "overlaid onto its flows of interpretation and meaning from the outset" (Marshall 2010, p. 42). As such, the concept of intercommunication helps us to map both the flow and modulation of presentational media practices largely organized around the remediation of legacy representational media, such as the creation and spread of memes. It is the mimetic qualities of digital objects that fundamentally enable the interpersonal, individualized, indexical, and internetworked components of intercommunication, as outlined in the previous chapter.

Persona studies is distinguished from prior forms of understanding the self through attending to the intercommunicative properties of digital objects. An online persona is a melange of digital objects. A social media profile, for example, is a collection of multiple types of digital objects, from personal information (names, dates, relationships, employment history, preferences, and locations) to images and video, and networks of connections to people, places, services, and applications. In this way, personas share some characteristics with what Timothy Morton (2013) describes as hyperobjects. Hyperobjects are "hyper" in their relation to some other entity; for example, atmospheric radiation is a hyperobject that results from nuclear testing (Morton 2013). Hyperobjects, says Morton, are sticky: they adhere to beings, but are nonlocal in their manifestation. The Facebook profile is a hyperobject because it is massively distributed in time and space. Facebook profiles cling to their users as a means for others to surveil them. Potential employers, parents, former partners, police, and government agencies can all make use of the way that Facebook profiles allow each of them to follow users around. Even when a user attempts to "hide" from their Facebook profile, the app leaves Internet "cookies" in the user's browser cache to monitor their online habits and movements across the web. Deactivated Facebook accounts spring into life when the user attempts to click on a Facebook link and, because they exist in Facebook's data-centers around the world stored on multiple Blu-Ray discs, it is almost impossible to physically "delete" all instances of the user profile.

Personas are hyperobjects because they are networks of digital objects with algorithmic components that have esthetic and affective properties that enfold us in a series of interobjective and subjective fields of relations and therefore they share a "lameness," to use Morton's term, in their fragility and asymmetry. There is an extensive degree of lameness to digital objects and our online personas which are created with technologies that endlessly surveil us but are distanced from us as objects that are owned, regulated, and modulated by institutions whose civic and corporate obligations to us as individuals are obfuscated. That is not to argue that personal monitoring and surveillance of these relations is without merit as the technologies of surveillance are individually redeemable and we, as humans, have always employed them for recording and reviewing our thoughts, processes, and activities. We have made prodigious use of self-surveillance techniques, including diary and letter writing, video cameras and photography, audio recording devices, and maps. However, the objects' ability to inform on both our public and private lives was previously limited to physical access and protected by restrictions and controls over material scarcity and the exclusive rights to reproduce: all these qualities begin to dissolve on contact with the digital.

Corporations like Apple, Amazon, Sony, Google, and Microsoft are characteristically hyperobjects; they are only corporations as much as they are devices, offices, warehouses, companies, brands, techniques, and personas. Each manifest at the macro and micro levels, having local interactions and global effects that are part of their individual user's physical and digital experience of networked activity. These hyperobjects exist in symbiosis with the digital objects that operate as nodes in the micro-publics of our personas (see Marshall 2013a, 2013b). The networked manifestation of persona as a digital and physical fragmentation of identity is a continuing performance of assembly, thus micro-publics are never static or stable. Micro-publics involve complex arrays of digital and material objects and their connections resemble networks of consumption, for example, participation in the intercommunication of popular and public figures: this might involve retweeting a celebrity's tweet about an upcoming film in order to perform a fan persona within an individual micro-public. A persona may be viewed holistically as a collection of micro-publics and observed over time as a series of digital traces, but it is never a complete identity frame, thus highlighting its lameness as a hyperobject. The persona in its entirety cannot be perceived, as is the case with any object, because it always recedes beyond the limited means in which we can interact with it (Harman 2011).

A persona is a collective interface to a range of micro-publics, it is a temporary summary of all the intercommunication between the digital objects attached to the referent, from user profiles, web cookies, and database entries, to other connections, processes, and interactions distributed across multiple locations and systems. Yuk Hui (2012) considers digital objects as objects that are composed of data and formalized by schemes of ontologies that can be generalized as metadata, in contrast to natural objects (such as the biological organism) and technical objects (tools). At the level of programming, digital objects are text files; further down the operating system they are binary codes; at the level of circuit boards they are signals generated by values of voltage and the operation of logic gates, and so on into the subatomic and quantum realms (Hui 2012, p. 387). Personas are hyperobjects because, as Morton (2010) explains, they disclose interobjectivity. Interobjectivity consists of interrelationships: by definition, a user's social media profile (see boyd and Ellison 2007) articulates a list to other users; it does not exist in isolation. A persona is an interobjective system and is made up of hardware and software, cameras, batteries, memory chips, data points, selfies, memes, and birthday videos that are also a part of, what Morton calls, the mesh (2010). The mesh is an important metaphor because it draws attention to both the hard edges and nodes of a network, but also the soft holes and gaps that appear in our social, scientific, and psychic "domains": "Each point of the mesh is both the center and edge of a system of points, so there is no absolute center or edge" (Morton 2010, p. 28). Because of the interconnectedness of the micro-publics of persona, there is no dividing line between where one user's micro-public begins and another's ends:

> A mesh consists of relationship between crisscrossing strands of metal and gaps between the strands. Meshes are potent metaphors for the strange interconnectedness of things, an interconnectedness that does not allow for perfect, lossless transmission between information but is instead full of gaps and absences. (Morton 2013: location 1467 of 4946)

This returns us to Bruno Latour's notion of the oligopticon from Chapter 2 and Facebook's bright light that only shines on the surface of the persona being lit; the surface does not reveal to the user the metadata of Facebook messenger app conversations, the psychometrics of Twitter hashtag use, or the metadata of Instagram images. This suggests that digital objects offer opportunities for comparatively different phenomenological modes of investigation and expression for describing an individual's persona, paying attention to the mesh and the relationships between code, data, and performance, where metadata serves as artificial memory. Facebook users are increasingly downloading their personal data, gaining access to a summary of likes, reactions, searches and location histories, and can even view deleted posts and comments (Matsakis 2018), and while these collections are pointing toward the interobjectivity of the individual persona, they are not the entirety of it, which is located both in the items and in the gaps between them. The interobjectivity of the digital objects, organized in micro-publics, provides the surface on which the persona can be perceived.

Digital Object and Autosurveillance

Digital objects are not bound entirely by the controls of their human referents or operators. Once in the public realm, digital objects can be directed but are already expert navigators of the systems to which they are native, mute and resolute as golems:

> In the poem, The Golem, Borges tells the story of the rabbi of Prague, who after long permutations, is able to find the key word that holds the secret life. A monster, the Golem, is created, but the process involves more than magic words. Borges describes how the rabbi modelled his puppet and then trained him, like an ancient virtual pet, into the mysteries of Time and Space. The Golem learned very much like an expert of the system. (Frasca 2003, p. 233)

Neither objects nor subjects, a persona is comprised of digital objects that, like golems, stand in and act for us as "quasi" objects with subjective qualities. Michel Serres's (1995) account of quasi-objects describes the relations between elements in a system, like the parts of an engine, the fonts in a meme, the characters in an alphabet, or the forces between human and nonhuman actors in a network. Our relationships and social bonds, argues Serres (1995, p. 87), would be intangible as vapor, were it not for the contact and contracts between subjects and objects. Objects stabilize our relationships as actors, even as others commodify our activities. The example Serres gives is the ball in a game of football, operating as the "nucleus of organization" and the gravity well around which all forces involved are organized as an intensively amplified signal confined to an extremely local time and space. The ball is a primary object in the game, it is the "sun of a system," where every signal and interaction must pass among its elements and across its vectors of attraction (Serres 1995, pp. 87–88). In the digital environment, however, every object, and every persona, has potential to be the ball.

The online persona is a galaxy of digital objects arrayed in micro-public constellations, competing for attention in a universe of other galaxies. The digital object is a "quasi" object-subject because it is simultaneously more than an object and less than one – it is a metaphor before it is a thing:

> The quasi-object is not an object, but it is one nevertheless, since it is in the world; it is also a quasi-subject, since it marks or designates a subject who, without it, would not be a subject. (Serres 1982, p. 225)

It is the quasi-objective and quasi-subjective lending capacities of digital objects that expand the tense field of relations with other objects and their ability to inform on our being. The qualities of digital objects equally lend themselves to quantification and qualification but are typically formatted for the former over the latter.

Surveillance techniques that provide quantified data about the persona, reformatting activity as a holistic unit via algorithmic analysis without the layers of qualified annotation that accompanies them, are at risk of being misinterpreted at best and used directly against us at worst. The use of metadata without permission and the contextual experience of its generation is always negative as the digital object cannot speak for the individual without the annotation required to modulate its signal and provide the golem with its voice. A key example is the use of wearable personal monitoring technologies including the FitBit, Garmin, and Jawbone-branded activity trackers. Responding to the warnings over the dangers of the predetermining frameworks of self-surveillance devices, Nafus and Sherman's (2014) ethnography of the quantified self (QS) movement identifies that users strategically adopt "soft resistances" to dominant modes of data formatting, that are "always necessarily partial" and "firmly rooted in many of the same social logics that shape the categories they seek to escape" (Nafus and Sherman 2014, p. 1785). First described by Gary Wolf and Kevin Kelly, the QS movement has focused on the use of personal tracking devices to provide a new perspective on the activity of the self and the objects of data that upon reflection may produce personal insight (Wolf 2010). Soft resistances are practices that users of these devices employ to modulate the persona signal as they are typically confined within the boundaries of predetermined categories, not to simply reject this remote and anticipatory control, "but as a productive way of creating an alternative mode of working with data" (Nafus and Sherman 2014, p. 1791).

The soft resistances of QS users produce a self that is both subject of, and subject to, digital objects which partially collapse the measurer and the measured in ways that Nafus and Sherman see, at the very least, as an attempt to escape Foucault's understanding of the disciplined body as it is oriented toward a hierarchically deterministic ordering of internalizing normative standards. Small degrees of agency are gained when users are dismissive of authoritative best practices, self-determining the disciplined body "idiosyncratically" and as "sense-makers" whose authority over the input is expressed in the communication of its output as the "narrative self" (Marshall 2014). However, such agency is always contingent on the systems provided, unless open and hackable or otherwise extended in different ways by the user. The failure of the Fitbit brand to enable the qualification of quantification, such as the expression of difference between categories of race and gender, is most telling: not having a function to follow menstrual cycles, for example, despite being popular products used by both males and females, reveals how the idealized user is formatted accordingly to a set of predetermined categories. The persona and micro-public that results from the public presentation of the self via the Fitbit app, for example, is a denial of basic elements of human nature. To address this gap, some apps that track female reproduction, such as Clue, have added application programming interfaces (APIs) to integrate with Fitbit systems; however, this augmentation opens even further the constellation of personal data being co-opted for the expansion of private capital as described by Andrejevic (2007).

In his short essay, "Postscript on Control Societies" (1995), Gilles Deleuze sets out an account of two historical periods. First, is the "disciplinary societies" as observed by Foucault, a result of Westernized modernity, emerging as a function of the rule of sovereigns into the "vast spaces of enclosure." The second is what Deleuze terms as the "societies of control" which are based around what he calls the logics of "modulation" and the "ultrarapid forms of free-floating control" (Deleuze cited in Galloway 2006, p. 87). Distributed networks and cybernetic power that operate under the endless threat of "indefinite postponement" enable the societies of control, as Mark Fisher observed:

> Education as a lifelong process ... Training that persists for as long as your working life continues ... Work you take home with you ... Working from home, homing from work. A consequence of this "indefinite" mode of power is that external surveillance is succeeded by internal policing. Control only works if you are complicit with it. (Fisher 2009, pp. 22–23)

The trend of social mediatization and intercommunication between all online platforms and services have pushed an identifiable change in the way surveillance has become a component of subjectivity in contemporary culture. The utopian and dystopian discourses accounting for these technologies and practices are attempts to wrestle with the clear cultural change that is an ongoing result of the new dynamics of communication between humans and machines. This has simultaneously produced an immense and exhilarating empowerment and its inverse, a growing sense of powerlessness and constant manipulation. What is missing in these polar oppositions that work within a technologically deterministic paradigm is a means for clearly articulating how both these elements are involved in the production of a public self that recognizes the performative dimensions of network citizenry, as consumer and politically, socially, and behaviorally active individual, as both audience member and content producer, and other characteristics of the public self that are qualitatively different to the discrete categories of identity permitted by social media profiles.

Mann, Nolan, and Wellman (2003) found potential for empowering subjective agency with the concept of "sousveillance," the inverse panopticism of surveillance that can be used to help observe those in authority. They argue for considering sousveillance as a form of "reflectionism," using technology to reflect its own bureaucratic organizational logic to confront the reality of situations and approaches to power, technologies, and performances that are integrated into technology and society:

> Reflectionism becomes sousveillance when it is applied to individuals using tools to observe the organizational observer. Sousveillance focuses on enhancing the ability of people to access and collect data about their surveillance and to neutralize surveillance. (Mann, Nolan, and Wellman 2003, p. 332)

Though it need not be overt, organized, or explicitly directed, sousveillance is a model of noncompliance and interference that relies on tactics of blocking, distorting, masking, refusing, and counter-surveillance functions by contaminating algorithmic analysis (Nafus and Sherman 2014). Respondents to Nafus and Sherman's study engaged in activities designed to dilute and reduce the accuracy and reliability of the data being collected. Such tactics are employed when using an activity tracker to record and analyze categories of activity that sit outside those defined by the manufacturer and app designer. Sexual activity, for example, is only rendered clearly by the user adding self-annotations to data that would otherwise be overlooked or reclassified. An anonymous Redditor shared with the subreddit /r/dataisbeautiful the visualization of heart rate data generated by a Fitbit while having sex. The application interface for the tracking device on the user's mobile phone only presented limited visual options for displaying the data. Further qualitative meaning was made by the Redditor overlaying comments on the graph, annotating the interpretation of the data for the observers, such as "Condom on," "I'm on top," "Knees give out, Him on Top," "I orgasm!," "He orgasms, I aftershock," and "Take a breather." Another anonymous Redditor created a sexual activity spreadsheet, charting sexual contact and their partner's hormonal cycle, generating a year of data which was graphed and annotated using the image-sharing website Imgur to present a visual analysis of the couple's self-reported "mismatched libidos." The user called on the expertise of the Reddit data analysis community to expand the interpretations of the intimate data in a very public way. The interpreted results quite possibly reinforced the negative normalizing stereotypes of sex and sexual activity that are replications of assumptions based on the consumption of mainstream pornography (see Van der Nagel 2013; Van der Nagel and Frith 2015).

The qualification and transmission of QS data as autobiographical elements of identity presentation serve as a digital dramatis personae; a mapping of a series of connections in the persona's micro-public of relations between public identity of the referent and the performative experience of the operator. The digital quasi-objects of persona connect the presentation of the public self to the imagined self, documented in the activity we call "autosurveillance."

Autosurveillance is the process of adding qualification to quantifiable data, digital objects, and content created as part of persona work. It is more than curation, it is annotation, making sense of the presentation of the public self for an anticipated audience, which includes the self. For instance, visualizing elements of data collected from a wearable device or third-party social media analytic service to assemble a graph, sociogram, or other image captures the "wires" of the persona micro-public "mesh," but it is the user's own annotations, descriptions, and attempts to make sense of the graph that begins to fill in the details that would otherwise be missing or overlooked. An act of persona autosurveillance attempts to expand the field of social relations in a persona micro-public, not as exhaustive topographical survey, but rather as a brief cross section or snapshot of a moment of the networks operation (Moore 2014). For example, a YouTuber sharing their subscriptions and likes with their viewers, and qualitatively detailing their personal response to the quantified data, is a good example of persona autosurveillance. In this type of response to quantitative information, the user takes control, reasserting agency over surveillance technologies. This is, however, not necessarily a liberation, because only the very surface layers are available to respond to direct inquiry, and much of the operations of the digital objects that comprise our persona online remain as a Latourian "black box" (see Latour 2005), obfuscated beyond our reach. However, we can access and interpret the top layers of data in such a way as to provide clues into the operation of others.

The visualization and interpretation of tweets, hashtags, and friend/follower relationships, and other social media activity, enables a user to modulate and transform the signals of the digital object involved in performance of the self in space and time. As Gehl (2011) argues, the activity of visualizing and sharing personal data is not meant to resist the homogeneity of mass individualized culture and intangible labor, but nonetheless this activity offers a means for the user to better understand the conditions under which they operate and consume products that are owned and controlled by corporations. The availability of publicly provided data via APIs means the persona micro-public can be sampled, visualized, annotated, and presented in what Zizi Papacharissi calls the "networked self":

> Consistent with practice of everyday expression and conversation, the form of connectivity on Twitter engages that which is privately imagined and collectively aspirational, personally defined and politically directed, individual motivated and civically inclined, phatically presented but also reflective of a deeply personal ideology of a networked self. (Papacharissi 2015, p. 101)

The performance of a networked self involves the acquisition and application of skill and style in public presentation that is self-broadcast to an anticipated potential set of heterogeneous audiences. The result can be surveilled as "small data" sets, capturing details of personal micro-publics which are revealing when coupled with the phenomenological contribution of an autobiographical response to the surveillance techniques involved.

In Gehl's (2011) critique of the "three-part logic" of personal branding literature, he identifies "autosurveillance" alongside the Deleuzian notion of the "dividual," Eva Illouz's (2007) concept of emotional capitalism, and Andrejevic's (2007) concerns over the digital enclosure. Gehl concludes that those individuals who brand themselves by adopting the logic of capitalism build their human capital without contributing to "an antidote for life in precarious times." Employing the terminology of autosurveillance to refer to the attention of the individual's image and others' perception of it, Gehl warns that it would be "unwise to easily dismiss this activity" because the personal branding advocates have "demonstrated a savvy understanding of our current mediascape and are simply making a rational choice to fully incorporate themselves into the network" (2011). Like Gehl, we understand that autosurveillance is not an unproblematic socially progressive use of social media, but argue at the same time, like Poster (2007, p. 136), that such activity has what de Certeau (1984) saw in all acts of consumption: a personal and local potential for resistance and a means for individuals to cope with the ever-increasing uncertainty of everyday life.

Branding, editing, staging, framing, lighting, narrativizing, pacing, nondiegetic cues, including music and text, and so on, are all fixtures of representational media that have been remixed within the presentational processes of persona assembly. Similarly, the structures of the web and the surveilling features of digital objects formed in the practices of everyday activity are incorporated in the distribution of this presentational content via multiple channels of intercommunication between the micro-publics of social media sites, between the new media and legacy media industries, and by the flows and connections of the networks that are obscured by the demands of commerce and security. Social media is made immensely useful and powerful by the techniques of surveillance, which have been incorporated within the user's presentation of the public self, particularly those in the niche, creative, and paratextual industries of blogging, podcasting, and video streaming. While it is necessary to draw attention to the potential for surveillance to enact harm via extensions of the command and control operations of the cybernetic interactions of the web (directing, controlling, and channeling user behaviors), the dystopian narrative is not one that has gained significant attention from users who are in the processes of negotiating a set of parameters and practices for dealing with digital objects in the ways that successfully manage their appearance to others.

The dystopian nightmare future of "uberveillance," Michael and Michael's (2010) term used to warn of the dangers of "tagging" humans with location tracking microchips, is Roger Clarke's (1999, p. 498) concept of "dataveillance" taken to an anticipated logical extreme. The individual, is already, in a very real sense, caught up in the pervasive circulation of digital objects with links and metadata pertaining to personal information enabling perpetual real-time tracking. The hyperobjectivity of digital objects makes them an always locatable entity that are subject to the informing powers of the network; take, for example, the "tag," including deliberate and aggressive mis-tagging and hashtag trolling behaviors, location tagging apps, and the ability to tag others, which suggests that we are already experiencing a heavily socially distributed "uberveillance." Unless we are permitted opportunity to respond to the tag without penalty, we are always subject to it, and other individuals and organizations who are capable of calling on these digital objects that identify and commodify us. Deborah Lupton (2016, p. 5) employs the concept of "lively data" in order to highlight the vitality of personal digital information that is generated continuously and capable of producing new forms of knowledge and insights into people bodies and selves.

Conclusion

In this chapter we have unpacked the dynamics of persona as the collective micro-public formations of digital objects in conjunction with concerns over state and corporate surveillance. We argue that by bringing together the social network analysis of small data with the phenomenological layers associated with the qualitative understanding of digital objects in a persona formation, it is possible to survey the new connections, overlaps, regions of similarity, difference, distance, and gaps and the unequal relations of power in the performance of a persona archive. Persona autosurveillance affords the potential of soft resistance utilizing small data as a response to the one-sided benefits of closed big data aggregated algorithmic analysis. It is not until we assemble the networked experience and annotate and present it for ourselves and for others that we begin to seek out a balanced field of relations with digital objects and corral them within meaningful narratives of the self.

An act of persona autosurveillance might be as simple as developing the digital literacy to search for oneself via a web search or setting up a Google Alerts notification, expanding our attention to the view of how we may appear to others. A more targeted investigation of the spread of a particular personal or private image across the web might start with Google image search and move on to Facebook's range of first and second party autosurveillance features. Both freely provided and for-fee services enable users with the means to visualize and annotate the role of digital objects in their micro-public formations that result from their movement across multiple networks. The Twitter API is very useful for collecting small data sets for visualizing recent micro-public activity and tweets are valuable contributions to the public sphere of communication; but their retention has been limited and access is extremely restricted in order for Twitter itself to monetize and maximize their potential value. The quasi-object–subject network that is produced is decentering as it requires locating the center of identity performance outside ourselves: it requires putting ourselves "on the line," online, to invest in our personas and to risk those public identities and the scrutinies they bring in order to enjoy the substitution of identity between object and subject (Serres 1982, pp. 228–299).

Personas require constant and consistent attention to navigate overlapping danger zones of activity. The digital objects that result from our computational and networked entanglements take on the properties of Serres's notion of the joker and the parasite: they bend and change direction and force independent connections, subliminating fixity under identity play. As with the photocopier and the zine, the VHS tape and the fan vid, the magnetic audio recording and the mix tape, vinyl and hip-hop, the affordances of these objects are wild cards, making possible new tokens of exchange. Personas are loose agents that affect users in unpredictable ways and point to the hypermediatization and intercommunication of the digital quasi-object–subject: a signal of identity that is always moving, non-unitary, circulating, trending via micro-public distribution, and becoming individual when stopped and isolated under attention as a particular node of expression.

References

Abidin, C. (2015). Micromicrocelebrity: Branding babies on the Internet. *M/C Journal* 18 (5): http://journal.media-culture.org.au/index.php/mcjournal/article/view/1022 (accessed July 15, 2017).

Abidin, C. (2016). "Aren't these just young, rich women doing vain things online?": Influencer selfies as subversive frivolity. *Social Media and Society* 2 (2): 1–17.

Agüera y Arcas, B., Todorov, A., and Mitchell, M. (2018). Do algorithms reveal sexual orientation or just expose our stereotypes? *Medium* (January 11).

https://medium.com/@blaisea/do-algorithms-reveal-sexual-orientation-or-just-expose-our-stereotypes-d998fafdf477 (accessed October 29, 2018).

Amin, A. (2002). Ethnicity and the multicultural city: Living with diversity. *Environment and Planning A* 34: 959–980.

Andrejevic, M. (2007). Surveillance in the digital enclosure. *The Communication Review* 10 (4): 295–317.

boyd, d. and Ellison, N.B. (2007). Social network sites: Definition, history, and scholarship. *Journal of Computer-Mediated Communication* 13 (1): 210–230.

Clarke, R. (1988). Information technology and dataveillance. *Communications of the ACM* 31 (5): 498–512.

Clarke, R. (1999). Person-location and person-tracking: technologies, risks and policy implications. *Proceedings of the 21st International Conference on Privacy and Personal Data Protection*, Hong Kong (September 13–15). http://www.rogerclarke.com/DV/PLT.html (accessed September 2, 2015).

Consalvo, M. (2007). *Cheating: Gaining Advantage in Video Games*. Cambridge, MA: MIT Press.

de Certeau, M. (1984). *The Practice of Everyday Life* (trans. S. Rendall). Berkeley: University of California Press.

Dredge, S. (2015). YouTube star PewDiePie responds to "haters" over $7.4m annual earnings. *The Guardian* (July 8). https://www.theguardian.com/technology/2015/jul/08/youtube-pewdiepie-annual-earnings-responds-haters (accessed November 12, 2018).

Fisher, M. (2009). *Capitalist Realism: Is There No Alternative?* Ropley: Zero Books.

Frasca, G. (2003). Simulation versus narrative: Introduction to ludology. In: *The Video Game Theory Reader* (ed. M.J.P. Wolf and B. Perron), 221–235. New York: Routledge.

Galloway, A. (2006). *Gaming: Essay on Algorithmic Culture*, Electronic Mediations, vol. 18). Minneapolis: University of Minnesota Press.

Gehl, R.W. (2011). Ladders, samurai and blue collars: Personal branding in Web 2.0. *First Monday* 16 (9): http://firstmonday.org/ojs/index.php/fm/article/view/3579 (accessed October 29, 2018).

Genette, G. (1997). *Paratexts Thresholds of Interpretation*. Cambridge: Cambridge University Press.

Gray, J. (2010). *Show Sold Separately: Promos, Spoilers, and Other Media Paratexts*. New York: New York University Press.

Harman, G. (2011). *The Quadruple Object*. Winchester: Zero Books.

Harris, S. (2017). #78 – Persuasion and control: A conversation with Zeynep Tufekci [podcast]. *Waking up with Sam Harris*. https://www.samharris.org/podcast/item/persuasion-and-control (accessed October 29, 2018).

Harris, T. (2016). How technology is hijacking your mind — from a magician and Google design ethicist. *Thrive Global*. https://journal.thriveglobal.com/how-technology-hijacks-peoples-minds-from-a-magician-and-google-s-design-ethicist-56d62ef5edf3 (accessed October 29, 2018).

Hayles, N.K. (2008). *How We Became Posthuman: Virtual Bodies in Cybernetics, Literature, and Informatics.* Chicago: University of Chicago Press.

Hindman, M. (2018). How Cambridge Analytica's Facebook targeting model really worked – according to the person who built it. *The Conversation* (March 30). https://theconversation.com/how-cambridge-analyticas-facebook-targeting-model-really-worked-according-to-the-person-who-built-it-94078 (accessed October 29, 2018).

Hui, Y. (2012). What is a digital object? *Metaphilosophy* 43 (4): 380–395.

Illouz, E. (2007). *Cold Intimacies: The Making of Emotional Capitalism.* Cambridge: Polity Press.

Ingram, D. (2018). Factbox: Who is Cambridge Analytica and what did it do? Reuters (March 20). https://www.reuters.com/article/us-facebook-cambridge-analytica-factbox/factbox-who-is-cambridge-analytica-and-what-did-it-do-idUSKBN1GW07F (accessed October 29, 2018).

Jenkins, H. (2006). *Convergence Culture.* New York: New York University Press.

Katz, E. and Lazarsfeld, P.F. (2009). *Personal Influence: The Part Played by People in the Flow of Mass Communications.* New Brunswick, NJ: Transaction Publishers.

Keane, J. (1995). Structural transformations of the public sphere. *The Communication Review* 1 (1): 1–22. https://doi.org/10.1080/10714429509388247.

Latour, B. (2005). *Reassembling the Social: An Introduction to Actor-Network-Theory.* London: Oxford University Press.

Lupton, D. (2016). *The Quantified Self.* Cambridge: Polity Press.

Mann, S., Nolan, J., and Wellman, B. (2003). Sousveillance: Inventing and using wearable computing devices for data collection in surveillance environments. *Surveillance and Society* 1 (3): 331–355.

Marshall, P.D. (2010). The promotion and presentation of the self: Celebrity as marker of presentational media. *Celebrity Studies* 1 (1): 35–48.

Marshall, P.D. (2013a). Personifying agency: The public–persona–place–issue continuum. *Celebrity Studies* 4 (3): 369–371.

Marshall, P.D. (2013b). Persona studies: Mapping the proliferation of the public self. *Journalism: Theory, Practice & Criticism* 14 (7): 153–170.

Marshall, P.D. (2013c). Recognition culture [blog]. *Persona Studies.* http://dro.deakin.edu.au/view/DU:30057246 (accessed October 29, 2018).

Marshall, P.D. (2014). *Celebrity and Power: Fame in Contemporary Culture,* 2e. Minneapolis: University of Minnesota Press.

Marshall, P.D. (2015). Intercommunication and persona: The intercommunicative public. *The International Journal of Interdisciplinary Studies in Communication* 10 (1): 23–31.

Marwick, A.E. (2015a). Instafame: Luxury selfies in the attention economy. *Public Culture* 27 (1): 137–160.

Marwick, A.E. (2015b). You may know me from YouTube: (Micro-)Celebrity in social media. In: *A Companion to Celebrity* (ed. P.D. Marshall and S. Redmond), 333–350. Hoboken, NJ: Wiley.

Marwick, A.E. and boyd, d. (2011). I tweet honestly, I tweet passionately: Twitter users, context collapse, and the imagined audience. *New Media & Society* 13 (1): 114–133.

Matsakis, L. (2018). What to look for in your Facebook data and how to find it. *Wired* (March 28). https://www.wired.com/story/download-facebook-data-how-to-read (accessed October 29, 2018).

Michael, M.G. and Michael, K. (2010). Towards a state of überveillance. *IEEE Technology and Society Magazine* 29 (2): 9–16.

Moore, C. (2014). Screenshots as virtual photography: Cybernetics, remediation and affect. In: *Advancing Digital Humanities: Research, Methods, Theories* (ed. P.L. Arthur and K. Bode), 141–160. Basingstoke: Palgrave Macmillan.

Morton, T. (2010). *The Ecological Thought*. Cambridge, MA: Harvard University Press.

Morton, T. (2013). *Hyperobjects: Philosophy and Ecology after the End of the World*. University of Minneapolis: Minnesota Press.

Nafus, D. and Sherman, J. (2014). Big data, big questions: This one does not go up to 11: The quantified self movement as an alternative big data practice. *International Journal of Communication* 8: 1784–1794.

Osborne, H. (2018). What is Cambridge Analytica? The firm at the centre of Facebook's data breach. *The Guardian* (March 19). https://www.theguardian.com/news/2018/mar/18/what-is-cambridge-analytica-firm-at-centre-of-facebook-data-breach (accessed October 29, 2018).

Papacharissi, Z. (2015). *Affective Publics: Sentiment, Technology and Politics*. New York: Oxford University Press.

Pariser, E. (2011). *The Filter Bubble: How the New Personalized Web Is Changing What We Read and How We Think*. Harmondsworth: Penguin Books.

Poster, M. (2007). The secret self: The case of identity theft. *Cultural Studies* 21 (1): 118–140.

Raessens, J. (2005). Computer games as participatory media culture. In: *Handbook of Computer Games Studies* (ed. J. Raessens and J. Goldstein), 337–388. Cambridge, MA: MIT Press.

Shifman, L. (2014). *Memes in Digital Culture*. Cambridge, MA: MIT Press.

Senft, T. (2008). *Camgirls: Celebrity and Community in the Age of Social Networks*. New York: Peter Lang.

Senft, T. (2013). Microcelebrity and the branded self. In: *A Companion to New Media Dynamics* (ed. J. Hartley, J. Burgess and A. Bruns), 346–354. Oxford, UK: Wiley Blackwell.

Serres, M. (1982). *The Parasite* (trans. L. R. Schehr). London: Johns Hopkins University Press.

Serres, M. (1995). *Genesis* (trans. G. James and J. Nielson). Ann Arbor: University of Michigan Press.

Tufekci, Z. (2014). Engineering the public: Big data, surveillance and computational politics. *First Monday* 19 (7): http://firstmonday.org/article/view/4901/4097 (accessed October 29, 2018).

Van der Nagel, E. (2013). Faceless bodies: Negotiating technological and cultural codes on reddit gonewild. *Scan: Journal of Media Arts Culture* 10 (2): http://scan.net.au/scn/journal/vol10number2/Emily-van-der-Nagel.html (accessed October 29, 2018).

Van der Nagel, E. and Frith, J. (2015). Anonymity, pseudonymity and the agency of online identity: Examining the social practices of r/Gonewild. *First Monday* 20 (3): http://firstmonday.org/article/view/5615/4346 (accessed October 29, 2018).

Wang, Y. and Kosinski, M. (2018). Deep neural networks are more accurate than humans at detecting sexual orientation from facial images. *Journal of Personality and Social Psychology* 114 (2): 246–257.

Wolf, G. (2010). The quantified self. *TEDTalks* [video online]. http://www.ted.com/talks/gary_wolf_the_quantified_self?language=en (accessed October 29, 2018).

Zuboff, S. (2015). Big other: Surveillance capitalism and the prospects of an information civilization. *Journal of Information Technology* 30 (1): 75–89.

Part II

Researching Persona

5

Analyzing Contemporary Persona

Methods to Reveal the Public Version of the Self

Researching persona is a study in the production, dissemination, and exchange of public identity. With very famous public personas, research is focused on finding the moments of consistency and inconsistency in the "personality" presented from public sources and then to determine the sources and origins for the various constructions of identity. However, because much of the production of contemporary persona is involved with much smaller micro-publics, studying persona means that the researcher must somehow enter into these smaller worlds and investigate how the individual produces a public version of him/herself. This chapter provides some of the ways that this analysis can be pursued via phenomenological interview approaches with actual individuals, through participant observation of online activity, and through engaging with the micro-publics connected to these individuals. We also provide examples from action research, where the researcher and participant(s) work together to investigate, build, and nuance personas.

There are some precedents to this research: ethnographic studies of fan communities and biographical and autobiographical research serve as two examples of how researchers have explored the construction of public personas indirectly. The chapter retools these approaches with phenomenologically informed methods to provide some useful ways to analyze contemporary persona. In addition, because persona is very much linked to self-branding and reputation, the chapter also explores how techniques derived from prosopography and its study of historical status can serve as a model for calibrating contemporary reputation and connections in various domains of online culture. Integrated into these analyses is the related research on affect: affect and resonance of persona defines the power and influence of public presentation. The work that has developed to study affect is also applied to the generation of a persona and its associated followers (Gregg and Seigworth 2010).

This chapter starts with the narrowest possible research focus – the self – and works out toward research methods aimed at understanding collections or

Persona Studies: An Introduction, First Edition. P. David Marshall, Christopher Moore, and Kim Barbour.

networks of personas. The methods and methodologies that are included are not exhaustive, nor necessarily limited to the targets we suggest here; rather they are a starting point from which to consider empirical research into the production and performance of the public self.

Researching Ourselves: Reflexivity, Autoethnography, and First-person Action Research

Reflecting on our own persona creation practices, we would argue, is an essential starting point to the development of any persona studies project. By no means are we suggesting that you need to do a focused research project on your own persona in every instance, but rather that personal reflection may be valuable in order to identify and engage with the methods, tactics, strategies, and intentions behind how you and others produce a persona. Taking a more methodological approach to this study could also be valuable, in which case either autoethnography – the focused research on the self in context – or first-person action research – a critical engagement with one's own behaviors and practices – may be suitable; indeed, many methodologies that focus on researcher-as-subject are implicitly or explicitly concerned with issues of identity and self-presentation.

Autoethnography, which Ellis (2008, p. 49) states "refers to ethnographic research, writing, story, and method that connect the autobiographical and personal to the cultural, social, and political," places the researcher within the field of study. This might occur through a framing of the exploration of the research topic through the experiences of the researcher, or by the construction of personal text that then becomes the research data to be analyzed as in traditional ethnography. Autoethnography can be performative, performed, creative, based around writing, images, or scripts, be fragmented or cohesive in form, and be reported in any of these (or alternative) formats. For the purposes of studying persona, you may simply turn your larger ethnographic study inwards, asking yourself the questions you intend to examine within a larger population. Alternatively, you could use an autoethnographic study to provide a basis, comparison, or pilot for a larger project, or as a standalone piece of persona research. Any and all of these are equally valid and useful approaches to the investigation of the self. Because the field of autoethnography is so broad, we will not attempt to provide detailed methods of research, but instead encourage you to read widely the existing literature in preparation for your own project. The work of Adams, Holman, and Ellis (2015), Bochner and Ellis (2016), Ellis (2004), Ellis and Bochner (2000), Hughes and Pennington (2017), and Reed-Danahay (1997) would all present useful starting points in this reading.

First-person action research can also provide a methodological framework with which to engage with one's own persona. In discussing the place of first-person action research within the wider social science field, Reason and Torbert state

> First-person "downstream" research/practice can involve critical examination of day-to-day behavior, drawing on qualities of mindfulness and self-awareness to notice critically the impact of one's actions in the wider world and the congruence or incongruence of one's behavior with purposes or espoused theories (Argyris and Schon 1974; Torbert 1973). Attending to our actions, we can ask whether they are achieving intended outcomes (single-loop feedback); whether they are congruent with the strategy or espoused theory (double-loop feedback); and whether the outcomes are congruent with our purposes (triple-loop feedback). (2001, pp. 17–18)

In this way, a first-person action research project, whether performed alone or with the support of a group of friends or colleagues, could allow you to interrogate your persona in relation to how you are perceived in particular contexts, how you consciously or subconsciously intended to be perceived, and/or whether any of these things are effective in achieving your purpose in creating and presenting the persona. The work of Reason and Torbert (2001), Reason and Bradbury (2008), and Marshall (1999, 2004) are all good starting points for direction and inspiration for conducting first-person action research.

Whether you approach the reflection on your own persona creation as a formal research project, complete with methodological guidance and clearly stated research methods, or as a personal exercise, the examination of your own practice can stand on its own or feed into more outward-focused projects. Even when studying a persona with which you have no personal connection, having a reflexive relationship with how you present yourself will provide some form of starting point in the analysis of the practices of others. More than this, however, you will be engaging in a similar type of self-analysis as your participants will do when participating in primary research, or that you will be performing for them when you do content analysis. To ask of others what you are unwilling to do of yourself is problematic in almost any research situation, but we believe particularly so when studying identity and persona.

Interpreting the Public Self: Interpretative Phenomenological Analysis

As researchers, we often seek to analyze how another person constitutes their public identity. However, our approach to this process needs to take into consideration the types of questions we are asking of the persona(s) we study.

Interpretative phenomenological analysis (IPA) comes from a research tradition that has not generally been closely aligned with media or cultural studies but nonetheless has links with structuralism and poststructuralism that have served as rich sources for the theoretical analysis of contemporary culture. Designed to understand "the individual's personal perceptions of their experiences" (Hinds 2011, p. 193), IPA is an applied research technique that has been associated with psychology and has been particularly successful in interpreting the experience of patients and caregivers in health settings (Smith, Flowers, and Larkin 2009). IPA's theoretical development as a research method draws on phenomenology and hermeneutics, in large part as they have been articulated by Heidegger and Gadamer (Smith, Flowers, and Larkin 2009, pp. 11–29). From Heidegger, we take the view that the production of meaning and reality is interpretative, even fictive, where a consistent and universal meaning or truth cannot exist. If we accept that a persona is a creation "comprised from an interpretation of one's identity and how that identity is made into a public entity" (Marshall, Moore, and Barbour 2015, p. 292), the relevance of a phenomenological approach that conceptualizes all understandings of reality as interpretation becomes clear. Through phenomenology, and more specifically IPA, we can explore persona as a construct, a strategic public discursive formation. From Gadamer's hermeneutics, IPA foregrounds the need to place interpretation within a larger context. Any text – whether a research interview, a media text, or a document – must be placed within its historical and cultural context. Equally, however, the researcher's interpretation must also be contextually located – this interpretation must be acknowledged as stemming from the positions and background of the person doing the interpreting.

Therefore, studying the experience of persona creation through interpretative phenomenological analysis goes beyond the study of behavior – observing what someone does, or asking them to report on their activities – and attempts to engage with what it was like to do something. Here, we offer a methodology designed to allow both researcher and participant (often considered co-researchers, as in action research) to uncover how the process of persona creation is understood by the person who is doing the creating. In applying IPA to persona studies, we must acknowledge first that when studying the personas created by other people, those people are the experts in what that persona is like, and what it is like for them to create it. Rather than attempting to prove or disprove their experience, or even their own relaying of their experience, we instead accept their interpretation of the experience on its own terms. Likewise, we must be clear in identifying our own interpretative processes and findings, marking them clearly as such rather than attempting to make grand claims to truth. An IPA approach would be most appropriate when a researcher has direct access to, and participation from, the creator of the persona that is under exploration. Smith, Flowers, and Larkin (2009, p. 51) emphasize the need for small samples to allow for deep analysis and interpretation, commenting that "IPA studies usually benefit from a concentrated focus on a small number of cases," arguing that more problems occur through a sample that is too large than one that is too small. A case-study approach is also possible, providing the researcher is experienced in qualitative research and analysis; this is less of an issue in persona studies, which seems to be attracting qualitative research scholars from the arts and humanities, than it is for IPA's home discipline of psychology.

To date, IPA has been used within persona studies to analyze the personas of particular fringe artists in their online settings (Barbour 2014; see also Chapter 6 in this volume). In these online locations, artists constructed public profiles, engaged with their followers, and expanded their visibility and presence. Three related research methods were employed in the intensive study of eight artists: an historical analysis of the tropes, stereotypes, and myths associated with artistness; a process of online listening to the personas being created by the research participants (considered co-researchers); and in-depth unstructured one-on-one interviews with the artists themselves. These three research methods worked together to provide comprehensive exploration of the artist's persona as it was experienced in these cases.

In order to locate a persona within its historical context, we must first understand that context. From that vantage point, we can then determine how this context might have influenced the creator's experience. In considering the artist's persona, this consisted of exploring and interpreting the various meanings of the artist historically and in the contemporary context. This kind of interpretation is an acknowledgment that the construction of a public self is always working with the material identity of previous discursive formations of identity. Integrating a phenomenological approach to this kind of research entailed acknowledging the interpretive and malleable dimensions of artistness, and recognizing that individual artists are interpreting these cultural formations in similar patterns, but also idiosyncratically. It is this foregrounding of the interpretative nature of contextual information, in line with Gadamer and the hermeneutic circle, which sets this type of analysis apart from a traditional literature review. When considering a persona as a type of role, such as an artist, a doctor, a soap opera star, a professional athlete, an academic, a mother, or any other identifiable "front," we must as researchers consider how that persona is located within a sociohistorical context of similar personas, and also how both our own and the participant's experience of that context will inform the way that persona is created, experienced, and interpreted.

The second technique used in the study of artists' personas was designed specifically to explore the online persona. Going beyond what would normally be recognized as a content analysis of representations of identity, online material related to the individual artist was collected for interpretation. Using Kate Crawford's work on how to research individual uses of social media as a guide (Crawford 2009), this phase of data collection involved "listening" to the way the artists engaged with others as well as "listening" to how their images and identity shaped their process of using online spaces. Screenshots of this online activity worked as records of this interaction and helped in constructing the narrative of persona. These screenshots were also useful in stimulating discussion through the interview stage of the research. We believe this online listening technique is of real value when exploring personas that are created, in part or in full, through digital means – without engaging with the personas in situ, interpretations by the researcher are hampered by a blinkered view of the experience. For the purposes of the study of artists' personas, the researcher followed her research participants for close to two years (both before and after the interviews) across a variety of platforms, including the social media spaces Facebook, Twitter, Tumblr, and Instagram as well as the artists' personal blogs. These spaces were checked daily, often multiple times a day, and this constant engagement gave the researcher a closeness and intimacy of understanding with the personas that would be difficult to achieve without being physically co-present. At times, the researcher interacted with the artists directly, commenting on posts or liking/favoriting status updates or images, or retweeting and sharing material posted to these spaces. Hundreds of screenshots were taken as records of posts or conversations, and these functioned not only as illustrative examples for the research, but also coded as data themselves. The screenshot is often overlooked as a research tool in and of itself: it is *looked* through. As a digital object, it is produced in the interaction between the researcher and their computer, whether a desktop machine, laptop, or mobile device such as a smart phone or tablet. Screenshots are "most often put to use in documenting unique visual evidence of an individual screen in a specific time and space" (Marshall, Moore, and Barbour 2015, p. 293), and are therefore interpretative objects in themselves: they capture the perspective of the researcher only, as platform algorithms offer increasing individualized online experiences. The use of online listening and screenshots will not be required of all persona studies projects that use an IPA methodology, but we would certainly recommend those studying digital personas to engage with this research method.

The third research method used for this IPA project into artists' personas was in-depth, unstructured interviews with the individual artists. These discussions aimed "to glimpse another person's experience of the world" (Barbour 2014, p. 118). Generating "narratives of experience," the interview process was designed to allow the artists to discuss their personas, both online and offline, through stories and anecdotes they felt were representative of their own experience. Although an unstructured interview was utilized in this study, other interviewers might equally choose a semi-structured approach, where an interview guide is used to provide general areas of focus or specific questions to be addressed. Similarly, if the online listening process has begun prior to the interview, screenshots that capture particular discussions or posts could be used as visual prompts for the interviewer, and as a way to get the interviewee to talk about and interpret their own experience of persona creation. Once again, the researcher must be clear about the interpretative nature of the research process: both the interviewer and the interviewee are engaged in a process of interpretation of experience, rather than the collection of verifiable truths. The researcher must also cede the status of expert to the interviewee, as the person who creates the persona is by definition the expert in that experience.

In the study of artists' personas, featured in Chapter 6, only one interview with each artist was conducted. However, it may be necessary or desirable to revisit the interviewees to ask them to reflect further or discuss a particular element of their persona in greater depth. Full transcripts of the interviews must be made (where possible by the researcher who will be conducting the analysis), and these transcripts coded for subordinate and superordinate themes. For a detailed and extremely practical description of the analysis of IPA interview data, we highly recommend the "Analysis" chapter of Smith, Flowers, and Larkin's *Interpretative Phenomenological Analysis: Theory, Method and Research* (2009, pp. 79–107). The thematic categories were also used to code the screenshots taken during the online listening process, allowing these to contribute usefully to the data analysis process.

These techniques – developing a context through a historical narrative, online listening to the personas under study, and in-depth interviews with the artists who created those personas – generated a narrative of the participant's experience of the creation of their artists' personas, while also connecting outward to broader conceptualizations of artistness as they have been discursively created. The IPA approach can be appropriated for the exploration of all types of public personas but is especially suited to those where the researcher can interview the creator of that persona. The key strength of this approach is the narrative depth of both the research data and the interpretation, while a key weakness is the struggle with scale: IPA produces ideographic profiles and is best applied when using small samples. For those researchers who wish to study larger groups, or who do not have direct access to the person who creates the persona under examination, action research, prosopographic field studies, or social network analysis (all explored below) may well be more appropriate.

Personas in the Making: Second-person Action Research

Researching personas can at times call for a hands-on approach. If you have access to a group of persona creators who are willing and able to become co-researchers, the capabilities to conduct longitudinal qualitative research, and an interest in the process of change as well as its results, an action research approach might be a way forward. Action research has similarities to IPA as described above – the focus on lived experience is phenomenological, the engagement with participants is interpretive, and the incorporation of findings into people's lives follows a hermeneutic cycle, as does prosopographic persona research described in the next section of this chapter. Stringer defines action research as "a systematic approach to investigation that enables people to find effective solutions to problems they confront in their everyday lives" (2007, p. 1), while Reason and Bradbury (2008, p. 4) state in part that it "seeks to bring together action and reflection, theory and practice, in participation with others, in the pursuit of practical solutions to issues of pressing concern to people." Whereas other forms of in-depth qualitative research, such as ethnography or participant observation, emphasize a hands-off approach from the researchers – even when encouraging a reflexive and responsive stance – the desire for change is built into the very nature of action research. The point is not to report on what is, but rather to explore together what could be. The participants in the project use the researcher much like a tool – perhaps to organize, to help resolve disputes in group situations, or to aid in accessing required resources. But as the facilitator, leader, or director (Stringer 2007, p. xvi) of the research, there is an explicit acknowledgment that the group members are the experts in their own experiences (Grant, Nelson, and Mitchell 2008, p. 589), and the researcher's key task is to empower the group to find and institute situationally appropriate solutions to problems or concerns.

Traditionally, action research has focused on disadvantaged or marginalized communities; some previous projects include educational programs for remote Aboriginal communities in Australia (Stringer 2007, pp. 3–4), support and development programs for young women in a multinational consumer goods company (McArdle 2008), the investigation into the effects of racism on the self-esteem of a group of African Americans, and the role of participation in health intervention research (Chiu 2008). While the emphasis on "improving the quality of … community life" through finding solutions to problems is the driver for action research (Stringer 2007, p. 11), the underpinning methodology and the practical methods can be adapted for the study of persona creation. Indeed, on reflection the Persona in Action pilot research project run at Deakin University in 2012 (Ng et al. 2012) provides a good example of how the facilitation of group exploration of persona can provide not only positive outcomes for the participants, but also research insights that extend existing knowledge.

Persona in Action (Marshall, Barbour, and Moore 2018) was a pilot project designed to empirically investigate the content analysis reported in "The Academic Online: Constructing Persona through the World Wide Web" (Barbour and Marshall 2012). A group of colleagues including doctoral candidates, lecturers, researchers, and members of the professoriate from the School of Communication and Creative Arts at Deakin University came together to develop their online academic personas within the context of the pilot project.

Having received ethics approval to study the process, we developed a series of workshops, questionnaires, discussion groups, and one-on-one consultations that were designed to guide the group through the process of examining, developing, and evaluating their academic personas according to each academic's personal goals. Although not designed as an action research project, Persona in Action does follow the same essential methods, and it was our evaluation of this project that allowed us to see the potential of action research as a methodology for persona studies.

Action research projects fall into three basic categories: first-person, second-person, and third-person projects. A first-person project might be somewhat similar to the methodology described above in the section "Researching Ourselves," where a researcher takes as the subject of inquiry their own life, "to act choicefully and with awareness, and to assess effects in the outside world while acting" (Reason and Bradbury 2008, p. 6). Second-person action research is what is described here, where the project is investigating issues of mutual concern, while third-person projects aim to influence large-scale, often geographically dispersed, groups by facilitating those involved in the research to become facilitators themselves of wider change. Where possible, a researcher should move from a small-scale project out to a larger one: the earlier engagement with one's own life experiences provides a starting point for the development of a small group project, while the insights provided in second-person research will aid in the facilitation of a large-scale intervention (Reason and Bradbury 2008, p. 6).

The creation of the inquiry group for second-person action research, what McArdle (2008) describes as "getting in," can be particularly challenging. You not only need to identify people who are creators of the persona you wish to investigate, but also ensure they are enthusiastic and understanding of what is involved in the process; participants must be willing to work alongside you as the researcher, put in the time and energy required to facilitate the change both you and they wish to see, and also work well together. It may also be necessary to include diverse stakeholders in the research group, along with the usual academic requirements of meeting funding, ethics, and institutional requirements for research conduct. Most important of these is the commitment of the participants. In the Persona in Action project, our initial wide call to participate was followed up by a seminar style group meeting, where we outlined our projected direction, as well as what would be required of our colleagues. We clarified that the research was not a matter of us teaching the group how to create an academic persona that would magically make them successful, but rather that we would facilitate their own development, providing resources and critical analysis that aided the group to experiment and determine for themselves what would be the best approach. Of the 20 or so colleagues who attended the initial meeting, 15 signed onto the project, and 10 made a significant contribution to the research throughout its 12-month duration.

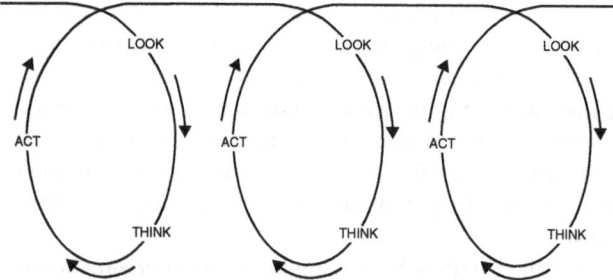

Figure 5.1 Springer's look, think, act spiral. *Source:* Stringer (2007). © SAGE. Reproduced with permission.

Determining how to approach action research will for a large part depend on what element of persona is being investigated, but the process itself follows a hermeneutic spiral. Stringer (2007) calls this the look, think, act interacting spiral (see Figure 5.1).

In the "look" stage, the group aims to see what is happening in the current situation, gathering information and describing how things are at present. This feeds into the "think" stage, where the aim is to determine what is happening and why things are this way. The third stage, "act," might include planning, implementation, or evaluation. We followed this structure with our group in investigating online academic personas, running through the spiral a number of times. In the first iteration of the "look" stage, we asked the participants to conduct a persona audit, identifying how and where they had an online academic presence. This led to the first "think" stage, which involved the participants engaging in what their current online presence meant, and how it had evolved in the way that it had. The first "act" stage asked the participants to put into place new strategies to develop their personas in the short term in order to reach their goals. The spiral then repeated, with a focus on how the initial strategies were working, why, and what skills needed to be developed to take things further in the next action cycle. At each stage, we asked the participants to complete audits or engage in recorded discussions, which allowed us to develop a variety of research data that could be used in traditional academic reporting structures (conference papers and journal articles). However, the key focus throughout the project was always on developing positive change in how this group presented themselves as academics in online spaces.

One area where our Persona in Action project was less successful was in the stage that McArdle (2008) called "getting out." Winding up a long-term project, particularly when there is not a clear way to end, can be tricky, and for us it was more a matter of tailing off rather than finishing up. We had intended the final contact would be a meeting of the whole group to debrief on what had been (or not been) successful for each of the academics, but as the end of the project coincided with the end of the academic year, we were unable to find a suitable time to get everyone together with people on leave and attending conferences. Instead, we arranged to have a one-on-one meeting between the participants and one of the lead researchers, but even this was a struggle, and the wrap-up discussions bled into the following year. Stringer (2007, p. 164) explains that celebrating the achievements of an action research project is an important part of the process, and advocates for informal events that allow participants to mingle and talk to one another. Most importantly, for Stringer, is the importance of saying "Look what we have accomplished together" (2007, p. 165).

When reporting on the project, whether through a dissertation, journal article, conference paper, or other formal academic document, it is necessary to foreground not only your own research findings, but also the voices of the participants. This can be difficult for those who are used to aiming for objective, highly structured writing styles; but obscuring the voice and experiences of the participants goes against the key principles of action research. The personas you are reporting on belong to persons and/or a group of people, and you must honor their engagement with the process of exploring and developing that persona throughout the research project.

Reputation and Inter-related Persona: Prosopographic Field Study

Persona studies can function as explorations of reputation. Reputation as an idea has been investigated by business analysts and marketing scholars. However, the field of prosopography from within historical studies provides persona studies with a way to engage with reputation, identity, and community of networks of individuals. Prosopography has been defined as "the investigation of the common background characteristics of a group of actors in history by means of collective study of their lives" (Stone 1971, p. 46), and is also called collective biography. The development of large, digitized, searchable databases of archival material has facilitated the production of prosopographic studies in a range of fields and historical time periods, giving the collective biography the power of computational networking capacities. By studying the connections between and related elements in the lives of groups of individuals who share a common element of some form, prosopography has given insight into the lives of those working in ancient Roman politics (Magdalino 2003) and medieval guilds (Verboven, Carlier, and Dumolyn 2007), British inventors born between 1650 and 1850 (MacLeod and Nuvolari 2006), the geographical spread of neo-Confucianism in twelfth century China (Bol 2012), and the study of French sporting elites in the twentieth century (Erard and Bancel 2007).

In Marshall, Moore, and Barbour (2015), we argue that prosopography ties in with Bourdieu's (1993) considerations of intersections between cultural fields, as it is the relationships between people, place, and activity that drive their inclusion in the collective being studied. Prosopographic studies focus on these relationships, examining how they influence an individual or group's political, social, and economic power. We see prosopographic field studies (PFS) as providing two important directions for persona research. First, tying back to the importance of providing a contextual basis for the study of persona as foregrounded in the previous section on IPA, prosopography requires that relationships between individuals can only be understood when one creates a comprehensive biography of the whole field under study. And related to this is the second direction: not only the power brokers should be studied as "cultural intermediaries" hold both significant influence over reputation and can translate their own and other's influence across fields of activity. Therefore, PFS can be utilized to study how status and reputation develops and spreads in the contemporary moment, making use of both traditional biographical information and digital network data. By utilizing both qualitative and quantitative methods of data collection and analysis, PFS becomes a powerful tool for "identifying fields of activity and influence as well as the most prominent intersections of fields" (Marshall, Moore, and Barbour 2015, p. 301), while also identifying the work and value of cultural intermediaries within a particular culture.

The proposed method that follows has been adapted for use in persona studies from the prosopography project in the History Department of the University of Oxford, and particularly their very useful guide "A Short Manual to the Art of Prosopography" (Verboven, Carlier, and Dumolyn 2007). As a methodology designed to make use of incomplete but potentially overlapping data sets, prosopography may seem nonsensical as a choice during a period of data abundance as is seen in the big data, computational research age within which we are working. However, by adopting the focused data collection strategies and analytical frame of prosopography, we have the potential to make sense of this data in useful and insightful ways.

Prior to conducting a prosopographic field study, you need to construct your sample population. This should be as comprehensive a list of names as you are capable of producing, including major players as well as their supporters. This list directs about whom you collect data. Consider not just the completeness of the sample, but also geographic and temporal limiters (from where and when your sample will be constructed), as well as what the common elements are that link them together to make an interesting cohort. Once you have a sense of the possible population (and you may well find additional people for your sample as you undertake the research), you determine whether you have access to their biographical data. The guiding document of prosopographical research is the questionnaire, which may include open and closed questions, multiple choice, and open fields. This list of questions needs to be flexible at the outset, and researchers should be willing to add (or possibly subtract) questions as the data collection continues, even when this results in the need to revise the rest of the cohort. This data should ideally cover personal and family life, career progression and achievements, material and social position, and cultural networks, as appropriate to the type of persona being studied. When studying historical samples, this type of material may be stored in hard copy only – that is, in yearbooks, council records, government archives, or personal and family history documents. Practical limitations, such as the need to travel to a location to access the archive, may frustrate the research at early stages, and it is best to be aware of and plan for these possible impediments. If studying a contemporary sample, this data may well be digitized, but inaccessible due to privacy restrictions, paywalls, or commercial agreements. As with physical records, it is important to determine prior to beginning the data collection whether the data is freely available for the sample you wish to study. A key requirement to maintain the reliability of prosopographical databases is to connect each fact to a source, so it is important to keep careful records as to where the data was retrieved as collection proceeds.

Once you have a comprehensive data set on your sample, it is necessary to give it a uniform structure in order to compare across strategies. This may mean developing generic titles for similar job roles or otherwise standardizing the information you have collected. Particularly when using computer-based analysis tools, this uniformity of codes and categories is important to allow comparison between individuals. Equally important is to keep track of these subjective coding decisions: being able to report on the data requires researchers to explain how and why they made these choices. Once coded and standardized, the data can be translated into graphs and tables, or more advanced computer visualization tools can be used, such as network analysis described in the following section of this chapter. The creation of these visualizations may be useful for the researcher to solidify their understandings and interpretations of the data but must be accompanied by explanations when presented to a wider readership – the visualization is a tool, not an end in itself. A "synthesis of the interpretations" (Verboven, Carlier, and Dumolyn 2007, p. 59), created by the researcher based on their reading of the data, will demonstrate insight into the persona(s) under examination, drawing from the correlations noted in the database as well as subjective understanding of the sample as a whole.

Prosopography offers a way forward for the study of historical personas, designed as it is for use with incomplete or fragmented data. However, we believe it also offers a useful methodological structure that can be adapted for big data sets, guiding the data collection and comparison stages of the research process. Additionally, a prosopographic field study can be a complementary method within a larger project, providing a mix of quantitative and qualitative data and analysis to support and extend other types of research.

Networked Selves: Information Visualization and Exploration

Cultural studies and celebrity studies have successfully incorporated and expanded on the tools of other disciplines and domains, including anthropology and social and political theory. Similarly, persona studies make use of the technologies and techniques of social network analysis and data visualization, originally derived from graph theory and network theory, and connected to a longer trajectory through the sociological traditions of Durkheim and the histories of mapping the social and spatial dynamics of networks and cultures. Networks are information-rich environments, from which, Lee Rainie and Barry Wellman suggest:

> Data mining, social network analysis, social-computing studies and user-generated folksonomies (collaborative creation of tags and catalogues) will make the web easier to navigate and allow information now scattered in various places to be pulled together in meaningful ways for networked individuals. (Rainie and Wellman 2012)

The rendering of computational and network information as visible and legible to the human also necessitates attention to the human agency in the mix of algorithmic and subjective meaning-making processes. This requires a "rapid shuttling" between the quantitative and the qualitative view of networks, and a constant movement back and forth between the automation of analysis and the hermeneutic close reading (Kirschenbaum 2004). This movement between interpretive and algorithmic analysis can be applied to the intercommunication of experiences of networked presentations of the public self. These experiences include the curation and management of digital objects, such as user profiles, online videos, memes, animated gifs, or screenshots that function as components in our multifaceted masks, and which compile to form the collective encounter of the individual online.

The labor of online identity formation and management involves important networked persona literacies, and a working out of the techniques of navigation and presentation of the self. Persona studies require the development of methods for dealing with both large and small degrees of activity and data, as well as conceptual tools for the articulation of specialized methodologies to visualize and analyze this material and assist in ways that do not require specific coding skills or great expense. The processes of investigating the power and influence of celebrities can be further applied to the broader analysis of networked celebrity activity, particularly the emergence of microcelebrities and the dimensions of their micro-publics. There are numerous applications and services available to map the individual micro-publics of social networking sites and for the individual's own self-surveillance of online persona, and the polarity of such an investigation can be inverted to study the self's interconnections to friends, peers, and celebrities via Twitter and Facebook and other social media platforms that make these data publicly available (Van Dijck 2014). The self-surveillance of the ordinary and everyday activities of social media are valuable "vernacular skills," argues Bennett (2010), and are demonstrated by celebrities such as television personalities whose public identity performance is organized around a vocational architecture of representational functions "in relation to cultural and ideological values" (2010 p. 29).

Users are already becoming familiar with the esthetics of the common visualizations of their own micro-public dimensionality, from basic Facebook plugins and apps through to more extensive social network analysis services capable of rendering and illustrating the various elements of network topologies for their users. One such example is the WolframAlpha (2015) "Personal Analytics for Facebook" exploration tool, which makes an extensive degree of forensic self-analysis possible by algorithmic summary of "curated data" and provides a powerful operationalizing of persona. The tool examines the degree of intercommunication involved in the public presentation of identity amidst the expansion of online semantic information in order to make sense of the unprecedented scale and heterogeneity of online content (Lopez et al. 2012). The free web-based tool reveals a detailed level of information, statistical analysis, and visualization of an individual's Facebook presence and micropublic. The results can feel like a macabre self-autopsy with the online persona laid bare across the screen. Highly compartmentalized tables, graphs, and summaries of Facebook activity and performance systematically account for the "work" of persona itemized down to the day, hour, and activity. WolframAlpha advertises its user-pay functions and the deeper levels of analysis available under its multiple subscription models, which attest to the anticipated value of these services.

The skills required to create, navigate, and effectively "read" visualized information and to make sense of network graphs are rapidly becoming an important set of persona network literacies for the types of informational work that will be fundamental to the successful management of the self online. Those making informed decisions about the intercommunication of mediated messages, taking stock of network activity patterns, or seeking to understand social roles and other features of networked cultural participation are going to rely on the ability to sample, render, and explore networks with the tools that simplify, automate, and help assimilate the collection, filtering, and analysis of the available data. Self-surveillance and autosurveillances activities, enabled by services such as WolframAlpha and others, reinvigorates individual user agency in a process that recaptures some of the value generated by the user in their investment in freely accessed and socially mediated platforms like Facebook. These platforms are privately owned and corporately regulated spaces whose automated processing of data operates on such an immense scale that even the most mundane or seemingly obscure act of persona formation translates to intellectual property to be sold to advertisers, investors, governments, security agencies, and others as metadata.

To approach the analysis of large datasets of images, Manovich turns to automated analysis, algorithmic visualization techniques, and new display technologies to generate visual descriptions to serve in the analysis (Manovich 2009, 2012a, b). Manovich comments on the need for multiple maps and cartographies of the cultural landscapes of large datasets: no one singular visualization is able to fully encapsulate a digital culture and reveal the totality of the territories of emerging cultural fields; rather, extensive and multiple mapping is required to appreciate its obvious diversity. Maps of cultural landscapes, argues Manovich, reveal "fuzzy" and overlapping clusters of intercommunication rather than highly discrete categories or rigid boundaries. Social media sites like Facebook, Twitter, YouTube, and Tumblr have cultivated complex networks of audiences and coproducers of hybridized forms of entertainment and information, where raw metrics are often less revealing to humans than their visual representations. Visualizations are the product of the researcher working to render the relational dimensions of the network visible, argue Rieder and Röhle (2012, pp. 70–74), and condense the representational complexities of networks into accessible forms that lend themselves to human analysis, interpretation, and explanation.

A practical approach to the visualization of individual micro-publics is possible with open source and freely available tools such as the Network Overview, Discovery and Exploration tool, NodeXL, a visualization plugin for Microsoft Excel created by the Social Media Research Foundation for the visualization of networked information and other data. Chief social scientist for the foundation, Marc Smith, describes the goal of NodeXL as the aspiration to be as simple and ubiquitous as the browser interface in terms of visualizing and navigating networks (Smith 2012). NodeXL reduces the time and expertise necessary in order to obtain useful graphs that can assist in the interpretation of complex network patterns. In Chapter 7, we provide a brief case study of the visualization of a Twitter hashtag relevant to the "indie" game developer persona as an example of this approach.

Conclusion

This chapter has explored and investigated some of the key methods we have privileged in the study of persona. It must be acknowledged that our work has highlighted the online transformation of persona and the techniques for analysis advanced are particularly valuable for this new and emerging generation of public identity. We also want to underline that our methods are not mutually exclusive and actually are useful when combined constructively. Thus, the idea of employing action research with its connection with IPA also acknowledges that network analysis and its visualization is equally a technique for individuals to understand the new ways in which the self is organized, shared, and reconstructed through its associations online. Prosoprographic field studies – or PFS as we have referred to it – can be valuably integrated into achieving a more comprehensive understanding of the complex contextual dimensions in the formation of persona. It can emerge with nuance from IPA-inspired interviews about how an individual strategically imagines their construction of their persona and what collective and preexisting constitutions of identity structure shape their conception and fabrication of their persona. As we have also identified, PFS can comfortably be an element in the way that we visualize connections through the large data fields of online public identity patterning and alignments.

In a vital sense, our methods highlight what we call persona *literacy*. How we approach literacy has multiple dimensions. First, it is important to understand our own individual intersection in the formation of a public self online or offline as these new generations of persona are instrumental in transforming the way in which our contemporary culture operates and our new positions within these shifted political/cultural/economic spaces. Second and equally, this understanding of persona helps us help others as our research can then expand to a networked reading of persona activity and interaction. Third, in the grander sense of larger data visualization, we can read the patterns of connection that are producing our personas and that are also the digital material which allow for the recalibrating of these public identities for other purposes that may or may not be in our interest. Along with an integration of our conceptual analysis in Chapter 3 of our registers and performativities of persona, our final three chapters identify the way our approaches and methods can be used to analyze our contemporary persona worlds.

References

Adams, T.E., Holman, J.S., and Ellis, C. (2015). *Autoethnography: Understanding Qualitative Research*. New York: Oxford University Press.

Barbour, K. (2014). Finding the edge: Online persona creation by fringe artists. PhD thesis. Deakin University, Australia.

Barbour, K. and Marshall, P.D. (2012). The academic online: Constructing persona through the World Wide Web. *First Monday* 17 (9): https://doi.org/10.5210/fm.v0i0.3969.

Bennett, J. (2010). *Television Personalities: Stardom and the Small Screen*. London: Routledge.

Bochner, A.P. and Ellis, C. (2016). *Evocative Autoethnography: Writing Lives and Telling Stories*. New York: Routledge.

Bol, P.K. (2012). GIS, prosopography and history. *Annals of GIS* 18: 3–15. https://doi.org/10.1080/19475683.2011.647077.

Bourdieu, P. (1993). *The Field of Cultural Production: Essays on Art and Literature* (trans. R. Johnson). Cambridge: Polity Press.

Chiu, L.F. (2008). Engaging communities in health intervention research/practice. *Critical Public Health* 18 (2): 151–159. https://doi.org/10.1080/09581590701771725.

Crawford, K. (2009). Following you: Disciplines of listening in social media. *Continuum* 23: 525–535. https://doi.org/10.1080/10304310903003270.

Ellis, C. (2004). *The Ethnographic I: A Methodological Novel about Autoethnography*. Walnut Creek, CA: Altamira.

Ellis, C. (2008). Autoethnography. In: *The SAGE Encyclopedia of Qualitative Research Methods* (ed. L.M. Given), 49–51. Thousand Oaks, CA: SAGE.

Ellis, C. and Bochner, A. (2000). Autoethnography, personal narrative, reflexivity: Researcher as subject. In: *Handbook of Qualitative Research* (ed. N.K. Denzin and Y.S. Lincoln), 733–768. Thousand Oaks, CA: SAGE.

Erard, C. and Bancel, N. (2007). Prosopographical analysis of sports elites: Overview and evaluation of a seminal study. *The International Journal of the History of Sport* 24: 67–79. https://doi.org/10.1080/09523360601005439.

Grant, J., Nelson, G., and Mitchell, T. (2008). Negotiating the challenges of participatory action research: Relationships, power, participation, change and credibility. In: *The SAGE Handbook of Action Research: Participative Inquiry and Practice* (ed. P. Reason and H. Bradbury), 589–601. Los Angeles: SAGE.

Gregg, M. and Seigworth, G.J. (2010). *The Affect Theory Reader*. Durham, NC: Duke University Press.

Hinds, J. (2011). Exploring the psychological rewards of a wilderness experience: An interpretive phenomenological analysis. *Humanistic Psychologist* 39: 189–205. https://doi.org/10.1080/08873267.2011.567132.

Hughes, S.A. and Pennington, J.L. (2017). *Autoethnography: Process, Product, and Possibility for Critical Social Research*. Los Angeles: SAGE.

Kirschenbaum, A. (2004). Generic sources of disaster communities: A social network approach. *International Journal of Sociology and Social Policy* 24 (10/11): 94–129. https://doi.org/10.1108/01443330410791073.

Lopez, V., Fernández, M., Stieler, M., and Motta, E. (2012). PowerAqua: Supporting users in querying and exploring the semantic web. *Semantic Web* 3 (3): 249–265.

MacLeod, C. and Nuvolari, A. (2006). The pitfalls of prosopography: Inventors in the *Dictionary of National Biography*. *Technology and Culture* 47: 757–776.

Magdalino, P. (2003). *Byzantinum in the Year 1000*. Leiden: Brill.

Manovich, L. (2009). Cultural analytics: Visualising cultural patterns in the era of "more media." *Domus*, Spring. https://drive.google.com/viewerng/viewer?url=http://softwarestudies.com/cultural_analytics/Manovich_DOMUS.doc (accessed November 11, 2014).

Manovich, L. (2012a). How to follow software users. http://manovich.net/index.php/projects/how-to-follow-software-users (accessed November 11, 2014).

Manovich, L. (2012b). How to compare one million images? In: *Understanding Digital Humanities* (ed. D.M. Berry), 249–278. New York: Palgrave Macmillan.

Marshall, J. (1999). Living life as inquiry. *Systemic Practice and Action Research* 12: 155–171. https://doi.org/10.1023/A:1022421929640.

Marshall, J. (2004). Living systemic thinking: Exploring quality in first-person action research. *Action Research* 2: 305–325. https://doi.org/10.1177/1476750304045945.

Marshall, P.D., Barbour, K., and Moore, C. (2018). Academic persona: The construction of online reputation in the modern academy. In: *The Digital Academic: Critical Perspectives on Digital Technologies in Higher Education* (ed. D. Lupton, I. Mewburn and P. Thomson), 47–62. London: Routledge.

Marshall, P.D., Moore, C., and Barbour, K. (2015). Persona as method: Exploring celebrity and the public self through persona studies. *Celebrity Studies* 6: 288–305. https://doi.org/10.1080/19392397.2015.1062649.

McArdle, K.L. (2008). Getting in, getting on, getting out: On working with second-person inquiry groups. In: *The SAGE Handbook of Action Research: Participative Inquiry and Practice* (ed. P. Reason and H. Bradbury), 602–614. Los Angeles: SAGE.

Ng, E., Barbour, K., Moore, C., and Marshall, P.D. (2012). Operationalising Persona: The academic public identity. Presented at the Celebrity Studies Inaugural Conference. Deakin University, Melbourne, Australia.

Rainie, L. and Wellman, B. (2012). *Networked: The New Social Operating System*. Cambridge, MA: MIT Press.

Reason, P. and Bradbury, H. (2008). *The SAGE Handbook of Action Research: Participative Inquiry and Practice*, 2e. Thousand Oaks, CA: SAGE.

Reason, P. and Torbert, W.R. (2001). The action turn: Toward a transformational social science. *Concepts and Transformation* 6: 1–37.

Reed-Danahay, D. (1997). *Auto/Ethnography: Rewriting the Self and the Social*. Oxford: Bloomsbury Academic.

Rieder, B. and Röhle, T. (2012). Digital methods: Five challenges. In: *Understanding Digital Humanities* (ed. D.M. Berry), 67–84. New York: Palgrave Macmillan.

Smith, J.A., Flowers, P., and Larkin, M. (2009). *Interpretative Phenomenological Analysis: Theory, Method and Research*. London: SAGE.

Smith, M.A. (2012). Charting collections of connections with maps and measures. Media X Stanford. [video online] http://www.youtube.com/watch?v=VwVvQhhLUqc (accessed November 9, 2014).

Stone, L. (1971). Prosopography. *Daedalus* 100: 46–79.

Stringer, E.T. (2007). *Action Research*. Thousand Oaks, CA: SAGE.

Van Dijck, J. (2014). Datafication, dataism and dataveillance: Big Data between scientific paradigm and ideology. *Surveillance & Society* 12 (2): 197–208.

Verboven, K., Carlier, M., and Dumolyn, J. (2007). A short manual to the art of prosopography. In: *Prosopography Approaches and Applications: A Handbook* (ed. K.S. Keats-Rohan), 35–70. Oxford: Occasional Publications.

WolframAlpha. (2015). WolframAlpha personal analytics for Facebook. http://www.wolframalpha.com/facebook/ (accessed November 12, 2018).

6

The Artist's Persona

Discussing persona studies in the abstract can only take us so far, and so here and in the following chapters we shift our focus to deal with specific case studies that work to exemplify the theoretical and methodological material we have presented thus far. In Chapter 7, the personas of people involved in digital games – both players and producers – are discussed, and in Chapter 8, the professional persona is analyzed with a specific focus on lawyers, academics, and medical doctors. We start our case studies, however, with an analysis of the persona performances of artists.

There can be no question that the development of the World Wide Web, and more recently social media, has allowed artists to promote their work to a much wider audience. The capacity to promote and sell work outside of a home city, region, or country is now available to anyone with Internet access, and a whole host of art-specific websites function as aggregators of artistic product. It is no longer necessary even for "fine artists" to develop a history of shows at reputable galleries in order to develop a reputation, although the art world as a whole still functions on the premise that this type of legitimization is necessary to sustain a career. For those who work on the fringes of the traditional art world, however, the creation of an online persona is an integral part of the legitimization and presentational process for the artist. It allows an artist to collect images of their work in a single space, develop support networks and a fan base, enter into dialog with followers, and promote new events and projects. In order for this persona to be effective, it must also be an engaging self-presentation. The artist must present themselves as "Artist," as someone who meets their audience's expectations of what an artist is. These expectations fall loosely into two categories: the artist as bohemian genius, commonly understood as the myth of the artist, and the artist as a producer of goods for sale, what can be called the "creative laborer." The balancing of these two contradictory sets of sociocultural expectations occurs in the space in which online personas are created by fringe artists. To examine this balancing act, we employ the term "artistness" (Barbour 2014, 2015).

Persona Studies: An Introduction, First Edition. P. David Marshall, Christopher Moore, and Kim Barbour.
© 2020 John Wiley & Sons, Inc. Published 2020 by John Wiley & Sons, Inc.

This is the institutionalized "collective representation" referred to by Goffman (1959, p. 37). The "artist" is a social role that exists outside of any particular individual creative practitioner; it is a trope, a descriptor, a construct, and any examination of artist's persona in the present context needs to engage with this social role as context for contemporary identity practices. This study takes an interpretative phenomenological analysis (IPA) approach, which requires this contextualization of the persona under investigation, along with a focus on how those artists who feature in this analysis experience the process of producing an artist's persona. In order to understand this construction of persona, and the social construct that underpins it, we draw on theories of the artist developed within art history (Codell 2003; Pollock 1980; Vasari 2005 [1551]) and the sociology of art (Becker 1982; Bourdieu 1993, 1996), in addition to poststructuralist theories of the author from Barthes (1977) and Foucault (1991), and recent research into creative labor and the creative industries.

The Artist as Subject

The performance of artistness is the performance of a socially constructed role, made up of identifiable elements drawn from historically grounded discourses of what it means to be an artist. These elements, explored below, combine to create the artist as the subject. This subject is then performed by creative practitioners enacting the role, performances which, in turn, reaffirm the discourse. Weedon (1987, p. 125) describes the subject as socially constructed through discourse and then inhabited by a "thinking, feeling ... social agent capable of resistance and innovation." We argue that as agents in their own presentational practices, artists perform artistness, drawing on elements of the discourse that created the subject through their performance in order to mold their identity to fit the discursive subject. This aligns with how Hall (2004, p. 3) describes the difference between identity and subjectivity:

> one's identity can be thought of as that particular set of traits, beliefs, and allegiances that, in short- or long-term ways, gives one a consistent personality and mode of social being, while subjectivity implies always a degree of thought and self-consciousness about identity, at the same time allowing a myriad of limitations and often unknowable, unavoidable constraints on our ability to fully comprehend identity.

In other words, a creative practitioner will have their own identity made up of beliefs and allegiances. In presenting themselves as an artist, however, they will enact the role of the artist-as-subject with some "degree of thought and self-consciousness." Therefore, it can be argued that one can, to some extent, actively engage with the artistic subject while one is performing the types and playing the role of artist. It is this active engagement that indicates a degree of individual agency within the performance. Hall goes on to state that "in probing agency, we are in effect, tackling the fundamental question of responsibility: in personal action, in aesthetic creation, in inter-personal norms, and social valuations" (2004, p. 5). The creation of online persona foregrounds the agency within the performance of a particular subject by encouraging (and in some cases forcing) choices in the presentation of the self. The choice of name, the choice of image or avatar, the personal description each online profile requests, and the choice of level of engagement through networks all demonstrate agency in self-presentation. At the same time, the people creating the personas are also responding to the pressure of expectation to create a representation of themselves that is consistent with discourses of the artist-as-subject.

As the discussion below will make clear, the elements that make up the role of the artist change over time and are built through discourse and representation. The current discourses that are most dominant in present constructions of the artist-as-subject stem from the "myth of the artist," and the artist as a creative laborer. By working through the historical development of these two discourses, we identify how artistness is currently represented. This understanding of artistness then provides a reference point for discussions of artistness as performed by the participants in the empirical portion of this study.

The Artist Myth

The roots of the hero, virtuoso, and magician elements of the artist's myth can be traced into stories of artists from antiquity, where the few Greco-Roman artists whose names and reputations have survived have surprisingly similar biographies attributed to them. Kris and Kurz (1979) traced a range of biographical stories related to these elements in the life stories of everyone from Lysippus, a Greek painter from the fourth century BCE, through Renaissance painters, to their own near contemporary, Picasso. These biographical anecdotes will be familiar to anyone reading the biographies of famous artists – the youthful genius, usually unrecognized; the struggle against close relatives who do not think that the child should pursue the arts; the teaching or patronage by a person in a position of authority in the arts; the extraordinary, even magical virtuosity; and so on. Despite the fact that many of the historical biographies were written many years, sometimes centuries after the artist's death (leading to serious questions about their accuracy), these stories form the basis on which our understanding of artistness lies.

Romanticism and the Arts

The "man with the black beret" artist stereotype that informs the myth of the artist in Western societies can be traced back to the early years of the Romantic movement in Paris in the late eighteenth and early nineteenth centuries. At a time of social, political, and artistic change, the Romantics inadvertently defined what it looked and felt like to be a creative practitioner even centuries later. Although the artist as an important individual in his or her own right began with the Enlightenment, prior to the Romantic movement the focus was on the artist as "intellectual elite" (Bain 2005, p. 28) along the same lines as mathematicians as holders of "higher forms of knowledge" (p. 43). The importance of the Romantic movement can be seen in the creation of a defined stereotype associated with bohemian lifestyles and withdrawal from society.

The myth of the artist requires those playing that role to demonstrate their outsider status, the trials and suffering they have overcome, and connect back to the history of their art form, all the while still maintaining a distinctive style. We see the stereotype trying to balance the virtuosic of the artist with some sort of pain – Van Gogh's brilliance with a brush is countered by his madness, supposed poverty, and self-mutilation; Beethoven wrote brilliant symphonies yet ended his life unable to hear them; Virginia Woolf was famous as a writer in her own time, but this was not enough to save her from depression and suicide. Of course, given the shift in the economics and education practices of the art world, most artists nowadays would not naturally meet many (if any) of these mythical defining features of a brilliant artist. In order to accept that an individual fits the criteria of "artist" set out by the myth, the one doing the claiming must bare their souls to a certain extent; they cannot simply claim the title, they must explain their troubled past, the works by acknowledged artists that changed their lives or otherwise influenced their style. Without this confession, how can we know what is made is art, or the person who makes things to be an artist? The requirement for **public** acknowledgment and acceptance of the confession also constitutes an element of **collective construction** of the persona, as described in Chapter 3.

Self-presentation in the Myth of the Artist

The myth of the artist is much larger than a confession of an individual's personal history. Gluck (2000) traces the history of the development of the bohemian artist and explores the physical manifestations of the desire to separate from the increasingly important middle class: "The young artists in historical costumes carefully distinguished themselves from the fashionable dandies or 'lions' of the time, who dressed according to the latest fashion imported from

England" (Gluck 2000, p. 357). However, the distinction was not only made through the adoption of contextually lurid clothing, but more importantly through behavior, as "the young bohemians were neither authoritarian, nor religious, nor hierarchical in orientation; they were, on the contrary, irreverent, antimoralistic, and transgressive" (Gluck 2000, p. 358). This worked in a **performative** and **intentional** fashion, and thereby contributing to the way artists are understood even now, even as the role was being performed in the first place.

Irreverence, transgression, and an antimoralistic stance can still be found in stereotypes of artists who are often perceived as loners. These perceptions are noted by Charland (2010), who described the stereotypes associated with artists, as described by the children in his study, as very similar with the most negative stereotypes accorded to African Americans – specifically links to poverty, drug use, unemployment, laziness, and promiscuity. Equally, Bain notes psychologists draw on these conceptions as well, describing the artistic persona as:

> hypersensitive, aggressive, autonomous, and independent, preoccupied with work to the exclusion of social activity, intolerant of order and seeking novelty and change, suffused with intense but chaotic emotions, and opposed to the conventional and banal. (Steptoe cited in Bain 2005, p. 30)

Charland believes this psychological description contributes to the underrepresentation of African American students in postsecondary art training, as "To adopt an artist's identity would be to simultaneously fulfil certain of White society's stereotypes of Black people, both groups stereotypically portrayed as destined to live in poverty simply by virtue of their group affiliation" (2010, p. 128).

Not all characteristics associated with artists are necessarily negative. Bain (2005, p. 30) goes on: "This tendency to rebel against established norms – to repeatedly question, challenge, and defy the limits of acceptability – may have become the defining feature of what it means to be an artist in contemporary society" (Bain 2005, p. 30). Bain posits that working artists play into this myth as it provides a collection of characteristics from which the artist can draw to "reaffirm their occupational identity" (Bain 2005). Thus, the myth is fed not only by the audience, who requires confession, but also by the artist, who accepts this need to construct a biography as a part of their practice.

Artist's Typologies

Pollock (1980) explores the idea of the construction of the artistic subject, within which specific types of artists' personas (including the bohemian, the genius, the magician, and so forth) can be located: "The construction of an artistic subject for art is accomplished through current discursive structures – the biographic, which focuses exclusively on the individual, and the narrative, which produces coherent, linear, causal sequences through which an artistic subject is realised" (Pollock 1980, p. 59). Similarly, Codell (2003) outlines a typography of artistic subjects that were either enacted by or imposed on artists through writing in her discussion of the life writing's – biographies, autobiographies, reviews, and journals – of British artists in Victorian England. Within a period of substantial focus on biographical publications, descriptions of the lives of artists became increasingly sought after and Codell comments that "The rise of British artists' celebrity was considered evidence that ... artists were thoroughly socialized, not alienated and suffering in garrets ... Biographically recognized artists were marked by conflicting and fluid identities between 1870 and 1920" (2003, pp. 2–3).

Codell's (2003) typology of these identities consists of four identifiable artist stereotypes: the bohemian (the vagabond adventurer, a playful rogue, although British bohemians were often considered gentlemen as well); the degenerate (which linked biology, creativity and madness, and where artists were constructed as dangerous, impulsive, and immoral); the uniquely Victorian prelapsarian (innocent, unworldly, humble, selfless, and unsocialized); and the professional (skilled, educated, economically established, and validated through membership to professional groups and societies). The degree to which an artist was associated with each of these types was dependent on who was doing the lifewriting. For example, while the bohemian stereotype was only occasionally written into British artists' biographies during this period, "some presented the benign Bohemian" as a connection of sorts to Continental artists, while still retaining moral superiority over French or Dutch counterparts (Codell 2003, p. 100). Codell offers satirical novelist William Makepeace Thackery as an example of this benign bohemianism in his characterization as a gentleman bohemian; similarly, the nonfiction of the time "emphasized Bohemians' playfulness, [which was] so unlike the solitary mad artist of degeneracy theories or the introverted Bohemians of Victorian fiction" (2003, p. 98). Perhaps the benign and somewhat twee rebelliousness of the hipster movement could be considered a contemporary reflection of this particular flavor of benign bohemianism.

Similar to the bohemian stereotype, the construct of degeneracy was only occasionally written into biographical literature from the Victorian period, and actively denied in artists' autobiographies and biographies written by family members. At a time when moral characteristics were thought to be visible and linked to physical characteristics, "most biographies and autobiographies denied artists' degeneracy through photographs of their bodies, homes, and families, including children and ancestors, to signal domestic, genetic, and biological normality" (Codell 2003, p. 103). Although the link between appearance and character has largely disappeared since its heyday in Victorian England, the traces of self-destruction evident in the appearance of singer Amy Winehouse could be a reflection of some continued persistence of the degeneracy stereotype. Hailed as "prodigiously talented and perennially wasted" (Heller 2007), Winehouse's talent won her five Grammy awards – the first British female to do so – and the album responsible, *Back in Black*, was the highest selling album of the twenty-first century in Britain shortly after her death in 2011 (McCormick 2011). The link between her drug and alcohol abuse, her talent, and her music is perfectly embodied by her hit song Rehab (which won Grammy awards for Record of the Year, Song of the Year, and Best Female Pop Vocal Performance), and this impassioned rejection of medical help for her addictions provided a soundtrack to the tabloid media's documentation of her physical degeneration. Bentley (2011) describes photographs which "caught her unsteady on her feet or vacant-eyed, and she appeared unhealthily thin, with scabs on her face and marks on her arms," and this external evidence of internal troubles shows the continued persistence of the link between creativity, talent, and mental illness.

Without the scale and ubiquity of photography and tabloid newspapers tracking artists' lives, Victorians used personal photographs in their autobiographies to deny the worst of the characteristics of the degenerate and the bohemian as described in fiction of the time. These images showed the artist as physically healthy, within stable family groupings, and showing thriving offspring. This worked to counteract the fictional depictions of creative people, where artist characters within stories were "divorced from the world by their excessive devotion to art [and] appeared disheveled, oddly dressed, spiritual, sloppy, and single" (Codell 2003, pp. 99–100). Here we can see the co-creation of the artistic subject through biographical, autobiographical, and fictional representations of the artist. The fictional exaggerates the stereotypes, while the biographical and the autobiographical minimizes and denies the worst stereotypes, with the agency of the artist contributing to the construction of a more socially acceptable artistic persona. House (2012) argues that some artists even worked to create a particular representation through their private letters, rather than only through public representations such as autobiography, as they were aware that letters were used extensively in the construction of biography both before and after the artist's death. Nineteenth century French Realist Gustave Courbet deliberately "used letters to propagate an image of his artistic identity, or rather to construct a public persona that would be used as a frame within which his œuvre might be viewed" (House 2012, p. 337), and postimpressionist Paul Gauguin used letters from his home in Tahiti to those in France, where his paintings were sold, as "part of his strategy of self-presentation and self-promotion" (p. 339). These artists, House argues, depended on personal connections through letters to help create an artistic persona that drew on the positive aspects of Romantic and bohemian stereotypes to explain and legitimize their marginalized artistic practice.

In addition to artist types seen in the bohemian and the degenerate, Codell (2003) describes the Victorians' development of their own unique artistic stereotype in the prelapsarian artist. She describes how artists of the time "were often revered for their unworldliness, cut off from social, commercial and professional demands" (Codell, 2003, p. 79). The innocent, childlike artist was seen to be capable of creating great art only if they were kept separate from the art market, and this separation would protect the artist's character and talent. By retrofitting famous artists of the time with this construct, the artistic gatekeepers – patrons and collectors – could maintain control over the market by excluding those who were actively involved in producing for that market. The growing celebrity of artists through the circulation of biographical materials was countered by the expectation that they would not engage directly with that celebrity and concentrate solely on their work. Codell (2003) explains that these expectations were particularly strong for the growing contingent of female artists, but others argue this conception of innocence-as-genius has also been co-opted into descriptions of brilliant people outside of the arts. Radcliff (2008) describes representations of Albert Einstein as artist which draw on understandings of the artist having "an incredible passion and a determination to follow a set path despite any possible consequences" (p. 67) and the "untainted genius who retains the innocence of childhood" (p. 68). Here, a figure of considerable public renown who is not involved in artistic practice has an artistic persona attributed to him through the use of the prelapsarian artistic subject. This attribution utilizes an existing shorthand the public can understand to present a figure "beyond the reach of average mortals" (Radcliff 2008, p. 70).

The use of prelapsarian expectations as reinforcement of existing control structures is seen in opposition to the development of estheticism and the desire for professionalism of many artists. Codell states that "Aestheticism, while advocating an anti-commercial preoccupation with art for its own sake, nonetheless shaped new professional identities for artists in opposition to the infantilizing didacticism of much Victorian art criticism" (2003, p. 93). It is in the development of these professional identities that the artists themselves contributed to the typology, as "In the face of stereotypes of degenerates, bohemians, or economically and socially naive prelapsarians, lifewritings intervened to construct mature artists embodying economic efficiency ... work ethic, and sociality" (Codell 2003, p. 272). Describing the autobiographical norms of the time, Codell states that artists endeavored to demonstrate that they "earned status by hard work and market acumen," presenting themselves as entrepreneurs (2003, p. 111). Just as Victorian artists proclaimed their professionalism through the creation of artists' societies and academies, so too do artists working today, including those working in the fringe practices that are discussed in the latter half of this chapter. Street artists create prints and canvas work both to sell and to exhibit in galleries; tattoo artists attend conventions and are interviewed for magazines discussing inspiration and training; craftivists work in collectives that engage with the process of legitimization of craft technique as art practice; performance poets distribute recordings of their shows (and often publish page poetry), to demonstrate skill and participation with the wider scene in which they are involved.

As introduced above, Codell describes artists of the Victorian era engaging with and contributing to the development of the artistic subject through their own lifewritings. These artists rejected elements that were not useful for their career (particularly from the degeneracy discourse, but also elements of the antisocial bohemian and the naive prelapsarian) and instead worked to construct an artistic subject which embodied the professional ideal. This analysis is particularly useful in discussions of the artistic persona. This professional identity, where the artist is represented as "an autonomous expert who determines the market value of his/her expertise and who produces for the sake of fulfilling a calling" (Codell 2003, p. 112) draws on the mythology of the artist as developed from the Enlightenment and through the Romantic movement. However, this representation of the artist also suggests a divergence from this mythology that allows us to consider the impact of creative industry and cultural economy discourses that emerged in the late twentieth century. This shift in discourse toward viewing the arts as a contributor to the financial economy provides additional complexity to our understanding of the artist-as-subject.

Authors, Auteurs, and Makers

The term artist is used broadly in this chapter, encompassing visual artists, including painters with brush and can, sculptors, photographers, filmmakers, writers of prose and poetry, musicians, actors, dancers, and performance artists, as well as those working in less traditional mediums such as tattoo, needlework, and fibrecraft. As can be seen in Codell's (2003) work, and in Charland's (2010) study introduced earlier, the term "artist" is most often used to describe those working in the "fine" arts such as painting or sculpture. We are less concerned with the medium used in the creation of an artwork than in the self-identification of the creator as an artist. In taking this broad view, we draw not only from the discourses developed within the visual arts, but conceptualizations of the literary author, auteur filmmaker, and maker. These last alternative understandings of author, auteur, and maker are explored briefly below.

Roland Barthes' "The Death of the Author" (1977) and Michel Foucault's "What is an Author?" (1991) are the two most seminal texts that discuss the role of the author in literature (Lamarque 1990). Both texts argue for the removal of the author from the text: the interpretation of the text should rest not with some all-knowing "Author-God" (Barthes 1977, p. 146), but rather should be interpreted without reference to either the author-as-person or the wider social construct of the author. However, in constructing their arguments for the death of the author, they also work to define and locate the concept of the author-as-person, which is instructive in our study. Both Barthes and Foucault describe the author as a "modern figure," created through ideology and discourse. This connects to Pollock's (1980) conceptualization of the discursive "artistic subject." The discussion of both the author as subject (what Foucault terms the author function) and the author as a specific individual, allows us to see the figure of the author as "a more weighty figure with legal rights and social standing, a producer of texts deemed to have value" (Lamarque 1990, p. 321). This separates the role of the author from all others who write, whose texts are not considered valuable; the identification as an author or artist is determined by whether their works are categorized as literature or art. A scientist who writes scholarly papers is not considered an author in the same way that a novelist is. The image of the author portrayed by Barthes and Foucault is one that holds back the interpretative process, informing and polluting the text with extraneous information. In Barthes's words "The image of literature to be found in ordinary culture is tyrannically centred on the author, his person, his life, his tastes, his passions, while criticism still consists for the most part in saying Baudelaire's work is the failure of Baudelaire himself, Van Gogh's his madness, Tchaikovsky's his vice" (1977, p. 143). This connects directly back to the role of the myth of the artist in determining whether a writer can be an author. The social role of the author/artist, and the specific elements of that role that are enacted by any specific individual, are integral to our understanding of the artwork that the specific individual has created.

Barthes and Foucault were, in Lamarque's (1990, p. 330) terms "prescribing the death of the author and by promoting the text over the work, both writers see themselves as liberating meaning from unnatural and undesirable restrictions." Whether or not you agree that this liberation of meaning is desirable, necessary, or even possible, the persistence of the role of the author/artist indicates we are by no means able to separate the work from its creator.

The development of auteurism and auteur theory in film is testament to the enduring need to allocate an artist to an artwork. Despite the reality that filmmaking is a collaborative endeavor, involving in many cases large numbers of highly skilled people who each contribute to the final product, the role of the director as auteur persists. Andrews (2012, p. 42) argues that auteurism and auteur theory persist despite having been debunked many times, with "critiques of auteurism generally condemn[ing] it for the false picture it provides of cinematic activity, which it simplifies at best and badly distorts at worst" (p. 42). Perhaps more than any other socially constructed artist's role, the role of auteur is not dependent on the individual's influence on the final creative product so much as it is granted by the audience. Andrews argues that "auteur status is hard and real while the authorship to which that status refers is subjective, negotiable, and marked by multiple contexts" (2012, p. 49); the role of the director as the sole author of the film is false, but that individual will still receive the credit and acclaim as author. By allocating a single author to a collaborative work, as with the auteur to the film, the artist-as-genius is enacted, and the film director becomes responsible for the beauty and depth of the film-as-art.

In a different vein, the craftsman (or maker, to use a gender-neutral term) may struggle to gain recognition as an artist. Whereas authors and auteurs are working in fields now accepted as "fine arts" – Risatti (2007, p. 90) argues that painting, sculpture, and architecture are the foundations of the fine arts, and that these three creative practices have been supplemented by "printmaking, photography, performance, happenings, film, installation, and video" – craft makers are most often excluded from this categorization. As a result of the outcome of their labor not being considered art, the makers are not considered artists. The distinction between craft and art can often seem arbitrary, as Becker (1982, p. 272) notes: "The same activity, using the same materials and skills in what appear to be similar ways, may be called by either title, as may the people who engage in it." A common way of determining whether an object is craft or art (and therefore its maker a crafter or an artist) is to consider the role of function: an object which places function at the core is considered craft or design, whereas an artwork may contain no function other than its own existence. Relating this back to the determinations of artistness explored above, the artist must have the capacity to explore their own creative impulse and vision, irrespective of whether the final result will be of use. Risatti explores the role of creativity as a driver of craft:

> If the maker is deprived of choice, of free will in the making process, he or she is also denied any chance at expression; there is no possibility to freely and wilfully "shape" the object so that it can be the bearer of the maker's intentions to artistic meaning. (2007, p. 221)

This requirement of freedom of expression and creativity does not in itself exclude makers from the realm of artistness, as many makers fully explore and test the boundaries of functionality and expression in the creation of objects. This is certainly not true of all makers, and Becker's (1982, p. 276) distinction between ordinary craftsmen, whose focus is on the practical and functional, and artist-craftsmen, whose focus is on the beautiful and expressive, is useful here. The former may be just as capable and skilled as the latter, but in focusing on function over appearance these makers do not engage with elements of artistness. By contrast, the artist-craftsmen may use the same materials and techniques as the ordinary craftsmen, but their focus on beauty and creative expression connects them to the discursively created artist.

These three conceptualizations of the artist – as author, auteur, and maker – all draw on and extend elements of artistness as described in the myth of the artist. However, despite its persistence, the myth of the artist is not the only discourse through which artistness is understood.

The Artist as Creative Laborer

Alongside the myth of the artist as a heroic individual, artistic identity can also be defined through a relationship with the labor market. The designation of artistness in economic terms has become more common since the shift in governmental policy in the Western world toward conceptions of a "creative industry" or "cultural industry" framework (Barbour 2006; Hartley 2005). The relationship between artists and the market is arguably as old as the art world itself, making recent developments in policy and marketing all the more interesting.

Karttunen (1998) investigates how "status-of-the-artist" studies – those conducting empirical studies into the arts for government – use the term artist. The author makes a distinction between how the term is used commonly – "a person who for a start paints, dances or sings, either as a job or as a hobby, or even someone who is instead simply very skilled at some activity, not necessarily art at all" – with how it is used in labor surveys, where the researchers are interested "in people who practise – or seriously endeavour to practise – the arts as an occupation" (1998, p. 3). Karttunen acknowledges the difficulty in determining who fits into these categories and recognizes that despite defining the artist on the basis of their "practice," including their economic success, the myth of the artist described above comes back to haunt researchers of creative labor, as "artists' occupational ideology ... portrays the 'true' artist as being indifferent to economic motives" (Karttunen 1998, p. 4).

Defining an artist in primarily economic terms does have some potential benefits over the Romantic mythology discussed earlier. For one thing, there is no need to look or act in a distinctively "artistic" manner to identify with this definition, which could help to remove damaging stereotypes that work against wider minority involvement in the traditional art world and which may be discouraging those artists in need of help from seeking it. Also, the explicit discussion of market, peer review, and economic reward may develop to the point that more professional artists are rewarded fairly for their labor.

One defining feature of the "artist-as-creative-laborer" understanding of artistness is that it tends to focus on what Becker (1982) calls the "art world" – the galleries, publishing/recording companies, distribution companies, and so on. Those operating outside of these systems might be caught by the labor market studies, but due to the requirement of self-identifying as an "artist" as an occupational category (rather than a vocation or identity), there may be many who simply do not see themselves as such even if they would fit the category. By contrast, the bohemian artist of the myth may fit some of those who work around the fringes of the art world, mimicking their forebears from the eighteenth century:

> Some Bohemians would be on the fringes of the commercial art world, or would actually receive an income from writing or the stage, but many, if not most, would receive little or no reward from their artistic endeavours and be forced to survive by borrowing, taking menial jobs, or by the use of their wits. (Campbell 1989, p. 196)

This historical and ongoing notion that artists have a "real job" in addition to their artistic endeavors does not seem to have challenged the economic designations of "primary occupation" according to the number of hours spent and the amount of money earned that form the basis of census questions.

Online Artistness

These two conflicting discourses of artistness have resulted in the expectation that artists must be simultaneously alternative and commercial, poor and well paid, a hero and an antihero, a loner and a social trendsetter. One way to deal with these types of contradictory expectations is for an artist to separate their persona as the *creator* from their persona as the *laborer* through the use of intermediaries such as dealer galleries, critics, publishers, and agents. By foregrounding particular parts of their self-presentation, the artist is able to symbolically distance themselves from the economic structures that allow them to continue to work. This can work well for those whose primary forms of creative expression can be hung on gallery walls and printed in books, where the artist is credited, *biographied*, and paid for their endeavors. Here, the laboring parts of artistness are less visible, with artists working with very little direct interference from their audience. When these artists are producing and maintaining their online personas, they can draw on the legitimizing systems and practices of dealers, critics, and publishers to demonstrate that they are, indeed, an artist.

However, for creative practitioners working on the fringes of the art world, who often struggle to have their creative practice seen as "art," the support structures that allow the musician, painter of canvas, or novelist to maintain a symbolic separation from their economics are not as available. For these artists, producing an online persona that demonstrates sufficient artistness requires a strategic performance of different elements of the myth of the artist and the creative laborer. In a study of street artists, craftivists, performance poets, and tattooists which utilized the IPA approach outlined in Chapter 5, the creation of an artist's persona online involved slipping between different "registers of performance" (Barbour 2014), giving the audience of fans, followers, friends, and family access to professional, personal, and intimate aspects of their lives. These artists used different parts of the collection of behaviors and beliefs that make up "artistness" as representative elements of their Goffmanian "front" (1959), **mediatizing** their role online through their use of photography, statuses, publically declared interests, and involvement in online communities.

Through photographs of their work, artists working in visual media demonstrate the skill and creativity required by the myth of the artist, along with the productivity required to meet expectations of the artist as laborer. Statuses speak to political causes and personal beliefs that align with bohemian interests or create a sense of an "in-group" where the artist demonstrates an involvement and commitment to the broader art world. Although demonstrations of mild social deviancy (drinking, smoking, socially acceptable drug use, avoidance of capitalist norms of consumption, work avoidance) might in themselves be commonly displayed on social networking sites, these can also be used to play into expectations of artists as bohemian. For example, demonstrating a profound level of skill through involvement in and recognition by the wider tattoo community, Benjamin Laukis reposted a photograph of himself with seven award trophies won at a single event in 2013. His accompanying text reflected a desire to downplay these accolades – "I couldn't be bothered posting all the Expo awards/tattoos" – while also utilizing them to build his fan base and thank his sponsors. Here, we can understand Laukis's post through the lens of VARP (value, agency, reputation, prestige): the posting of awards demonstrates reputation and external validation of prestige, while the post helps the artist add value to his persona and demonstrates his agency in how he is presenting himself publicly.

Rayna Fahey is a craftivist whose work speaks to environmental issues. Her involvement in permaculture and community gardens, as demonstrated in the Facebook post shown in Figure 6.1, reflects a personal commitment to the issues that inform her work, and connect to an understanding of artistness relating to anti-consumerism.

By inviting his audience into his musings on happiness and relationships, a stencil artist performs a sense of vulnerability and loneliness through the post presented in Figure 6.2, while also acknowledging mildly deviant behavior – "random stoned deep status"; both are elements associated with the myth of the artist. By contrast, tattoo artist Amanda Cain expressed feelings of being misunderstood or persecuted. Leaving Australia for a trip to Japan, she posted a comment to Facebook that she'd "never been stared at so much!" as she had while in Melbourne Airport. Despite the fact there was, presumably, no way for those staring at her to identify Amanda as a tattoo artist in this context, she interpreted the stares as related to the tattoos she wears, and so the experience of mild persecution remained.

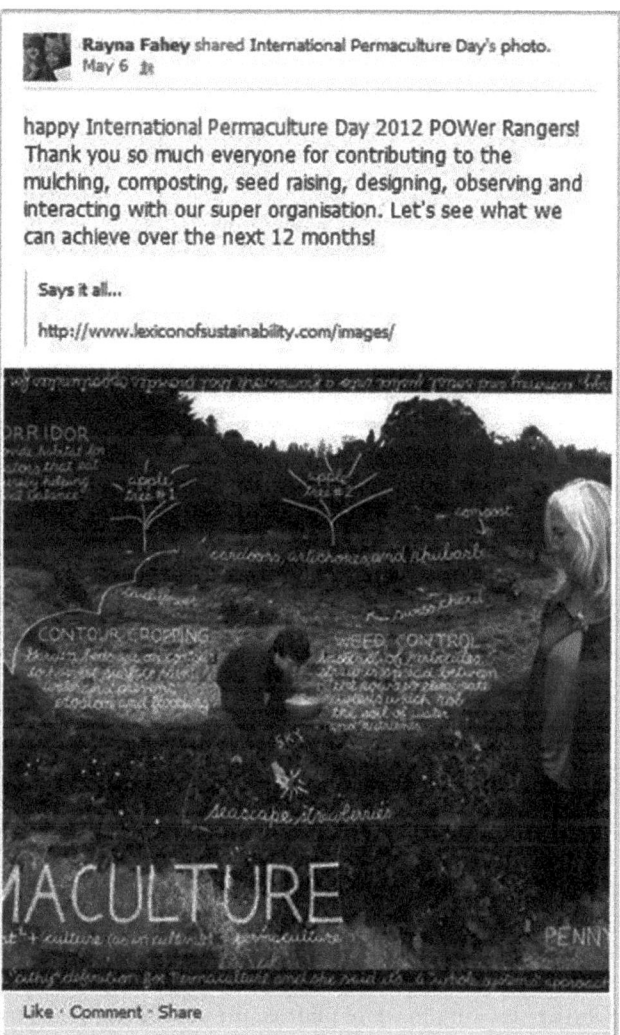

Figure 6.1 Rayna Fahey "Happy International Permaculture Day 2012," Facebook post.
Source: Reproduced with permission of Rayna Fahey.

The range of spaces where artists network, promote, create, and play online are diverse, running from personal and professional websites (either self-created or made by others), collective spaces such as online galleries or sites such as DeviantArt, and increasingly in the past decade social networking sites such as Facebook, Twitter, Tumblr, and Instagram. Each of these spaces is encoded with its own set of presentational expectations: Facebook encourages the sharing of many elements of one's life; Twitter rewards brevity and wit;

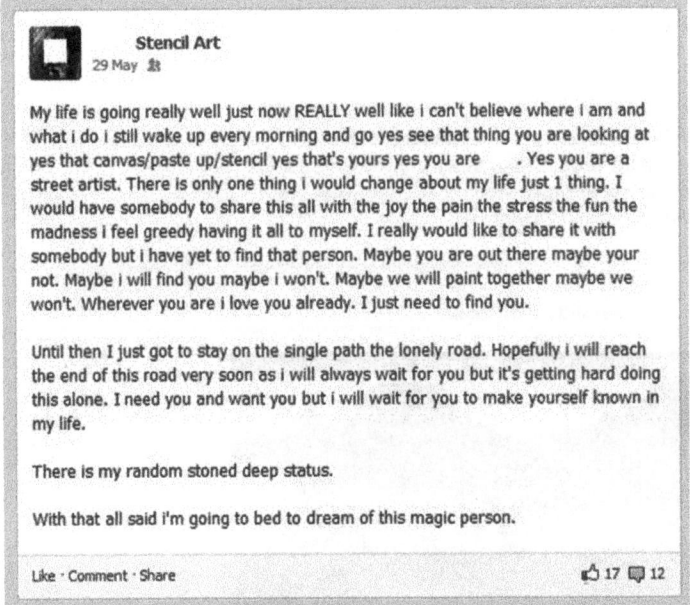

Stencil Art
29 May

My life is going really well just now REALLY well like i can't believe where i am and what i do i still wake up every morning and go yes see that thing you are looking at yes that canvas/paste up/stencil yes that's yours yes you are   . Yes you are a street artist. There is only one thing i would change about my life just 1 thing. I would have somebody to share this all with the joy the pain the stress the fun the madness i feel greedy having it all to myself. I really would like to share it with somebody but i have yet to find that person. Maybe you are out there maybe your not. Maybe i will find you maybe i won't. Maybe we will paint together maybe we won't. Wherever you are i love you already. I just need to find you.

Until then I just got to stay on the single path the lonely road. Hopefully i will reach the end of this road very soon as i will always wait for you but it's getting hard doing this alone. I need you and want you but i will wait for you to make yourself known in my life.

There is my random stoned deep status.

With that all said i'm going to bed to dream of this magic person.

Like · Comment · Share   👍 17 💬 12

Figure 6.2 Stencil artist, Facebook post. *Source:* Reproduced with permission of the artist.

Tumblr and Instagram have a core currency of sharable content (particularly photographs). The successful adoption of these spaces for the creation of an artist's persona requires some acknowledgment and acceptance of these encoded expectations. For the tattoo and street artists in our research, the visual nature of Instagram was a boon, but came with downsides: images quickly left the artist's control, or photographs, such as those taken by tourists in subcultural hotspots, were posted to the platform and circulated without acknowledgment of the artist. Here the benefits of the medium – access to a worldwide audience who are looking for cool photos, the capacity to network with and learn from other artists – are balanced by the desire to have one's efforts and skills recognized and attributed. These are ongoing issues in both these types of creative practice, however – tattoo art is almost exclusively unsigned and can never be replicated or returned to the artist, and street art is both pseudonymous and deliberately ephemeral.

The need to distance his legal identity from his artist's persona means that a stencil artist must shield (or in some cases pixelate) his face in photos posted to his social media accounts, as demonstrated in Figure 6.3. This deliberate framing demonstrates the artist's agency in producing his persona, as he selectively engages with identifying practices and the norms of engagement in different social media platforms.

Figure 6.3 Stencil artist, identity obscured, Facebook cover photo. *Source:* Reproduced with permission of the artist.

By contrast, the embodied nature of the work created by performance poets and, to a lesser extent, craftivists, connects the work tightly to the artist who created it. Rather than concern over the loss of control, performance poets were concerned about sharing *too much* of their work, to the detriment of attendance and participation at live events. One poet avoided sharing audio or audiovisual recordings of her performances as she wanted people to engage with her work in person. Another made use of audience recordings of the performances but struggled with the fact that some pieces from his repertoire – audience favorites – were recorded and uploaded far more frequently than others. In contrast, the content and purpose of craftivist work can prove problematic in online spaces. For one artist, the use of specific language around female genitalia breached platform use terms and conditions, requiring her to rename pieces of work in order to share them with audiences. For another craftivist, the determination to connect to others, to be a node in a network or a member of a community rather than a loner artist, deliberately plays against ideas of the artist as a heroic genius.

Ben Mellor's website includes a "10 of the Best" collection (Figure 6.4) of fan recordings of his live performances. While he saw this as a useful way to introduce online audiences to his work, Ben struggled with the fact that many of the recordings uploaded by audience members were of the same popular pieces, rather than reflective of the breadth of his poetry.

While Ben Mellor's work can be recorded and shared online by fans, some artists have found online engagement with their performance work to be less complementary. The tag NSFW (not suitable for work) is often applied to Casey's work (see Figure 6.5) and although in the case of *Casting off my womb* this led to international coverage of a small piece of performance art as well as

Figure 6.4 Ben Mellor's "10 of the Best," webpage. *Source:* Reproduced with the permission of Ben Mellor.

the impetus for several follow-on works (Barbour and Mansfield 2019), it also meant that potential audience members may not have engaged directly with her art practice due to the framing of the piece as "gross" or potentially sexualized by online commentators.

Conclusion

In selectively engaging with some elements of the myth of the artist, and balancing these with elements of the creative laborer, the participants in this study demonstrated remarkable flexibility and intention in the presentation of

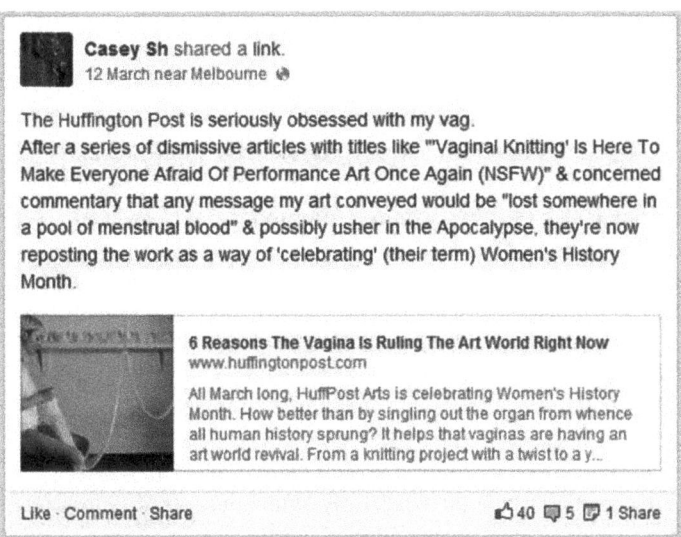

Figure 6.5 Casey Sh, "obsessed with my vag," Facebook post. *Source:* Reproduced with permission of Casey Sh.

artistness through online spaces. We can see all five of the dimensions of persona represented here, as the artists produced personas that were public, mediatized, performative, collectively constructed, and were produced intentionally to create some form of value for the artist. Social media spaces were used to build particular micro-publics of audiences that enabled the artist to connect to the myth of the artist as creator, while legitimizing the persona of the artist as laborer. This mediatizing of their persona demonstrated the elements of VARP – value, agency, reputation, prestige – that empowered the artist to claim ownership of the relationship between the work and the persona. Utilizing their agency in self-presentational practices, the artists played within the stereotypical expectations of artistness, using the platforms strategically to create an online persona that demonstrated they were, in fact, artists, despite not working in the fine arts. By taking an IPA approach to investigating artists, it is possible to locate the current practice of specific artists within a broader history of the role of the artist as bohemian, genius, mad man, laborer, and tax payer.

References

Andrews, D. (2012). No start, no end: Auteurism and the auteur theory. *Film International* 10 (6): 37–55.

Bain, A. (2005). Constructing an artistic identity. *Work, Employment and Society* 19 (1): 25–46. https://doi.org/10.1177/0950017005051280.

Barbour, K. (2006). Constructing artistic integrity: An exploratory study. Masters thesis. The University of Waikato, New Zealand.

Barbour, K. (2014). Finding the edge: Online persona creation by fringe artists. PhD thesis. Deakin University, Australia.

Barbour, K. (2015). Registers of performance: Negotiating the professional, personal and intimate in online persona creation. In: *Media, Margins and Popular Culture* (ed. E. Thorsen, H. Savigny, J. Alexander and D. Jackson), 57–69. Basingstoke: Palgrave MacMillan.

Barbour, K. and Mansfield, L. (2019). Intersections between corporeal performance and distributed digital audiences: Casey Jenkins and remediated artistic practice. *TDR/The Drama Review* 63 (1): 125–140.

Barthes, R. (1977). *Image Music Text*. London: Fontana Press.

Becker, H.S. (1982). *Art Worlds*. Berkeley: University of California Press.

Bentley, P. (2011). A death foretold: The rapid rise and tragic fall of Amy Winehouse, the deeply flawed soul prodigy. *Mail Online* (July 25). www.dailymail.co.uk/tvshowbiz/article-2018025/Amy-Winehouse-dead-Before-rise-fall-deeply-flawed-prodigy.html (accessed June 24, 2013).

Bourdieu, P. (1993). *The Field of Cultural Production: Essays on Art and Literature* (ed. R. Johnson). Cambridge: Polity Press.

Bourdieu, P. (1996). *The Rules of Art: Genesis and Structure of the Literary Field*. Cambridge: Polity Press.

Campbell, C. (1989). *The Romantic Ethic and the Spirit of Modern Consumerism*. Cambridge, MA: Blackwell.

Charland, W. (2010). African American youth and the artist's identity: Cultural models and aspirational foreclosure. *Studies in Art Education: A Journal of Issues and Research in Art Education* 51: 115–133.

Codell, J.F. (2003). *The Victorian Artist: Artists' Lifewritings in Britain, ca. 1870–1910*. New York: Cambridge University Press.

Foucault, M. (1991). *The Foucault Reader* (ed. P. Rabinow). London: Penguin Books.

Gluck, M. (2000). Theorizing the cultural roots of the bohemian artist. *Modernism/Modernity* 7 (3): 351–378. https://doi.org/10.1353/mod.2000.0059.

Goffman, E. (1959). *The Presentation of Self in Everyday Life*. New York: Anchor Books.

Hall, D.E. (2004). *Subjectivity: The New Critical Idiom*. New York: Routledge.

Hartley, J. (2005). *Creative Industries*. Oxford: Blackwell.

Heller, K. (2007). The ruin of a talent, shrilly told by tabloids. *The Philadelphia Inquirer* (December 12). http://web.archive.org/web/20080206083621/http://www.philly.com/inquirer/magazine/20071212_Karen_Heller___The_ruin_of_a_talent__shrilly_told_by_tabloids.html (accessed June 24, 2013).

House, J. (2012). Working with artists' letters. *Word & Image* 28 (4): 335–339. https://doi.org/10.1080/02666286.2012.740182.

Karttunen, S. (1998). How to identify artists? Defining the population for "status-of-the-artist" studies. *Poetics* 26 (1): 1–19.

Kris, E. and Kurz, O. (1979). *Legend, Myth, and Magic in the Image of the Artist: A Historical Experiment*. New Haven: Yale University Press.

Lamarque, P. (1990). The death of the author: An analytical autopsy. *British Journal of Aesthetics* 30 (4): 319–331. https://doi.org/10.1093/bjaesthetics/30.4.319.

McCormick, N. (2011). Amy Winehouse had talent to burn. Instead, it burned her. *The Telegraph* (July 23). www.telegraph.co.uk/journalists/neil-mccormick/8657146/Amy-Winehouse-had-talent-to-burn.-Instead-it-burned-her.html (accessed July 1, 2013).

Pollock, G. (1980). Artists, mythologies and media – genius, madness and art history. *Screen* 21 (3): 57–96. https://doi.org/10.1093/screen/21.3.57.

Radcliff, M. (2008). Absentminded professor or romantic artist? The depiction of creativity in documentary biographies of Albert Einstein. *Journal of Popular Film and Television* 36 (2): 62–71.

Risatti, H. (2007). *A Theory of Craft: Function and Aesthetic Expression*. Chapel Hill: University of North Carolina Press.

Vasari, G. (2005 [1551]). *Vasari's Lives of the Artists: Giotto, Masaccio, Fra Filippo Lippi, Botticeli, Leonardo, Raphael, Michelangelo, Titian* (trans. J. Foster (ed. M. Aronberg Lavin). New York: Dover Publications.

Weedon, C. (1987). *Feminist Practice and Post-structuralist Theory*. Oxford: Basil Blackwell.

7

From Player to Persona

In the previous chapter we began the process of examining the practice of the public presentation of the self through our conceptualization of persona, demonstrating the interpretative phenomenological analysis approach to understand the construction of the artist persona better. This chapter continues our application of persona studies to consider the relationship between play and persona. We begin with an historical overview of the ways video games have provided players with the opportunity to experiment with identity. This experimentation was initially confined to the internal virtual worlds of role-playing games and the use of avatars, which became public as game play was connected by early Internet technologies. This chapter highlights the historical shift, from the play of identity within games, to the externalization of player identity via the social networking features of digital distribution platforms. We consider the ways games culture has been classified and distinguished in the past and look to recent developments within games culture and document the tensions that a particular persona, that of the "gamer" has generated through public campaigns of harassment and "toxic" behavior. The chapter then deploys the methodology of analysis introduced in Chapter 3 in which we use five dimensions of persona – **public, mediatized, collective, performative**, and **intentional value** (summarized as **VARP**) – to examine the rise of a new persona type, the "gâmeur," among independent video game developers currently challenging the normativity of the mainstream video game industry. The approach includes an example of network visualization of collective activity within the "indie" game community (described in Chapter 5).

The slightest review of the history of digital or "video" games reveals an outright hostility toward the medium. In the past, games were dismissed as childish diversions, and today they are commonly labeled as dangerous tools for promoting violence and inactivity. However, games are no longer on the borders of the mainstream; they are at the center of popular culture and one of the most successful global entertainment industries. As Danish game designer

Persona Studies: An Introduction, First Edition. P. David Marshall, Christopher Moore, and Kim Barbour.

and theorist Jesper Juul (2009) suggests, games are everywhere, and they are becoming "normal." The rise of the digital games industry, reportedly worth US$109 billion in 2017 (McDonald 2017), has meant a competing narrative to the negative attitudes of disregard, hostility, and contempt the industry has faced over the past four decades. However, despite the massive success of the medium, concerns about the effects of mobile, console, and PC games, especially on children, still linger in the representation of games in cinema, television, and print media.

Accompanying this global rise has been a steady evolution in thinking about the relationship between players and their games. At first, games were considered as entirely consumable and disposable diversions, unconnected to the broader presentation of the player as an individual. Except for one important element of arcade game culture: players were able to add three initials to their top scores on arcade cabinet machines. This was the first iteration of the player's public persona; however, it was subject to erasure with a simple unplugging of the cabinet. Nonetheless, it marked the first important point of difference of games as a form of media that empowered the user to express the five dimensions of persona. The simple initializing of the player's identity was a mediatized public performance of the self among a collective of players that represented an investment in the value of personal reputation (one coin at a time). As games became more familiar and moved into the home, colonizing the lounge room and the family television, as well as personal computers previously framed purely as office-at-home devices, new types of experiences emerged which required players to invest intensive amounts of time and energy (see Mitew and Moore 2017). As the technologies expanded, games increased in scope and complexity and were able to incorporate the player more directly into the action and narrative of the experience.

Early role-playing games, like the prototypical *Colossal Cave Adventure* (1977) provided players with a way to take control of a character through a textual interface. It was followed by the graphical era of the 1980s, which brought a visual dimension to role-playing games with *Mystery House* (1980) for the Apple II and Sierra's highly successful *King's Quest* series. LucasArts' *Maniac Mansion* (1987) introduced the command interface, which provided an onscreen list of commands for the player to interact with the game world. Role-playing games (RPGs) began to increase the sense of adventure and player control over the narrative as well as the player's sense of in-game identity through customization of the playable character. With the expansion of the Internet from universities into the home, multiplayer RPGs called multiuser dungeons (MUDs) became accessible in the late 1980s. This trend expanded with the availability of increased graphical processing power in the 1990s and the success of games like the multiplayer RPG *Neverwinter Nights*, which continued the popular integration of the pen-and-paper RPG franchise Dungeons & Dragons. The massively multiplayer online role-playing games

(MMORPGs) were popularized in the 1990s by *Ultima Online*, and the genre became dominated by Blizzard Entertainment's *World of Warcraft* (*WoW*), which launched in 2004.

Until very recently, online RPGs afforded players a high degree of anonymity. This ended with Blizzard's real name policy in 2010, which forced players to use their real names when participating in the company's online forums designed to support and discuss the games *StarCraft II* and *WoW*. Anonymity has been further eroded by games publishers encouraging players to connect their social media accounts to their game accounts. The popularity of MUDs and MMORPGs had previously been driven by players who enjoyed virtual spaces where they could refashion their identities and reinvent themselves in fantasy and science fiction settings. Sherry Turkle's work on gender and identity manipulation through role-playing in *Life on the Screen: Identity in the Age of the Internet* (1995) investigated MUDs and other text-based worlds. Turkle viewed these places as semiprivate and digitally networked spaces that afforded the player unique opportunities to bend and blend their player identity, personalizing the way they presented themselves to others online. Turkle's analysis of the conditions of anonymity in early Internet-enabled computer game spaces found them to offer the player new means of gaining control over the presentation of their subjective selves. Between the repertoire of a game's choices and the player's abilities, the assembly of a gendered in-game performance was explained by Turkle (1995, p. 49) in postmodernist terms as being decentered and multiple; an analysis which highlights the fractured experience of everyday identity (Kendall 1998) and which saw the gender-swapping practices of players as identity formations exploring the conflicts of biological gender.

The Role of Avatars

As players became more familiar with the experience of computer, video, and mobile games, they gained familiarity and cultural literacy with the manipulation of the in-game self as an avatar. In Hinduism, an avatar is a concept that refers to a deity's appearance on the earthly plane of existence. The 1979 game *Avatar* was one of the earliest graphical multiuser role-playing games to experiment with the concept in which players selected the race, gender, ability scores, and name for the in-game version of themselves. In 1985, the designer of *Ultima IV: Quest for the Avatar*, Richard Garriott, took inspiration from the Hindu meaning and sought to make the in-game characters as explicit in-game version of their "real" selves, thereby promoting an ethically driven narrative. It should be noted that in-game avatars are not only limited to one style of representation: they have been simple text characters, 8- and 16-bit graphics, and fully 3-D rendered polygons. Avatars can have an over-the-shoulder perspective or position the player to see through the eyes of their character, as is typical in the first-person view of contemporary "shooter" games. The avatar has become the primary means for controlling both the player's point of view and subjective identity within games and serves as the interface for both game narratives and mechanics.

Beth Coleman (2011) suggests that player engagement with a game's simulation of the world expresses an agency that is otherwise considered abject. She argues that unlike legacy broadcast media models, the networked media format of online games enables a new form of situated agency through alternative technical affordances and cultural practices, including the perception that the individual can affect change in the world.

> In effect, the primary purpose of using an avatar is to conjure presence. They mark our sense of being there together when we are physically apart. And, in this sense, avatars are a product of computational simulation that gesture toward a state of the actual – an effect across sites of engagement. (Coleman 2011, p. 117)

The situated **agency** of the avatar is a resistance, argues Coleman, against mediation as obfuscation. Avatars are a co-presence which externalizes our personal experiences, interactions, utterances, and gestures within digital objects (save files, images, and algorithms): "As an avatar may have a face, so too, our emails, IMs, and SMS create an archive of our expressions and days" (Coleman 2011, p. 117). This is an important recognition of the way avatars, like any other digitally networked activity, have begun to persist online as digital objects and are no longer purely isolated within individual game existences; rather they are now frequently connected to publicly available profiles. This marks a crucially important shift from the idea of a player identity inside game worlds to a player persona that exists and persists external to those individual game instances.

Much has changed in the video game industry since Chan and Vorderer (2006, p. 98) suggested that one of the major affordances of avatar-mediated communication is anonymity. There are still some online spaces where players can create virtual selves that are unconnected to their physical identities. The virtual world of *Second Life*, which now looks dated compared to current generation games, is still popular because it provides user-programmable options for players' in-game identities, and complete anonymity. There are also multiple contemporary MUD experiences which provide spaces for users to experiment with identity presentation, but these are now in the minority of online game worlds connected to digitally distribution platforms that require players to manage their relationship to the game via social networking style interfaces. A different type of identity play has emerged, one in which player avatars are connected to player's public personas and Turkle anticipated this change when she wrote *Life on the Screen* (1995), arguing it is not just that computers change, but the "times" also change. There is no direct causal link between the two, but the result of the change is new ways of thinking, and new ways of being open to that change.

From Avatar to Persona

Castronova (2005) coined the term "avatar capital" to refer to the massive investment in time and money that players commit to in perfecting their online representations. Games like *Minecraft* have a peripheral market in player "skins," and many games have entire economies based on cosmetic items and costumes for personalizing an avatar's in-game look. Substantial structural changes have occurred to support the rise of these niche and paratextual industries that are associated with avatars and video games more generally. The primary change has been the move away from bricks-and-mortar retailers as the primary locale for the sale of digital games and games-related content as digital distribution platforms have fundamentally remade the games industry (Moore 2009). The ubiquity and ease of online purchasing and content management have been coupled with social networking services and platforms, which involve individual user profiles and pictures acting as a static avatar to represent the player outside of the games they enjoy. Similarly, online games platforms which function as digital distribution services have adopted the interfaces of social media as part of the paradigm shift from representational to presentational media. Players now have the tools to create online personas attached to the games they play, thereby inverting the avatar–player relationship. Where previously the avatar represented the player in-game, the player now has a social media profile linked to their individual collection of games and in-game activities (such as achievements, cosmetic items, and other digital objects) that represent the player outside of any particular game to their micropublic of friends and followers (see Moore 2011a, b).

This inversion of the player–avatar relationship has been an important change and has allowed for the development of an **intercommunicative** player persona that is distinct from a player's singular avatar identity within specific games. In a study of *WoW* and *Eve Online* (*EO*) players, Oskar Milik (2017) identifies the traditional twin trajectories for the approach to the study of player identity. He notes that attempts to understand the identity work of players usually either focus on the representational (attention to characters and choices of gender, class, race, and so on) or the psychological (attention to motivation and individual expression). Milik proposes a combined approach which understands player persona as a methodological concept that is useful for considering the expression of play as a public relationship between character and player. Milik's approach does not constrain a player's persona to particular individual instances of play but views it as generated holistically across and between games, social networks, eSports, live streaming events (on platforms like YouTube, Twitch, and Facebook), web forums, and other online activity. Milik (2017, p. 68) argues that persona studies offer a method for understanding player expression of the self publicly across multiple characters, roles, and games as multiple facets that create complex social interactions across and between different **micro-publics** (see Marshall, Barbour, and Moore 2018; Marshall and Barbour 2015). In MMORPGs, such as *WoW* and *EO*, players manage multiple characters, usually possessing one or two "main" characters, and a range of other characters known as "alts." Some of these characters serve utility purposes for storing and trading items, while others are used to fill in missing roles during group activities known as "guild raids."

> The primary character is the persona, regardless of the avatar or embodied entity that exists within the game world. Therefore, to only observe active characters as the focus of research, as is customary in linguistic approaches or studies of power relations, may lead to incomplete data and ignores the complex relationship an individual may have with their alt and main characters. (Milik 2017, p. 70)

As Milik suggests, guilds often require players to choose between different characters, each with their own specific roles, powers, and abilities, to maximize the team's chance of success during an encounter. In *EO*, this can include players using multiple instances of the game running simultaneously, which forces us to consider the individual as a series of presentational elements initiating representational actions performed across a series of avatars. Players often have naming conventions which connect different avatars together, while many others do not adopt similar names and have wildly different avatars, choosing different races, genders, as well as classes to make a complex persona formation.

The major games platforms offer social networking dimensions to their digital distribution services. XBox Live, Nintendo online, PlayStation Network, and the Apple iOS, all provide ways for players to create online profiles, adopt nicknames (often referred to as "gamer tags"), and display custom profile images to represent themselves and produce a player persona. These platforms still allow for a degree of anonymity, but many require connectivity to other social media accounts and other forms of identification through email, mobile phone, and credit card verification. The digital distribution platform Steam, owned and operated by Valve Corporation, was the first to integrate an online game management service with a player profile and social network features in 2003. It later added a digital storefront, screenshot features, video streaming, and an application programming interface (API) to integrate with micropayments and support for user-generated content. Steam has had a major impact on the global games industry since its launch by replicating Amazon.com's "long tail" approach to sales, which overcomes the limited shelf space of retailers making titles available in perpetuity that sees an increase in sales over their expanded lifetime (see Anderson 2004; Shirky 2000). Because Steam largely removed the distribution cost from the retail process, it was able to support the release of games from small "independent" games companies and producers previously locked out of the expensive in-store market. The Valve Corporation significantly contributed to the rise of the "indies"; this term identifies games which are often created by hobbyists and small groups of developers that tackle serious and challenging concepts and gameplay as well as represent in-game worlds that are not reliant on the latest 3-D technology. Perhaps most importantly, indies are not forced to hand over their intellectual property to large publishers. Later in this chapter, we will return to the independent games sector and examine what these changes mean for the persona of the game developer.

The embedded forms of social networking in digital distribution platforms require players to manage and present their personas through game-related biographical information, personal preferences, game collections, player networks, and in-game achievements. Blizzard's service platform, which is required to access games like *WoW*, *StarCraft II*, and *Overwatch* offer players a way to integrate their player accounts with their Facebook profiles. This creates a merger of the player's identity with their Facebook self, bringing together two previously separate personas, which is an increasingly common phenomenon in the age of **intercommunication**. Facebook itself has become a massive digital games service, with more than a quarter of its users (375 million) playing games each month on the platform (Taylor 2014). The increase of real name policies on Blizzard, Facebook, and many other platforms, have narrowed players' opportunities to anonymize their online activities, a move predicted by Deleuze in *Postscript on the Societies of Control* (1992). The anchoring of a player's online persona within the broad social media complex and thereby pointing toward a singular identity ensures the potential for monetization of the player's activity through advertising revenue and data surveillance.

The Rise and Fall of the Gamer

The games industry and game scholars have long wrestled with ideas of classifying players and establishing taxonomies of interests to comprehend and better understand player motivations. Richard Bartle's (1996) taxonomy of player types is one of the earliest attempts to describe the motivations and interests of players investing time in MUDs and early MMO (massive multiplayer online) games. A programmer with a PhD in artificial intelligence, Bartle was an active MUD developer who saw common patterns of behavior in four primary types of players – achievers, explorers, killers, and socializers – which are monikers based on the four suits of a deck of cards. Bartle used taxonomic descriptions of these categories to suggest how game developers might maintain a balance in their game design to cater to all different player types. Achievers, represented by a diamond in Bartle's model, are those players who seek to "beat" the game, working to complete all the missions, fulfill every quest, collect every item or set of items, and earn every award. The allure of multiplayer environments for this type of player is the top rank on the leaderboard or the victory of their team. Explorers – spades – enjoy digging into a game to uncover its secrets, exploring new areas, filling in the empty map provided to players at the start of the game or uncovering game glitches, bugs, and secrets often described as "easter eggs." The explorer uncovers the best way of playing a character class, especially in multiplayer games, and seeks to learn as much about the game's "lore" and narrative as possible. In Bartle's taxonomy, socializers are the hearts and are the players who are present in the game for its social dimensions and connection to other players. As socializers, they usually run guilds, manage group websites, coordinate, and organize in-game play for others. The final player type is the killer or the clubs, a group of players who specialize in competitive battle. Killers are often experts in defeating in-game monsters (described in MMORPGs as "mobs") but they are more notorious for their expertise in player-versus-player combat (PVP), seeking out other humans in-game purely to defeat them in battle.

Expanding on Bartle's taxonomy, Nick Yee (2002) plotted further variations in player activity mapped to five different intrinsic and extrinsic motivations: relationship, immersion, grief, achievement, and leadership. Yee's model reduces the emphasis on categorizing players into different types and instead offers a spectrum of different vectors along which player motivations are mapped. James Gee (2003) provides an alternative account of three player identity categories: "real-world" identity, "virtual world" identity, and "projective" identity. Gee's (2003, p. 55) projective identity is the closest to the notion of a meta-player identity, or player persona, as it highlights the depth of investment that occurs between players and their avatars. As the player projects values and desires onto their virtual characters, collecting and purchasing items to personalize them, the "projection" extends beyond the game. Players use their game experiences, through screenshots, video streams, stories, and discussions to frame their online persona across Facebook, Reddit, Instagram, YouTube, Flickr, Tumblr, DeviantArt, and other social media sites and services. This projected identity allows the player to both strongly identify with their in-game character and sees them using the virtual experience to compose their player persona external to the world of the game environment. However, Taylor (2006, p. 70) reminds us that regardless of a type of behavior, motivation, or expression which might describe patterns of play, the outward expression of a public player identity as a "gamer" is nonetheless performed and perceived differently, with extensive variation. For reasons to be detailed in the following, the moniker of "gamer" has been avoided in this chapter. Although a common way to refer to individuals who identify themselves publicly as someone who plays games, the term "gamer" is not a neutral reference point, and it has become a contested public identity and one that points to a particular moment in the development of video game culture more generally.

Mackenzie Wark (2007) defined a gamer as someone who comes to understand the world through quantifiable failure, but this account does not take into consideration the broader cultural activity of online play. Due to increased online activity and media attention, global "gamer" culture has come to represent extremely antisocial behavior, including misogyny, homophobia, racism, and even domestic terrorism. There are many reasons for this negative turn, and one of the most prominent is the collective attitude of "gamer" culture toward women. Until recently, argues Mia Consalvo (2012), even the very fact that women play games has been newsworthy. The game industries' top-tier games titles (typically known as AAA releases), which can cost hundreds of millions of dollars to make and advertise has been predominantly marketed at men. This is despite regular studies in the United Kingdom, Europe, United States, and Australia that women now make up between 45% and 52% of the global gaming audience (Brand and Todhunter 2015; Statista 2018a; Sullivan 2014). Although video games are played by people of all ages, races, and genders, there is still a significant lack of women working in the video game industry, which Adrienne Shaw (2010, p. 408) suggests contributes to the absence of diverse narratives and representations in the broader video game market.

The "toxicity" of gamer culture drew the attention of the mainstream media following the success of feminist critic Anita Sarkeesian's crowd-funded project in 2012. Titled "Tropes vs Women in Video Games," Sarkeesian (2012) raised approximately US$160 000 for a series of videos to be hosted on her Feminist Frequency YouTube channel, examining tropes in the depiction of female video game characters. This prompted an immense outpouring of hate and online harassment directed at Sarkeesian, including threats of personal violence, sexual assault, rape, and death made against her and her family, across all of her social media accounts. This type of behavior metastasized dangerously with the GamerGate controversy in 2014, which dramatically increased hostility toward women in the global gaming community. The Twitter hashtag #GamerGate was first tweeted by actor Adam Baldwin, linking to two videos by the YouTuber InternetAristocrat in August 2014. The videos attacked indie game developer Zoe Quinn on the basis of a blog post from her ex-partner that accused Quinn of having affairs with other men in the video game industry. Together the tweet, the blog post, and the Internet videos went viral and triggered a campaign of hate directed at Quinn under the guise of concern about integrity in the relationship between games development, marketing, and review journalism. In her book, *Crash Override* (2017), Quinn identifies that this wave of hatred was not only popularized by gamers: it also pointed toward a disturbing new online persona.

GamerGate wasn't really about video games at all, so much as it was a flashpoint for radicalized online hatred that had a long list of targets before, and after, my name was added to it. The movement helped solidify the growing connections between online white supremacist movements, misogynist nerds, conspiracy theorists, and dispassionate hoaxers who derive a sense of power from disseminating disinformation. This patchwork of Thanksgiving-ruining racist uncles might look and sound like a bad joke, but they became a real force behind giving Donald Trump the keys to the White House. (Quinn 2017, pp. 4–5)

Quinn and Sarkeesian continue to be harassed online and are often the victims of bomb and death threats when they appear at venues to speak. The culture war over gamers continues. Gamer culture and gamer persona were declared to be "dead" by a series of blogs, news posts, and scholarly articles in August 2014. Gamers are over, according to video game culture critic Leigh Alexander, who describes gamers as a dated demographic that no longer referred to a new generation of consumers:

the industry has changed. We still think angry young men are the primary demographic for commercial video games – yet average software revenues from the commercial spaces have contracted massively year on year, with only a few sterling brands enjoying predictable success. It's clear that most of the people who drove those revenues in the past have grown up – either out of games, or into more fertile spaces, where small and diverse titles can flourish, where communities can quickly spring up around creativity, self-expression and mutual support, rather than consumerism. There are new audiences and new creators alike there. Traditional "gaming" is sloughing off, culturally and economically like the carapace of a bug. This is hard for people who've drank the kool-aid about how their identity depends on the ageing cultural signposts of a rapidly-evolving, increasingly broad and complex medium. (Alexander 2014)

Dan Golding (2014) adds nuance to Alexander's criticism, framing the gamer as a consumer identity that has been stretched to breaking point. Golding recognizes that although the traditional gamer persona is now "culturally irrelevant," the gamer as a consumer identity will still be targeted and exploited as long as it remains profitable. Gamer typologies continue to be prevalent, and the term "hardcore gamer" is still a frequently deployed moniker online to distinguish between casual players and the traditionally young white male dominated identity formation. Other troubling tropes have become popular in gamer culture, such as the PC "master race" which is the name given to a popular forum on the website Reddit, used to separate PC users from the more casual focused console "peasants."

There are, however, positive signs of evolution of the negative gamer persona due to the increased popularity of the transmedia and paratextual industries associated with games media. The popularity of cosplay, or costume play, has generated a new persona, that of the cosplayer, which is expressed across social networking platforms Twitter and Facebook, and image-intensive sites like Instagram, and financially supported via crowdfunding services like Patreon and Kickstarter. The labor of cosplay, argues Suzanne Scott (2015), is a form of mimetic fan production, borrowing Matt Hills's (2010, 2014) term, which involves complex negotiations of ongoing gendered anxieties over the professionalization and commercialization of fan labor. Another area of concern is the massively popular domain of eSports, which has developed an audience via streaming services on sites like YouTube, Facebook, and Twitch. Although men gain none of the traditional physical advantages of women in the digital sporting arena, they still are dominant in the industry. However, as Seo and Jung (2016) point out, eSports fandom is a participatory identity that takes on multiple roles and demonstrates unique competencies in spectatorship, online competition, community building and management and other forms of participation that result in a unique persona formation.

Gâmeur: From Modder to Indie Game Developer Persona

Prior to the availability of digital distribution platforms, open access tools, and developer-friendly platforms like Unity and Unreal, game development was almost exclusively conducted by replicating the Hollywood and television production "studio" system. The studio system of games development has made personalities and celebrities out of leading figures in the industry, including John Carmack, Peter Molyneux, Satoshi Tajiri, Will Wright, Sid Meier, and Shigeru Miyamoto. These luminaries have all had a very similar developer persona, not unlike film directors, with teams of highly capable programmers, artists, interface designers, and playtesters working under the creative vision of a singular public figure. In many ways, game development has now welcomed back the garage and bedroom developers of the type that first helped to make the studio system a reality in the late 1970s and early 1980s before the first industry recession in 1983. In the following section, we will examine the alternative game developer persona, commonly referred to as "indies," made possible by new software tools and digital distribution; but first, it is essential to highlight the public persona type which made independent video game development possible: the modder.

Prior to the game industry's recognition of independent game designers and developers in the late 2000s, the games modder was seen as a fan persona, not a developer persona. A "mod," short for modification, is any kind of alteration applied to an element of a video game. Some mods are very minor, effectively just small changes to the behavior of a game element, such as rate of fire of a weapon, or the jump height of a character. Other mods are total transformations of a game, such as *Counter-Strike*, by Minh "Gooseman" Le and Jess "Cliffe" Cliffe, which took the game *Half-Life* by the Valve Corporation in 1999 and transformed it into one of the most played FPS (first-persona shooter) multiplayer games of all time. Mods are a form of participatory media culture (see Jenkins 2012; Raessens 2005) in which the consumer becomes a co-contributor, adding new and original content to the commercially available product. As Barry Ip (2008) explains, the participatory media practice of games modification represents a major shift in power within the games industry toward that of the consumer. The emergence of the game modder persona in the late 1990s and early 2000s represented a major step forward for user-generated content with a different culture of consumption organized around highly social communities of users who challenged the linear distribution model of traditional content developers (Ip 2008, p. 220). The modder persona had a very public presence on games forums, websites, and social media, and has since become a major contributor to the content of games via Steam.

Modding has been around since the early days of digital games. The first mod was a variant of the text-based role-playing game *Adventure* in 1976, and *Ms. Pac-Man* was the first mod to receive a retail release in 1981 (Kushner 2004). Modding became more accessible to computer game users in 1993 with the release of *Doom*. When Id Software published *Doom*, the game was organized by lead programmer John Carmack to be modding friendly; the code and file system enabled modders to add new sounds, graphics, and game levels with greater ease than previous titles. Although the game was released as a complete work, it was not hermetically sealed, and its production deliberately encouraged user-contributed content. The Steam platform brought modders and the modding community into the mainstream, making it easier for players to load mods purchased on the platform into their games. Steam was followed by other platforms such as the PlayStation Network, the Nintendo eShop, and Xbox Live, as well as sites like Itch.io. Modders articulated a public presence across these sites and services, often in ways that differentiated them to studio- and publisher-funded game designers. Steam attempted to monetize the modding community in 2015, confusing the modding persona with a developer persona, and met strong resistance from modders and consumers.

The indie game developer persona is a merger of the game modder and the studio developer persona. The indie game developer persona does not have the backing of the studio system and relies heavily on the social connections, community support, and networking practices pioneered by game modders. Some indie games and their developer personas, like *Minecraft* and Markus "Notch" Persson, have reached mainstream status in terms of sales and popularity, but others remain much less known by broader game audiences. In the following, we are going to draw on the five dimensions of persona, as identified in Chapter 3 as public, mediatized, performative, collective, and intentional value (VARP), in order to examine the intertwined relationship between indie games and their developer personas.

Public

Stefan Werning (2017) and Mata Haggis (2016) have both brought attention to the autobiographical dimension of the indie game developer persona. Thanks to digital distribution via Steam and Itch.io there has been a dramatic increase in commercially available games that are publicly revealing personal stories inspired by life events or are in some way autobiographical. Games like *That Dragon, Cancer* by Ryan and Amy Green, which deals with the experience of childhood cancer and mortality, are deeply autobiographical. Itch.io is the most prominent website for indie games sales, featuring a "pay what you want" model, and at the time of writing has 18 titles tagged as "autobiographical." The collection includes *Memoir En Code: Reissue* by Alex Camilleri, which explores episodes of the developer's life divided into "tracks" and structured like a record album to be explored by the player. Mata Haggis (2016, p. 21) describes the indie game scene as the most experimental area of video game publishing, and "where the extreme focus on narrative, and specifically autobiographical games, is most likely to appear."

This is an important turn for the videogame industry that has been historically overpowered by "blockbuster" AAA titles with stereotypical representations of gender and violence, and whose main attraction is the complete break with reality. The term "indie games" mostly refers to games that are both developed and published independently by individuals and small teams of developers, but as Haggis suggests, it also describes an important range of alternative gameplay experiences.

> Not a conventional "genre" in its own right, indie games have what might be better described as a "persona," a characteristic set of styles that are typically situated outside the mainstream, including games that are short, limited in scope or diversity of interaction, or lacking typical gameplay features, such as scoring or increasingly difficult challenges. (Haggis 2016, p. 21)

We are in essence dealing with two distinct but intimately connected **public** personas. First is the persona of the indie game, which is not a comprehensive genre but an expression of an experience that includes a unique set of publicly distinguishing features that refer to nonmainstream activities. A good example of an indie game persona is *Cuphead*, a 2016 title developed by two brothers, Chad and Jared Moldenhauer, as StudioMDHR. *Cuphead* has two obvious

Figure 7.1 Characters Cuphead and Mugman featured in the 2016 indie game by StudioMDHR, Cuphead. *Source:* Reproduced with the permission of StudioMDHR.

features that are part of its public persona; the esthetics and the mechanics. The art style is based on the "rubber hose" animation technique featured in cartoons of the 1930s, most notably Disney and Fleischer studios, with hand-drawn cell animation and watercolor backgrounds. The game's soundtrack is an original 1930s style jazz recording by composer Kris Maddigan and includes a 13-piece big band, 10-piece ragtime ensemble, and solo pianist and singers (StudioMDHR 2018). The two protagonists, Cuphead and Mugman, are unique character designs (see Figure 7.1), emulating Mickey Mouse style bodies with tea-cup heads, making the visual elements entirely original but familiar, contributing to the games public persona in a way similar to the Creepers of *Minecraft*.

The game's' persona is also publicly constructed as a reaction to its difficulty, which provides a high-level sense of accomplishment and reward. The "run and gun" mechanics require players to memorize and execute a different set of moves for each of the boss characters which have their own unique attacks and characteristics (see Figure 7.2).

In what might otherwise be described as a brand, *Cuphead* had success without a mainstream publisher or marketing budget, selling one million copies in the first two weeks after release. However, the game was not an overnight success and, like many indie games, *Cuphead* was in development for three years; during this time StudioMDHR worked on identifying and promoting the *Cuphead* persona to the industry and the broader public by presenting at multiple game developer conferences, including E3 in 2014, after which the

Figure 7.2 A screenshot of the 2016 indie game Cuphead by StudioMDHR. *Source:* Reproduced with the permission of StudioMDHR.

developers secured Microsoft funding to release the game on Xbox One. This long production time is typical of the indie game sector, where developers often have to support themselves with other work. This process leads to promoting unfinished games to the indie game-playing public and amassing a micro-public of friends and followers via social media who become instrumental in sharing the game's persona intercommunicatively via their own networks at the game's eventual release.

Mediatized

If the first persona type we are dealing with is the persona of indie games as discrete digital objects, the second type of persona we are interested in is the **mediatized** public presentation of the self that is central to the role of the indie game developer. Moore (2011b) previously described the modding persona as a "gâmeur" for their ability to shape, resist, and change the commodified experience of play, and this moniker should be extended to encompass the mediatized self of the indie game developer. The gâmeur is modeled after the figure of Charles Baudelaire's flâneur, who is identified in Walter Benjamin's *One Way Street* (1979 [1928]) as an important social type, a stroller of the arcades and streets of Paris, interested in the experience and perception of urban landscapes and crowds. Unlike the flâneur, however, the gâmeur is not satisfied with pure spectatorship, and as an indie game designer, the gâmeur is able to challenge the dominant forms of expression commonly found in the mainstream video games industry. The gâmeur persona is mediated in two ways. First by the individual expression of identity, which is frequently a non-normative identity as indie game developers often express themselves through alternative identity politics, nonheteronormative sexualities, as well as nonwhite, non-masculine, and non-Western cultural tropes. Of course, not all indie personas fit within these categories, but the indie game space exists as a domain of game development where alternatives to the mainstream are celebrated.

Second, the gâmeur is mediated by the indie developer's social media presence, which is often crucial to the success of their indie game titles. The gâmeur's social media accounts are the primary locations for generating an audience as the lack of a publisher also typically indicates the absence of a marketing campaign. The gâmeur is an "ur form," as defined by Susan Buck-Morss (1986) as a phenomenological fragmentation which serves as a means to critique the games industry and to speak back against regressive phenomena such as homophobia, transphobia, misogyny, racism, ageism, as well as issues of class, labor, and migration. The indie game designer as the gâmeur is one way the games industry is challenging the problems experienced as a result of toxic gamer culture. One example of the gâmeur is Anna Anthropy and her indie games, *Mighty Jill Off*, *Sex Cops of Tickle City*, and *Lesbian Spider-Queens from Mars*, which are made using freeware – free versions of software – such as Game Maker and Twine, an open-source app which uses the visual structure of hypertext to make interactive narratives and games without any need for coding or programming. Anthropy describes her games "as transmissions of ideas and culture from person to person, as personal artifacts instead of impersonal creations by teams of forty-five artists and fifteen programmers, as in the case of Gears of War 2" (Anthropy 2012).

Another example of the indie game developer persona as gâmeur is Christine Love, whose interactive game novels gained attention in 2010 when *Digital: A Love Story* was mentioned in the website Gamasutra's Best Indie Games of 2010 list. Love's work features LGBT characters with non-normative genders and sexualities and she portrays individuals identifying as "queer" in meaningful relationships, storylines, and adventures. Her most recent work, *Ladykiller in a Bind*, received the Excellence in Narrative award at the Independent Games Festival in 2017. Love has a highly active game developer profile on Twitter and is a strong advocate for mature depictions of sex and love in games, where sex is not a prize to be won by the player but a vehicle for telling complex stories and exploring adult relationships. Her social media activities involve a highly intercommunicative mediatized presence featuring hashtags, screenshots, video clips, memes, and gifs.

Performative

The public identity of Christine Love, presented via social media, is also a clear example of the **performative** dimension of the gâmeur persona. To perform an indie developer persona is to engage in public interaction, which makes social media the most important vector for publicizing and marketing indie games. By performing themselves across platforms, such as Facebook, Twitter, Tumblr, and Reddit, indie game developers support the micro-publics of interest that emerge around their games. Derek Yu is a gâmeur whose Twitter profile @mossmouth has 35 000 followers, all potential consumers of his indie games which include *Spelunky*, *Aquaria*, and *Eternal Daughter*. Yu's public persona became well known through his active participation on the website TIGSource, where he took on a leadership role and contributed to a culture which promoted indie games as a unique art form (Yu, cited in Bradley 2018). Yu performed his persona as a champion of indie games and indie developers, a role which he continues via his Twitter profile.

It is important to note that the gâmeur is not restricted to indie game developer personas, but also includes the players of indie games, who perform their persona via streaming media sites like YouTube and Twitch.tv. Dan "The Diamond Minecraft" (DanTDM) is a successful YouTube persona with 18 million subscribers, who first became popular for his live playing of *Minecraft* in 2012. DanTDM and other YouTubers and Twitch streamers, belong to the enormously popular "let's play" (LP) genre. The LP genre includes recorded video shared via YouTube, live streaming of play via Twitch.tv, and the documenting of play through screenshots and texts shared via blogs and websites (White 2013). YouTubers and Twitch streamers engaging in LP have generated a global audience by performing the role of the indie game player, signaling to audiences an affinity for alternative, different, unusual, and nonmainstream play activities afforded by indie games.

LP streamers and YouTubers, like DanTDM and the infamous PewDiePie, are performative characters, whose play lives are shared with an active audience. Like indie game developers, YouTubers and streamers rely heavily on social media platforms to support their micro-publics of fans and followers. This expands outwards from YouTube comments and Twitch chat dialogs, to Twitter, and Facebook, and on to voice-operated hangouts like Discord servers and Teamspeak channels. Live streaming audiences are consuming an entirely different form of televisual entertainment, that is, without the typical broadcast features, especially editing. While the streams are an "amateur" style of television, there is an increased pressure to manage interactions with fans and followers professionally in order to support a community of viewers. This increased need for professional public performance obviously extends to the competitive eSport industry, which is modeled on branded sporting genres.

Collective

The **collective** dimension of the indie game persona means that the gâmeur is not merely an individual node in a network, but part of an evolving and changing arrangement of multiple overlapping organizations, communities, and micro-publics. Like the flâneur in Benjamin's (1928) account, the gâmeur is a social figure, continually looking for new encounters. The gâmeur's mediatization, publicness, and performativity means conveying new perceptions about those experiences to an audience of friends, fans, and followers. Keith Tester (1994) notes that the flâneur was a spectacle for the "teeming crowds" whose meanderings were completely visible to the metropolitan public of Paris. Tester suggests that the knowledge of being in the crowd gave the Baudelairean poet the ability to make meaning out of the metropolitan spaces and spectacle of the public. For the gâmeur, however, the ontological basis of the collective is not the active doing of nothing (as is the case with the flâneur), but the active contribution to the assembly of public interactions. A key example of this is the indie game developer community which participates in the use of the hashtag #screenshotsaturday. Each week, indie game developers take a screenshot of a game design being worked on and share their progress in public.

Figure 7.3 is a visualization of the hashtag #screenshotsaturday for the weekend of March 5–6, 2016, made using NodeXL, as described in Chapter 5 (see also Hansen, Schneiderman, and Smith 2010; Smith 2014; Moore 2014; Turnbull and Moore 2017). The software has been used to "cluster" similar patterns of activity and map the relationship between nodes, which are the gâmeurs and their micro-publics. The red lines indicate connections between individual nodes, specifically comments, replies, and likes.

The visualization (Figure 7.3) illustrates the activity of interconnected indie game developer personas and their overlapping micro-publics, expressed as key clusters in the left-hand side of the graph. The unconnected nodes on the right-hand side of the graph represent users of the hashtag that are separate to the major groups and are yet to develop their micro-publics and their interconnections to other gâmeurs and followers in the network. What is difficult to determine from this example is the two distinct micro-publics, the indie developer community and their supporters; however, the three large clusters and the dozen smaller clusters reveal the different degrees of intercommunication between the two. The visualization tells an interesting story about the collective expression of hashtag usage. In this example, the gâmeur shares a screenshot of an indie game in development and responds to feedback, criticism, and commentary, all forming different nodes in the network. The shared screenshot is obtained from the often-solitary process of game development and used to create and enhance an active and collective interest.

Intentional Value (VARP)

Finally, the fifth dimension of persona that is conducive to the idea of the indie game developer persona as gâmeur is the concept of **value**, which can be considered regarding raw value, as well as agency, reputation, and prestige (summarized in Chapter 3 as VARP). In pure sales terms, thanks to platforms

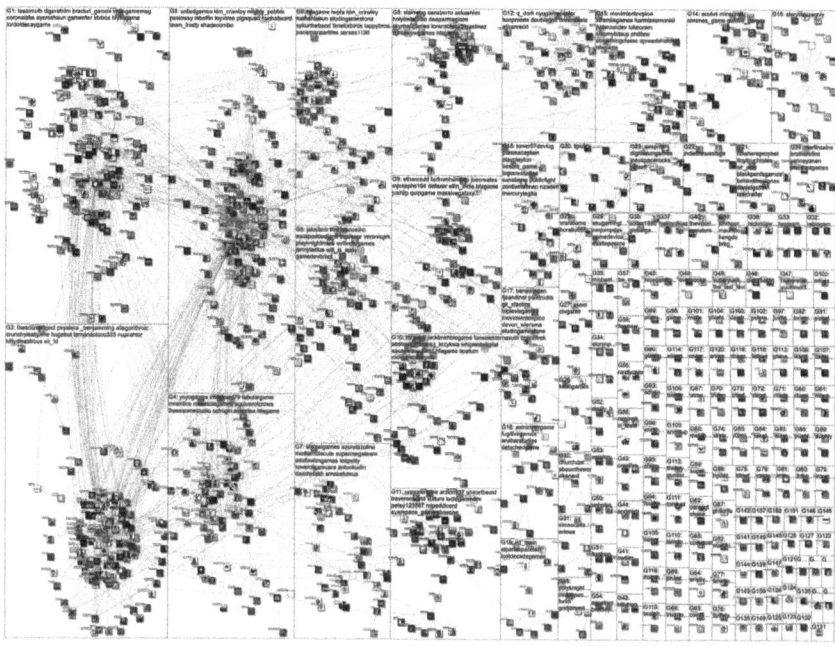

Figure 7.3 A network visualization of the Twitter hashtag #screenshotsaturday taken using NodeXL on March 6, 2016.

like Steam, Facebook, Apple iOS, Xbox Live, and the website Itch.io, the development and publishing of independent games have never been easier. This has produced immense competition for indies and, although the process of development is still complex and laborious, the number of independent games released each year continues to grow. In the month between June 13 and August 13, 2016, 685 indie games were released on the Steam platform worldwide; in 2017 during the same period, that number of indie games jumped to 1017. However, the cost of indie games for the consumer at their launch significantly decreased in that same time period (Statista 2018b). While more and more gâmeurs are making indie games, the competitive nature of the industry has made it harder for those developers to succeed financially in the industry. It is important to also understand that the indie game space is particularly well suited to experimentation in term of sales and consumer availability. *Minecraft*, for example, popularized the "early access" payment approach in which early adopters, who are testing out beta versions of the game, pay less for their copies than later players of the game following its official launch. The Steam platform has stabilized this approach by enabling developers the ability to offer "early access" titles at reduced costs while automating the upgrade feature. This early access model helps developers foster the collective nature of their audience playing the game while it is still in development, and this adds further value to the developer who receives feedback from players and a constant stream of bug reports enabling more rapid development. This also provides significant agency for both consumers and indie developers, which supports the formation and maintenance of entire communities of players who are not simply enjoying the game but being part of the development process itself. Similarly, the crowdfunding space of sites like Kickstarter has given new agency to developers and consumers who are (and have been) seeking financial backing for the development of unique, novel, and interesting game ideas that would otherwise not be developed through lack of funds and publishing deals. Becoming a Kickstarter backer offers a new level of prestige to players who get to contribute to the direction of development via the game's website and forums as well as having a direct line of contact to the game developers. Being a successful Kickstarter and early access game developer also has a major impact on the reputation of the indie game persona, both in relation to the game itself and the gâmeur developer behind the title.

Conclusion

In this chapter, we have presented a historical overview of the relationship between games and persona not as an identity theory, but as a means to account for the way games provide opportunities for the public presentation of the self. Games, more than any other entertainment medium, have provided the tools for audiences to present themselves publicly to others in various networked ways, both from within the multiplayer game environment and through games distribution services and digital platforms. Games have made available spaces for players to experiment with identity formations and the ability to share those experiments with others in small communities and large public gatherings as part of their persona, especially as fans. Games have also encouraged us to develop confidence in creating a self that was exterior to the person, to essentially invest in avatars as a way of presenting ourselves anew in a context that we controlled and manipulated. Games effectively furnished the means for sharing those experiments with networked public platforms. Games have proven to be the source of important digital objects, like scores and achievements, which have been communicated via screenshots across bulletin boards, web forums, social media, and digital distribution platform profiles to assist in collective persona formations that exist outside of the characters or avatars from any one game. In its short history, the global games industry has shifted away from offering players anonymous "safe" spaces in which to experiment with gender, race, and sexuality, to massively public spaces connected to real-world identities through social media profiles that have greatly reduced the anonymity of players, without eliminating it entirely. We have become familiar with the concept of the avatar, but the player character has become one of many digital objects that are used to construct the player's persona. The public presentation of the self now includes entire virtual games libraries, associations with various communities called guilds and clans, networks of friends and playing companions, and detailed records of hours played and achievements won. These personas are entirely intercommunicative, being linked to and from and across multiple social network sites. The YouTube and Twitch streaming of games and the rapid increase in popularity of eSports, has made these personas incredibly valuable as brands, channels, and as public figures. This chapter has sought to reflect on the documented changes occurring within gamer culture and the difference between a public persona that identifies the individual as a player of games compared to that of a "gamer." We have documented both the gradual demise of the "toxic" gamer persona and the subsequent flourishing of alternative player identities, such as the eSports personality and the cosplayer. Perhaps most significantly, the chapter has mapped the emergence of two persona types unique to the digital games industry, the indie game and the indie game developer, or gâmeur, across five of the most significant dimensions of persona.

References

Alexander, L. (2014). "Gamers" don't have to be your audience. "Gamers" are over. Gamasutra (August 28). http://www.gamasutra.com/view/news/224400/Gamers_dont_have_to_be_your_audience_Gamers_are_over.php (accessed February 23, 2018).

Anderson, C. (2004). The long tail. *Wired* (January 10). https://www.wired.com/2004/10/tail (accessed February 19, 2018).

Anthropy, A. (2012). *Rise of the Videogame Zinesters: How Freaks, Normals, Amateurs, Artists, Dreamers, Dropouts, Queers, Housewives and People Like You Are Taking Back an Artform*. New York: Seven Stories Press.

Bartle, R. (1996). Hearts, clubs, diamonds, spades: Players who suit MUDs. MUD (August 28). www.mud.co.uk/richard/hcds.htm (accessed February 22, 2018).

Benjamin, W. 1979(1928). *One Way Street and Other Writings* (trans. E. Jephcott and K. Shorter). London: NBL.

Bradley, A. (2018). Being Derek Yu: A chat with the creator of "Spelunky," "UFO 50": From Aquaria to "Spelunky 2," "UFO 50." *Rolling Stone* (February 8). https://web.archive.org/web/20180208195225/https://www.rollingstone.com/glixel/features/derek-yu-interview-ufo-50-spelunky-2-w516498 (accessed March 19, 2018).

Brand, J. and Todhunter, S. (2015). Digital Australia Report 2016. Interactive Games & Entertainment Association, Bond University. https://www.igea.net/wp-content/uploads/2015/07/Digital-Australia-2016-DA16-Final.pdf (accessed February 23, 2018).

Buck-Morss, S. (1986). The flaneur, the sandwichman and the whore: The politics of loitering. *New German Critique* 39: 99–140.

Castronova, E. (2005). *Synthetic Worlds: The Business and Culture of Online Games*. Chicago: University of Chicago Press.

Chan, E. and Vorderer, P. (2006). Massively multiplayer online games. In: *Playing Video Games: Motives, Responses, and Consequences* (ed. P. Vorderer and J. Bryant), 88–101. Mahwah, NJ: Lawrence Erlbaum.

Coleman, B. (2011). *Hello Avatar: Rise of the Networked Generation*. Cambridge, MA: MIT Press.

Consalvo, M. (2012). Confronting toxic gamer culture: A challenge for feminist game studies scholars. *Ada: A Journal of Gender, New Media, and Technology* 1 (1): http://adanewmedia.org/blog/2012/11/11/issue1-consalvo (accessed February 23, 2018).

Deleuze, G. (1992). Postscript on the societies of control. *October* 59: 3–7.

Gee, J.P. (2003). *What Video Games Have to Teach us about Learning and Literacy*. Basingstoke: Palgrave Macmillan.

Golding, D. (2014). The end of gamers (August 28). http://dangolding.tumblr.com/post/95985875943/the-end-of-gamers (accessed February 23, 2018).

Haggis, M. (2016). Creator's discussion of the growing focus on, and potential of, storytelling in video game design. *Persona Studies* 2 (1): 20–25.

Hansen, D., Schneiderman, B., and Smith, M.A. (2010). *Analyzing Social Media Networks with NodeXL: Insights from a Connected World*. Burlington, MA: Morgan Kaufman.

Hills, M. (2010). As seen on screen? Mimetic SF fandom & the crafting of replica(nt)s. Media Res (September 10). http://mediacommons.org/imr/2010/09/06/seen-screen-mimetic-sf-fandom-crafting-replicants (accessed October 29, 2018).

Hills, M. (2014). From Dalek half balls to Daft Punk helmets: Mimetic fandom and the crafting of replicas. *Transformative Works and Cultures* 16: https://doi.org/10.3983/twc.2014.0531.

Ip, B. (2008). Technological, content, and market convergence in the games industry. *Games and Culture* 3 (2): 199–224.

Jenkins, H. (2012). *Textual Poachers: Television Fans and Participatory Culture*. New York: Routledge.

Juul, J. (2009). *A Casual Revolution: Reinventing Video Games and their Players*. Cambridge, MA: MIT Press.

Kendall, L. (1998). Meaning and identity in "cyberspace": The performance of gender, class, and race online. *Symbolic Interaction* 21 (2): 129–153.

Kushner, D. (2004). The mod squad. Popular Science (July). https://www.popsci.com/gear-gadgets/article/2002-07/mod-squad (accessed August 8, 2005).

Marshall, P.D. and Barbour, K. (2015). Making intellectual room for persona studies: A new consciousness and a shifted perspective. *Persona Studies* 1 (1): 1–12.

Marshall, P.D., Barbour, K., and Moore, C. (2018). Academic persona: The construction of online reputation in the modern academy. In: *The Digital Academic: Critical Perspectives on Digital Technologies in Higher Education* (ed. D. Lupton, I. Mewburn and P. Thomson), 47–62. London: Routledge.

McDonald, E. (2017). The global games market will reach $108.9 billion in 2017 with mobile taking 42%. Newzoo (April 20). https://newzoo.com/insights/articles/the-global-games-market-will-reach-108-9-billion-in-2017-with-mobile-taking-42 (accessed March 25, 2018).

Milik, O. (2017). Persona in MMO games: Constructing an identity through complex player/character relationships. *Persona Studies* 3 (2): 66–78.

Mitew, T. and Moore, C. (2017). Histories of Internet games and play: Space, technique and modality. In: *The Routledge Companion to Global Internet Histories* (ed. G. Goggin and M. McLelland), 448–460. New York: Routledge.

Moore, C. (2009). Digital games distribution: The presence of the past and the future of obsolescence. *M/C Journal* 12 (3): 1–5.

Moore, C. (2011a). Hats of affect: A study of affect, achievements and hats in Team Fortress 2. *Game Studies* 11 (1): 1–14.

Moore, C. (2011b). The magic circle and the mobility of play. *Convergence* 17 (4): 373–387.

Moore, C. (2014). Screenshots as virtual photography: Digital media objects and the production of online persona. In: *Repurposing the Digital Humanities: Research, Methods, Theories* (ed. K. Bode and P. Arthur). London: Continuum.

Quinn, Z. (2017). *Crash Override: How Gamergate (Nearly) Destroyed My Life, and How We Can Win the Fight Against Online Hate*. New York: Public Affairs.

Raessens, J. (2005). Computer games as participatory media culture. In: *Handbook of Computer Game Studies* (ed. J. Raessens and J. Goldstein), 373–388. Cambridge, MA: MIT Press.

Sarkeesian, A. (2012). Damsel in distress: Part 1 – tropes vs women in video games. Feminist Frequency [video online]. https://www.youtube.com/watch?v=X6p5AZp7r_Q (accessed March 25, 2018).

Scott, S. (2015). "Cosplay is serious business": Gendering material fan labor on heroes of cosplay. *Cinema Journal* 54 (3): 146–154.

Seo, Y. and Jung, S.-U. (2016). Beyond solitary play in computer games: The social practices of eSports. *Journal of Consumer Culture* 16 (3): 635–655.

Shaw, A. (2010). What is video game culture? Cultural studies and game studies. *Games and Culture* 5 (4): 403–424.

Shirky, C. (2000). Open source and Quake. Shirky.com. http://www.shirky.com/writings/opensource_quake.html (accessed February 19, 2018).

Smith, M.A. (2014). NodeXL: Simple network analysis for social media. In: *Encyclopedia of Social Network Analysis and Mining* (ed. R. Alhajj and J. Rockne), 1153–1170. New York: Springer.

Statista. (2018a). Share of female video game players in Australia from 2005 to 2017. Statistica.com. https://www.statista.com/statistics/784972/australia-female-video-player-share (accessed February 23, 2018).

Statista. (2018b). Number of indie games released on Steam worldwide from 2015 to 2017. Statista.com. https://www.statista.com/statistics/809258/number-indie-games-steam (accessed February 7, 2018).

StudioMDHR. (2018). FAQ: Cuphead. StudioMDHR.com. http://studiomdhr.com/faq (accessed March 12, 2018).

Sullivan, G. (2014). Study: More women than teenage boys are gamers. *The Washington Post* (August 22). https://www.washingtonpost.com/news/morning-mix/wp/2014/08/22/adult-women-gamers-outnumber-teenage-boys/?utm_term=.485940010148 (accessed February 23, 2018).

Taylor, C. (2014). Facebook: 375 million users play games each month. Mashable Australia (March 20). https://mashable.com/2014/03/19/facebook-games-stats/#l5ytVnVQYiqc (accessed February 19, 2018).

Taylor, T.L. (2006). *Play Between Worlds: Exploring Online Game Culture.* London: MIT Press.

Tester, K. (1994). Introduction. In: *The Flâneur* (ed. K. Tester), 1–22. London: Routledge.

Turkle, S. (1995). *Life on the Screen: Identity in the Age of the Internet.* New York: Simon & Schuster Paperbacks.

Turnbull, S. and Moore, C. (2017). Teaching with Twitter: A case study in the practice of audiencing. In: *Studying Digital Media Audiences: Perspectives of Australasia* (ed. C. Hight and R. Harindranath), 173–192. London: Routledge.

Wark, M. (2007). *Gamer Theory.* London: Harvard University Press.

Werning, S. (2017). The persona in autobiographical game-making as a playful performance of the self. *Persona Studies* 3 (1): 28–42. https://ojs.deakin.edu.au/index.php/ps/article/view/650 (accessed October 29, 2018).

White, P. (2013). Fan fiction more creative than most people think. *The Collegian* (April 18). https://www.kstatecollegian.com/2013/04/18/fan-fiction-more-creative-than-most-people-think (accessed 25 April, 2018).

Yee, N. (2002). Facets 5 motivation factors for why people play MMORPG's. http://www.nickyee.com/facets/facets.PDF (accessed February 22, 2018).

8

The Professional Persona

In our previous two chapters, we have examined personas as they have emerged in artistic (online) practice and the digital games industry. This chapter is a closer investigation of the "professional" persona and, ultimately, how various professional personas are being transformed through online culture and activities. Our intention in this chapter is to develop the methods and means for understanding the transformation of professional **public** identities. Our work will ultimately draw on exemplifications of professional identity in the specific milieus of academics, lawyers, and medical practitioners. To make sense of these identities, it is worthwhile exploring the backstory of "the professional," and what we think of as "the professions." Our approaches and methods used for making sense of persona, outlined in Chapter 4, support the approach here in identifying what we call the **cultural context** of persona and its dependence on preexisting models of public comportment. From this vantage point, the rest of the chapter will investigate how our online world intersects with the meaning and transformation of professional public identity through a focus on what we have called a **VARP** (value, agency, reputation, and prestige) analysis.

Work, Public Identity, and the Concept of the Professional

Throughout the long arc of human culture, work and identity have been closely linked. Indeed, historical worker identities have informed the way we identify ourselves as individuals, with the words used to identify a specific skill, activity, or job becoming a part of many language systems. Indeed, work-bounded names are the third most common origin point for names, following location and relationships (Hanks, Coates, and McClure 2016). For example, names such as "Smith" in English are linked to the activity of the Smithe or smithy – a coppersmith, a locksmith, or an ironsmith would be three examples and date

Persona Studies: An Introduction, First Edition. P. David Marshall, Christopher Moore, and Kim Barbour.

back to the Middle Ages. In the English language, roughly 8% of names are linked to occupations and names such as Smith, Cooper (those who make wooden barrels), or Weber (related to working with textiles and weaving) are some of the most common or popular (Hanks, Coates, and McClure 2016). Surnames in China, although generally determined by the region or origin (Koon 2016), also had links to very high-level professions such as a Chang (ancient judge: 常) as well as lower level such as Tu (a butcher) (Yutopian Enterprises 2000). The tradition of identifying individuals through their tasks or work, eventually becoming family names, underline deep patterns with which we differentiate ourselves and adopt shortcuts for that form of distinction. As this linguistic research reveals, location, relation, and occupation shape the organization of our named identity in many cultures.

The concept of professional as it is deployed in a number of cultures represents a further sign and designation of some sort of augmented **prestige** and **value** that has clear relationships to divisions of work and labor particularly over the last 400 years. "Professional" has come to mean a generic marker of distinction and expertise which connects professions to distinguished positions such as medical doctor or lawyer back to Antiquity and the societies of Ancient Greece and Rome. Its etymological origins point to this relationship of prestige and expertise. For instance, according to the *Oxford English Dictionary*, one of the roots of "professional" distinguishes it specifically in an elevated way from what became trades or **crafts**. Professional skill demanded even further training. Indeed, professions were seen as a calling, with vaguely religious connotations of a "vow" for acknowledged and accredited entry into its work "mission." Being a professional has always had a connection to being able to profess in a certain discipline (which has led to its close alignment with the idea of professor) and perhaps a capacity to demonstrate skill and expertise as much as practice of those skills.

Professions have been explored in great detail in sociology with equally great debates. For Émile Durkheim, professions identified a social glue that fostered a **collective** service beyond the individuality of commerce and trade. They built a form of consensus, where these professions "should become so many moral milieux" for industrial society (Durkheim, cited in Johnson 1972, p. 12). Talcott Parsons (1939, p. 463) identified this collective value of professions further in contemporary society, and likewise separates the rationality of professional expertise from the forms of decisions made in business. Others such as C. Wright Mills saw the gradual bureaucratization of professions into managerial positions, where the proliferation of the title of profession was an extension of the power of the "white collar" worker as Mills described the managerial class in the middle of the twentieth century (Mills 1951). Max Weber has been similarly influential in the study of professions particularly in the way that they identified a form of social stratification: knowledge, expertise, and the accreditation this demanded created the distinctions that became prized values in an increasingly industrially and technologically sophisticated society (see MacDonald 1995).

Although there are many other researchers that have investigated professions and professionals that could be explored in this chapter, here we focus on the kinds of public identities that the professions manifested, and how these identities are perhaps becoming less stable. To advance on this, it is important first to underline the way that the term professional has migrated in its usage.

The most common use of the term in the contemporary world – paradoxically for professional classes perhaps – is in sports. "Turning professional" implies that the individual athlete/performer has accepted an income for their specific role in the sport. Being paid as a professional athlete is contrasted with the unpaid amateur. In many team and individual sports, the term professional athlete identifies skill, prestige via income and renown, and the capacity to comport oneself appropriately. Professional athletes, because they are sponsored by corporations, by the very leagues and associations in which they compete – and by proxy the fans and **audiences** who are drawn to watch and support them – live within an expectation that they will comport themselves appropriately in order not to shame themselves, their sports, their myriad of sponsors, or their fans.

This idea of professional comportment is something that has been appropriated from this longer history of value associated with professions. In professions such as medicine and law, this comportment is linked to accredited knowledge acquisition. Guilds, societies, and associations have been the manner in which professions have maintained their public identity and value as a form of expertise, as well as to determine who is included as a legitimate member of the profession. Aspiring lawyers are "called" to the bar, a phrase that identifies their official status and that their legal practice is somehow linked to something almost spiritual in its purity of purpose. Accountants in various countries are called "chartered" to identify the legitimacy of their work. The Hippocratic Oath remains intriguingly core to the profession of the medical physician and further identifies the ways in which thresholds are achieved in order for an individual to appropriate a profession as part of their public identity and status. At least historically, those individuals who considered themselves "professional" were not expected to be driven by the financial reward: calling oneself a professional was, at least up until the nineteenth century, often an **indexical** sign that one was of the propertied classes in the European context.

There is no question that the institutions of higher education have been critical in the maintenance of professional identities. Professions are wedded to knowledge in a parallel way that a professional athlete has acquired visibly superior skill in their performance of their sport or game. Universities have situated themselves as the pathway to accreditation for many professions. For most working in the medical and legal professions, diplomas are a required adornment of their offices, a kind of ambient comportment as they construct their authenticated personas. Other occupations are also accredited through university degree diplomas: teachers, engineers, and nurses represent three professions that require a university qualification, the first step in professional identity. However, it has to be acknowledged that "professional" identity has also proliferated as a term that has been taken into occupations not normally linked with higher education institutions or elite knowledge. Being "professional" in trade occupations such as plumbers or electricians is often linked with holding a very formal public identity while working: it is indexically linked to the apparent elite quality of what constitutes a professional identity. Likewise, The National Secretaries Association (founded in 1942) changed its name to the International Association of Administrative Professionals in 1982 at least partly to underline the value of administrative tasks and connect it with the esteem of being a professional. In a 2009 survey conducted by the British Government, 11 million people, or roughly half of the UK working population identified as professionals, a number that included the creative industries as well as many other economic sectors (Susskind and Susskind 2015, p. 285).

As much as there has been an inflation in the designation of professional in contemporary culture, the most prominent professions have developed public displays of authority to differentiate themselves and their expertise. Dress styles, for instance, further configure the public identity within professions: the lab coat or the surgical scrubs interestingly do not reduce the identity of the doctor and surgeon but reinforce it. The robes and wigs of barristers and judges in the legal systems of many countries look absurd and derive from outmoded identity traditions outside of their courtroom environments; nonetheless they serve as markers of professional identity and dignity within judicial systems. One can even identify dress styles among the academic profession at universities: there is no question at formal graduations, academics are obliged to wear their robes, "hoods," and caps that identify and verify their certification and their "home" university. Perhaps the casual dress of the contemporary academic in the classroom is a further sartorial style that tries to acknowledge that they somehow transcend the demands of other more business-driven professions.

Based on this overview of the public identity of the moniker of "professional," it is safe to assume that professional in all its manifestations identifies a position of status, a role that is believed to be superior to other roles and tasks in society. The appropriation of "professional" in recent commercials by the automobile manufacturer General Motors (GM) Canada highlights this idea of status and guarantor of quality and expertise, while linking it to wider public aspirations. The 2017 ad entitled "Like a Pro" asks the question "how do you want to live your life?" and links GM trucks to striving for uniqueness and the top echelon. Through a montage of examples of reaching beyond "good" toward the exclusivity of "best" by individuals – and by vehicles – it concludes with how GM links to this professional level:

> One of a kind, the centre of their world, the lynchpin, undeniable, like a boss, like a rebel, like a standard-bearer, LIKE A PRO. We couldn't agree more. WE **are** professional grade. GMC. (GMC 2017)

The ad clearly identifies the value of the notion of professional, and how that status operates in our contemporary world on all sorts of metaphorical levels. It dangerously links a driven-masculinist-gendered identity to its trucks via the term professional and thereby identifies superior achievement and authority to this value-laden term. Nonetheless, what the GM Canada commercial expresses is how the notion of professional is imbued with the key methodological/analytical elements of persona that the commercial deftly links with its truck products: **Value, Agency, Reputation**, and **Prestige** are what we call **VARP** (see Chapter 3). What follows is a VARP analysis – a series of steps we have developed to analyze personas – of the personas of professionals that recognizes that the very term professional has deeply embedded high-status monikers of value, agency, reputation, and prestige. Our analysis focuses broadly on the concept of professional, but will exemplify this through the professions of law, medicine, and academia through a study of how these identities are being conveyed, expressed, and transformed by their migration into online culture in various public pathways, forms, and formats.

Step 1: Identify Online Culture's Destabilizing Effect on Professional Personas

In his *The System of Professions*, Andrew Abbott attempts to synthesize what constitutes a profession: they "are exclusive occupational groups applying somewhat abstract knowledge to particular cases" (1988, p. 8). Through a structure usually supported by government and sustained through their professional bodies, professionals control the distribution and application of knowledge and expertise. We perceive professionals as stable configurations through their associations and accreditations. However, because they are fundamentally involved in some form of regulating the use of knowledge, Abbott makes the valuable point that their "jurisdictional boundaries are perpetually in dispute" (1988, p. 2). There are many implications that Abbott's research explores in his study of this expert labor, but we now focus on how professionals are particularly vulnerable, specifically because they attempt to control monopolies of knowledge in the era of online culture where the actual information and the knowledge economy are fundamentally being transformed. Abbott's insight that professionals are always patrolling, maintaining their "jurisdictional boundaries," is very much connected to the recent research by

Susskind and Susskind (2015) that identifies how new technology and a related new online information economy is breaking down the structures and enclosures of knowledge that professionals have so powerfully maintained over the last 300 years.

According to Susskind and Susskind, the most prominent professions' (which in their research included law, medicine, education, journalism, religion, accounting, and architecture) knowledge enclosure and role in the "sharing of expertise" was dependent on "print-based industrial society" (2015, p. 20). They argue that

> in a "technology-based Internet society," we predict that increasingly capable machines, operating on their own or with non-specialist users, will take on many of the tasks that have been the historic preserve of the professions. We anticipate an "incremental transformation" in the way that we produce and distribute expertise in society. This will lead eventually to a dismantling of the traditional professions. (Susskind and Susskind 2015, p. 20)

Professions, they argue, are "intermediaries" (2015, pp. 155–156) in the process of knowledge application. Contemporary online culture challenges the necessity of their exclusivity through a dramatic shift in the knowledge economy in terms of machines that can perform, through various forms of aggregation and data analysis, many of the analytical, interpretive, diagnostic, and explanatory tasks of professionals. An equally significant challenge to the expertise of professionals is the sharing economy of online culture. Because knowledge does not operate like other commodities and products, any sharing of formerly – and exclusively – professional knowledge in our online worlds makes the knowledge move in "non-rival," "non-exclusive," "cumulative," and digitally reproducible and potentially transformed ways (Susskind and Susskind 2015, p. 229). In other words, the former exclusive domain of **private** consultations with professionals becomes something that many of us, as well as many online entities, applications, and corporations such as Google, can distribute with no relationship to professional bodies. For Susskind and Susskind, this new knowledge economy, derived from the effect of machine learning through large data related to professions as well as the culture of sharing of information online through billions of users, is leading to a "disintermediation" and "decomposition" (2015, pp. 155–157) of these many professions into new labor models. The authors note that the manner in which this is occurring resembles the transformation of certain trades and crafts that were disintermediated into the assembly lines of the factories of industrialization (2015, p. 141).

As Susskind and Susskind persuasively argue, the implications of technology are profound for the future of professions, and their research deals with many issues and possible pathways for professions that could play out over the next three decades. What is critical for our study of professional persona is how professionals are actively working to "reintermediate themselves … [and] to insert themselves in new places in the supply chain" (2015, p. 156) in the transformed knowledge economy. This reintermediation may involve many new directions for professionals. Fundamentally, it also demands a transformed presentation of the self with what traditionally would have been clients and patients in the old face-to-face or "bespoke" (Susskind and Susskind 2015, p. 59) professional model to incorporate "new models of communication" (2015, p. 149) that play actively in the spaces of how information is acquired, shared, validated, and transformed in online culture.

Our second step in this investigation of the professional persona and its online transformation looks specifically at these new modes of **communication** that are shaping the public display of professional selves through a VARP analysis. We begin with a look at the formation of value within the three professions of law, medicine, and academia.

Step 2: The Instability of Past Value and the Push to New Value

As we have developed in Chapter 2, there has been a shift to a **presentational media** and cultural regime that has very direct implications for professional persona. Professional identity has been predominantly dependent on a hierarchical structure of identity that has been derived from a **representational media and cultural** regime that in its emergence roughly parallels the historical preeminence of identity and value of the three professions we are exploring in this analysis. As identified above, professionals in their various disciplines have constructed systems or relative monopolies of knowledge, an elaborate filtering system where the public identity of their work is generally understood with great consistency across its occupation and in the wider notion of the general public. Through their offices, visible diplomas, dress, comportment, and their professional associations, they have produced a representation of a public role that allows the rest of the culture to implicitly identify their social and cultural value as well as identify individuals as members of these exclusive occupational clubs. This consistent public persona also has been conveyed through popular culture: the public has been tutored through centuries of novels, films, and television programs what have become stereotypical notions of academics, doctors, and lawyers. Our three professions similarly rely on these identity tropes as a kind of identity safety net.

Along with this representational system of differentiation of their public identities, a related structure of value has been maintained in these professions. In particular, lawyers and doctors have been able to construct, through their monopolies of expertise, a high economic value for their services. This construction of value is sustained through a number of communicative processes. First of all, the expert identity beyond their professionally supported identity is maintained through **interpersonal** or one-on-one communicative consultations. For lawyers, these consultations with clients are literally metered to every six minutes of activity; for doctors with specializations there is an elaborate system of personal referrals from general practitioners through a communicative chain of expertise that identifies the norms of communication of value. For our third profession, academics, a slightly more complex communication system of public performance via lectures and tutorials is wedded with other performances of the **public self** through private consultations with students and formations of public presentation as well as academic publications and conferences. Academics construct a public form of value through their accreditation – doctoral degrees, of all the measures, establish cultural value – and these various forms of communication operate as a way in which that value is regularly and positively mediated into the contemporary world with perceived and publicly validated legitimacy. At the very center of value in each of these professions, there is an emotional connection with patients, clients, and students of what could be thought of as *trust*. We trust professionals individually through their professionally constructed and conveyed persona and this trust produces their base economic and cultural value.

The presentational nature of online culture and its pervasive restructuring of our knowledge economy has also led to a transforming construction of value and validation for these professionals. What we are observing is a gradual integration of different forms of communication by professionals into their constitution of public selves. In some ways, the best way to understand this shift in professional persona is to observe how certain members of professions have been used in **legacy media** for almost a century to explain things to a wide public. For academics, these experts are often called "public intellectuals" and represent their disciplines in the media by making themselves available for news commentary and other programs and stories that deal with their specialized knowledge (Marshall and Atherton 2015, pp. 69–70). Similarly, certain medical practitioners and lawyers have occupied commentary spaces on news, current affairs, morning programs, and talk shows throughout most of the twentieth century and in some form on legacy media into the twenty-first century.

In the new knowledge economy provided by online culture, information related to these professional disciplines breaks down, to varying degrees, the disciplinary knowledge monopolies that the professions and their associations maintained and modestly extended by visible experts through the legacy media of television, radio, and newspapers. Two parallel transformations of information are occurring online that are having regular and direct impact on some professions.

First, there is more widespread sharing of information and much of this information is the kind and substance that might have been formerly housed under the control of professions. Online sharing of information and news has reconstructed our forms of media and communication foundationally; in contrast to very few media entities controlling the flow of information, online culture produces a culture of media and communication production and exhibition among its billions of users. The transformed knowledge economy that we have identified is being profoundly transformed by an ethic and economy of sharing. In Chapters 2 and 3 we used terms such as "**intercommunication**" to describe this transformative moment where people regularly moved between and blended the activity of sharing something highly mediated and something that could only be described as predominantly an interpersonal form of communication. The implications for professions of the ethic and economy of sharing is that there is a new lack of control in the movement, dissemination, and acquisition of profession-related knowledge that is unparalleled to anything of the last two centuries. For the individual professional there is an imperative perhaps to engage in this new distribution of knowledge in some way. This engagement and embracing of sharing information is, of course, fraught; nonetheless, what we are observing is an experimental foray of individual professionals and their companies in some instances making themselves visible via **social media** platforms through their professional and public identities: their personas.

Second, this form of information is being collected in a variety of ways by entities and companies that have their own expertise related to the contemporary information economy. Websites sharing information related to medicine began appearing in the 1990s with WebMD emerging to have over 179 million visitors by 2016 (WebMD Annual Report 2016). Its Medscape service, an information source and education platform for doctors, also has 675 000 practicing physicians registered and 404 000 of those active each month (WebMD 2016). Some of these medical-related services, such as Doximity (https://www. doximity.com), work to provide professional and research sources and information for doctors: by connecting active searches to equally engaged interest groups on specific issues allows medical professionals to work out best strategies in their own practices (Becker's 2016). Likewise, Zocdoc services the connection between patients and doctors in its attempt to link practitioners and those in need of consultation within 24 hours. What they add to their service are reviews of doctors and, through this technique, the attempt to match patients to best-practice physicians and clinicians (Becker's 2016).

Similarly, in the legal profession, certain applications such as the American-based Avvo actively rank the quality and value of lawyers, allowing potential clients to delve into what kinds of expertise these professionals can bring to their cases and legal needs. In 2008 (and with limited success), Esqchat was designed as an American internal lawyer-based social media site to allow legal professionals to exchange information (Henry 2008). Nonetheless, lawyers have used LinkedIn, the social network that is associated with professional activity, with enormous regularity: according to Nicole Black (2016) in her

American-focused infographic, 57% of American law firms use LinkedIn, with only 35% using some official Facebook profile. A total of 76% of American law firms maintain what she calls an "online presence" (Black 2016).

In academia, the service RateMyProfessors (www.ratemyprofessors.com) has served as a means for university and college students to not only express their likes and dislikes of their instructors, but also a place where the actual academic observes the various criteria being used to evaluate them. Academic life has naturalized this relationship to ranking, credibility, and value for many years through both official, metricized student evaluations and citation tracking. The online conversion of this tradition of valuing citation metrics has led to the formation of identities for academics on particular sites such as Academia.edu where, according to their official website, 58 980 041 academics are subscribers (Academia.edu 2018). The site itself is a locus for the sharing of research and outputs, as academics are encouraged to follow other academics to boost the impact of their own work, as well as to develop social media-like communities. ResearchGate is another powerful academic network particularly with scholars in the sciences and social sciences and professes a subscriber base of 14 million (ResearchGate 2018). Both of these subscriber-based academic networking and research-sharing sites generate an incredible amount of data that has the potential to reposition individual influence to a degree, but perhaps with greater force, the power of Academia.edu and ResearchGate to control the flow of academics' research that they wish to share.

These are two parallel transformations of information, where

1) individuals are exchanging information that includes what could be described as interpersonal forms of communication connected to their personal and professional identities along with widely shared and mediated information and;
2) the development of web-based platforms that are both servicing this information/communication exchange but also compiling valuable data in and about these professionals as well as actively infiltrating the monopoly of information and potentially knowledge.

These transformations allow us to see the particular ways in which a shifting and personalized formation of professional persona is advancing.

Through both the communication dimension and information gathering/ organizing dimensions of these new online practices in the professions, what we can discern is the way that value is being differently constituted. Traditionally, professionals' constitution of value was collectively held in check by the way that the profession held its monopoly of knowledge in conjunction with their social mission at imparting that knowledge to a wide – and needy – public. It was individualized in medicine and law through recognized and unquestioned (through their acknowledgment by governments and their recognition of the professional governing bodies) practices of fees for service. For academics, a longer connection to a higher purpose (in the tradition of the Church and monasteries), and thus separate from the direct exigencies of economic value, has linked them to a system of guaranteed reward for service as the individual climbs into positions as tenured or permanent members of the university.

In the current information environment, there is a new requirement emerging in the professions: whether in the medical, legal, or academic realm, professionals now need to actively support their perceived public value. This requires them to manage much more widely their public identity to maintain and/or fit into the new structures of value of the individual in the online knowledge/information/sharing economy. As Sundararajan's (2016) research on the sharing economy identifies, individuals are building new systems of "trust" with other individuals who may be only known through their online activity. With trust being the essential economic and cultural value for the three professions we are exploring, a new imperative of building online trust is emerging. Individuals, as evident through their massive presence online, are advancing this protection and maintenance of value, as are the companies and institutions that ultimately employ these professionals. Professional *online* visibility is now part of the mélange of what could be thought of as value for each of the professions. Our next step is to explore how professionals are engaging in this production of value through their activities or, what we call **agency** in our VARP analysis.

Step 3: Agency, Active Visibility, and the Professional Persona

In Chapter 3, we explored the way that agency is central to online persona. It is a particular incorporation of celebrity-developed public identity that now informs the comportment of persona across online culture. In some of our research into online culture, we have called this new form of activity of the self **industrialized agency**, as its integration of some of the models for the public self resembles the work of major corporations (Marshall 2017). In addition, we have integrated Bruno Latour's more inclusive conceptualization of agency through understanding agency in its capacity to be both human and nonhuman and a challenge to the way that we have traditionally thought of social change in much of the social sciences.

Online culture's transformation of the agency of the professional is in many ways the production of an identity that must now be visible on all sorts of platforms for the individual professional. There is a conversion dimension to this new agency that demands a familiarity with the online mediatized transformation of various versions of ourselves, including our work-oriented public identities.

For academic professionals, they have inhabited a space of online profiles for a very long time. Because universities were instrumentally connected to the establishment of the World Wide Web from its origins, they became some of the earliest institutions to establish public profiles online. By the late 1990s, thousands of universities expected their academics to present their course material such as syllabuses on the university website; roughly at the same time, it also became standard practice for academic profiles to be publicly accessible through these university portals and websites. In our own research, we explored the patterns through which academics have produced a kind of blend between institutional agency and something that is connecting to the wider dimensions of industrialized agency and that the engagement by academics with actively constructing online personas is both expanding and nuancing in interesting ways. In our earlier study, we identified five different types of academic personas online.

- The "static self" and institutional frame where nothing more than a university bio with links to perhaps related teaching and research.
- The "teaching self" that used online platforms to connect to their cohorts of students as well as those platforms such as "Blackboard" that set up discussion-related sites for enrolled students.
- The "networked self" that defined the new active but professional agency where academics engaged with other academics and also used social media to construct professional and public profiles.
- The "comprehensive self" with a blend of professional and private identity mixed through social platforms such as Facebook and Twitter.
- The "uncontainable self" which identified the academic who without much forethought and a high degree of professional risk moved between private, public, and potentially **intimate** along with forays into political and cultural spaces where their academic professional expertise was nowhere nearly aligned (Barbour and Marshall 2012).

In our follow-up study through an **action research model** (as identified in Chapter 5), where we worked with academics in and through their uses of online platforms, we learned further variations in the practices of academics as the participants were faced with the possibilities and potentials of expanding their professional public profile through online and social media platforms. There is no question that some academics identify for themselves how different forms of social media could expand their impact. The pressure in academia is to ensure that research has impact, particularly through citation counts because of the ease with which that metric is measured. Connecting regularly to other academics and developing the skills and digital literacies for understanding how different forms of social media such as Twitter or Facebook can make one circulate with higher visibility in a community was a growing rationale among contemporary academics (Marshall, Barbour, and Moore 2018, pp. 56–57). Nonetheless, the time pressure to reconstruct another public version of one's professional self in many instances led to inconsistent management of these online personas by the participants in our study (pp. 59–60).

Academics represent a profession that constantly has to produce a public identity outside of their primary workplace. In many ways, this key element of their job – mainly related to their research and publications – has generated a flurry of activity and engagement in producing some sort of validating visibility. Although perhaps not to the same degree as entertainment performers in film, television, and popular music, academics have invested in mapping and producing for this new and pervasive **attention economy**.

It is interesting to see that the legal profession is beginning to experience a similar push to be more visible, but their professional starting point in terms of the agency of persona is markedly different and worthy of a short explanation. Importantly, the concept of persona as an agent and a form of agency is actually foundational to the operation of the legal profession. Not only has the term persona been used by lawyers and the law to express how corporations and commercial entities can be individualized into "legal personas" (Nijman 2004), the term has also been deployed as a way to express intellectual property issues around identity management in entertainment law. More comprehensively than either of these uses of persona in different legal fields, the core activity of the lawyer–client relationship is the production of a persona: A lawyer, in documents as much as in court hearings themselves, is already a representation of a client – an embodied and active translation of another being. Lawyers are already not themselves in their actual job and role. They recognize that their role is strategic in the fabricated world of law and courts. How this representative persona is reconfigured in online culture presents a relatively uncharted dimension of a lawyer's professional identity formation. The online environment provides unique challenges to the legal persona, presenting vast opportunities for breach of confidentiality and the unique lawyer–client relationship. Lawyers must navigate their own need to establish an identity, to present themselves as professional and reliable service providers, while balancing the need to appear as a neutral advocate and officer of the court.

In our recent research, we have investigated the Twitter activity of the Australian legal profession. To uncover this material, the data we have gathered were derived from the public profiles of Twitter users. Thus, when people self-identify in the biography section of their publicly accessible Twitter profiles through the keywords of "lawyer, barrister or solicitor" they have been included in this study. The source of this material is the database of TrISMA, the Tracking Infrastructure for Social Media Analysis, which has collected self-identified Australian users of Twitter (Bruns et al. 2016). According to the Law Society of Australia, in 2014 there were 66 211 practicing solicitors/lawyers in the country (Urbis 2015). In contrast, on Twitter in May 2016, only 3785 Twitter users self-identified as either lawyers, barristers, or solicitors, although there could be many others who do not identify their profession. Overall, of the 2.8 million Australian identified account holders in May 2016, the legal profession's Twitter activity is both small in comparison to the total number of lawyers, but also a small part of what could be called the Australian Twittersphere. Indeed, over the period surveyed (from May 2015 to May 2016), 2866 of those 3785 or 75% self-identified Australian lawyers actually tweeted.

From this preliminary investigation, we can see that even in this group of Tweeting lawyers, relative activity varies greatly as they express their constructed online identities and public personas. For instance, it becomes obvious that certain lawyers are more active than others are and dominate this part of the online world. In our one-year survey, the most active lawyer had the screen name davidbewart with 36 731 tweets and a further 14 727 retweets or 5.41% of all the legal worker tweets (see Figures 8.1 and 8.2). Cumulatively, lawyers tweeted 952 764 tweets from May 2015 to 2016; but it should be added that the top 10 accounts collectively tweeted more than 25% of the entire activity (see Figure 8.2).

In terms of content and themes, a study of hashtags and keywords (with the elimination of common "stopwords" such as "and," "a," or "the," etc.) was also conducted. It is difficult to interpret the meanings of these isolated words without mining down further into the context of the individual tweets: for instance, the most common word used was "good" (21 263 appearances – see Figure 8.3) with other words such as "people," "great," and "Australia" following with high usage levels. However, hashtag usage – keywords beginning with # – quickly identifies a pattern of government and legal engagement: the hashtag #auslaw that identifies direct legal interest (7281 tweets) and the popular television current affairs debate program in Australia *Q and A* signaled by the hashtag #qanda (5969) can be identified as some of the leading

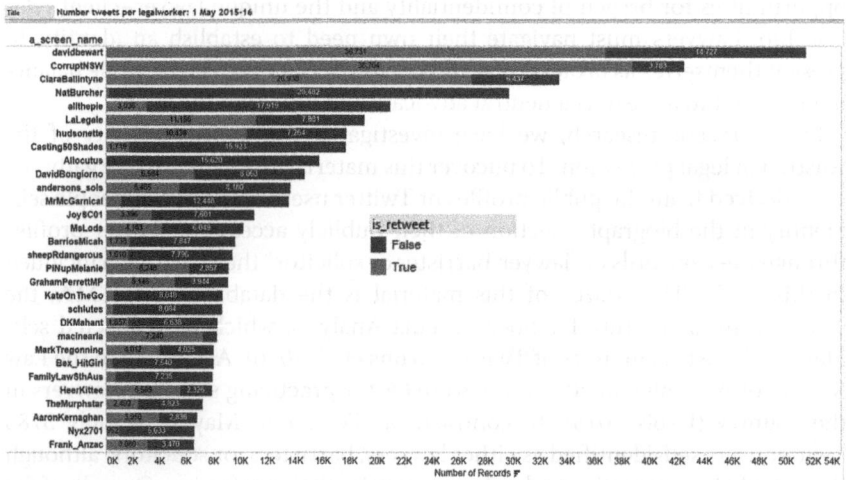

Figure 8.1 Number of tweets per legal worker – tweets versus retweets, May 1, 2015 to May 1, 2016.

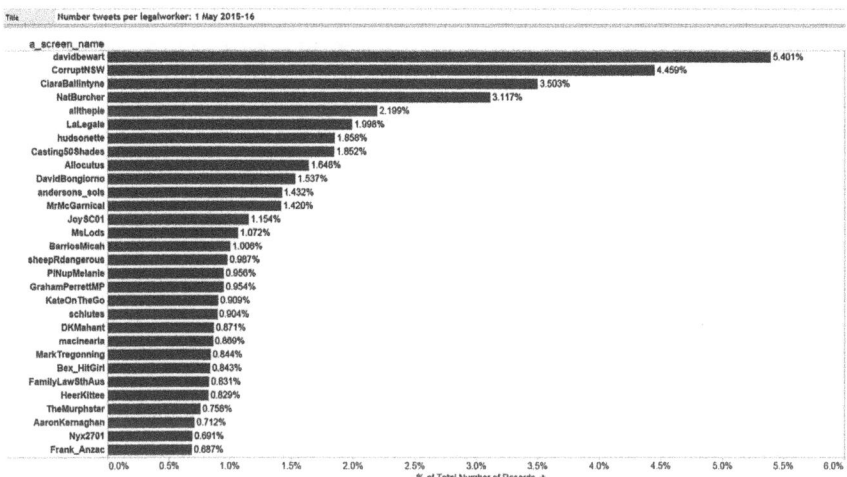

Figure 8.2 Number of tweets per legal worker, as proportion of total.

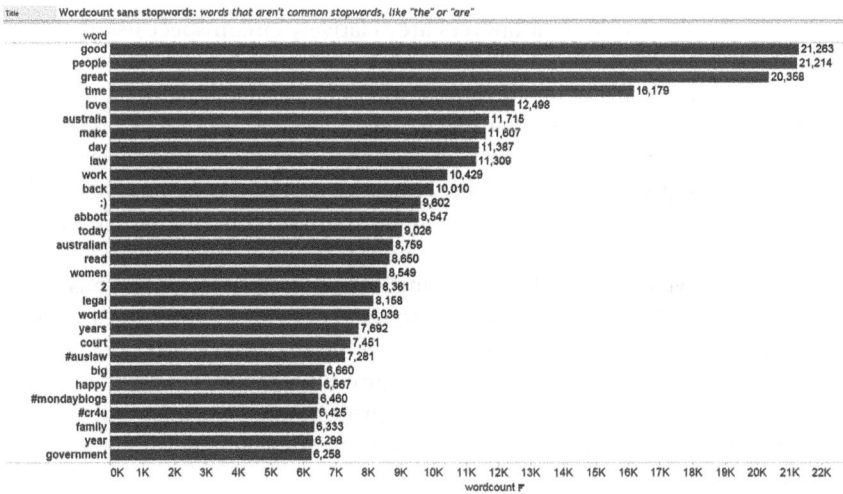

Figure 8.3 Frequency of word use in legal worker tweets, sans common stopwords.

topics among legal workers (see Figure 8.4). Other tags such as #letthemstay, which refers to the political issue around asylum seekers and refugees attempting to come to Australia, further implicate legal workers in particular political but also legal debates.

In this preliminary investigation of the professional activity of Australian lawyers/legal workers, it is difficult to make a firm conclusion. Provisionally,

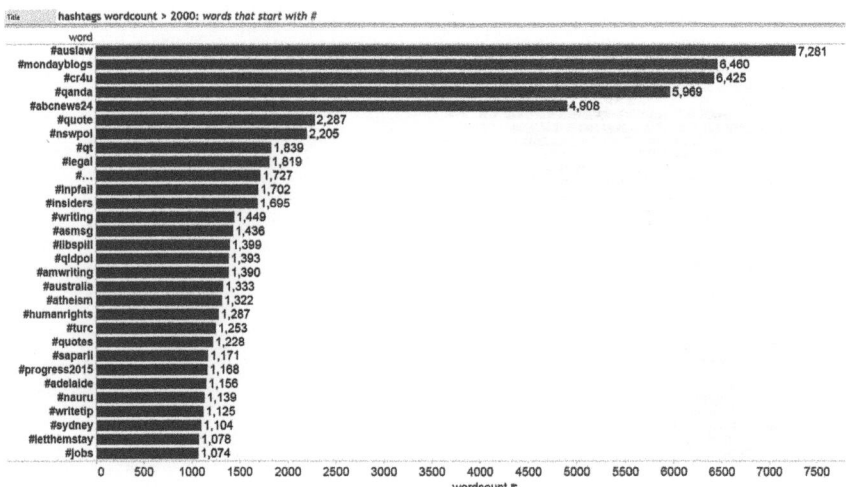

Figure 8.4 Frequency of hashtag use in legal worker tweets.

however, we can identify that lawyers are relatively circumspect users of this form of social media with a small minority of active participants. About a third of the self-identified Australian legal workers are either lurkers or inactive. Because they have identified their place of work in their profiles, a large number who are active also construct a professional identity on this social media site that is synergistic with their jobs. However, it is interesting to look at the variety of screen names that are used by legal workers. In this simple survey, some of the most active Twitter users who self-identify as legal workers have quite provocative names such as "Casting50Shades," "SheepRdangerous," and "PINupMelanie." It is equally important to see that institutional names such as "Roseattorney," "FamilyLawSthAustralia," and "GrahamPerrettMP" (a member of parliament) are also prominent (see Figure 8.5). Much like other users of social media, legal workers blend their professional identities with some aspects that are perhaps humorous or identify some private dimensions of their lives.

Of our three professions, it is interesting to find that doctors are the least engaged professionally with producing a new form of agency through online persona reconstructions. In contrast to lawyers, doctors are rarely perceived as businesses by their patients and this differentiation in wider professional persona has led to an even more nuanced reconstruction of doctor identity online. Despite this apparent reluctance to engage with producing an online persona, social media use has become of significant interest in the medical community. In a 2014 national survey of Australian doctors, Brown, Ryan, and Harris (2014) identify that most physicians use social media in some form with Facebook the

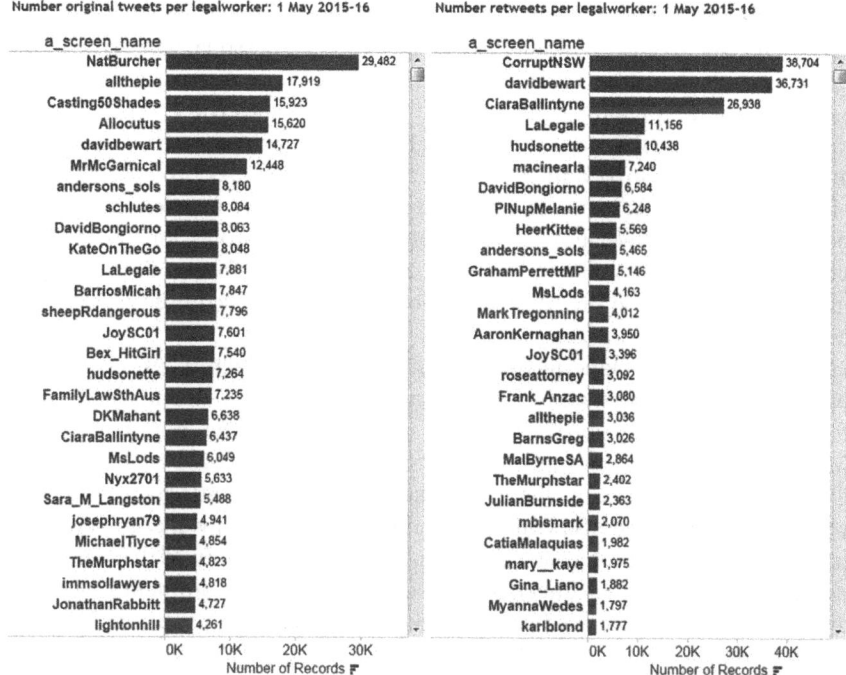

Figure 8.5 Number of original tweets per legal worker, and number of retweets by legal worker, listed by Twitter handle.

most popular platform. Moreover, 38% of the research participants have used social media during their work hours (Brown, Ryan, and Harris 2014). The blending of identities represented the most difficult element for physicians and their activity in online culture. For example, 19.4% of "participants had received a friend request from a patient they only knew and interacted with professionally" and felt that these kinds of connections were worrying (Brown, Ryan, and Harris 2014). Other researchers that are part of the medical profession have counseled doctors to pursue developing a "duality of citizenship," where physicians hold two completely distinct online identities through social media and, through careful curating, regularly monitor their online profiles to ensure that risks do not bleed into their professional identity (Mostaghimi and Crotty 2011, p. 561).

As much as this fear of online activity runs through the medical community, there is no question that doctors perceive that their role as being both the source of medical knowledge and the pathway for counseling patients is shifting into a partially electronic form of communication. A form of empathetic agency has become part of health-related information websites, where doctors have relayed types of advice that always conclude with the urgency with which these potential patients need to make a real appointment with a practicing physician. Doctors are working through a negotiated persona, where they realize according to a now dated Pew survey that 61% of American adults had searched online for information related to health issues (Lu et al. 2017) and know that they must engage at some level in this movement toward connection and need for their involvement and engagement online. As Brown, Ryan, and Harris's research also reveals, it is definitively younger, female, and general practitioners who have allowed their practice and their professional persona to be visible online, as well as pursuing a more earnest effort to deal with and interpret the online information that their patients have acquired before their in-person consultation (2014).

What we are observing in the medical field is that doctors are involved in online communication and are adapting a differentiated identity. Through text-mining and keyword extraction of 20 years of the popular website MedHelp.org, as well as the site's chat forums, Lu et al. (2017) were able to discern an emerging and distinctive medical persona that was a persistent voice of caring and advice, while remaining less emotionally charged than the patients who were asking for help and advice. In their study of three medical ailments (diabetes, lung cancer, and breast cancer) where comments were collected on the website, medical practitioners' involvement represented only 7.43% of comments, compared to patients at 61.68% and caregivers of patients at 30.88% (Lu et al. 2017). This indicates that not only did medical practitioners develop a specific type of persona through the site, but also that they were selective in deploying it, with conversations dominated by patients and carers.

The push to engage in online movements of expert information is expanding across the medical-related professions. Practices and clinics are increasingly comfortable with websites and visible profiles of their physicians. However, what is creating instability for the medical professions is where they exercise their expertise and the new boundaries of public, private, and personal that both they and their patients as well as their potential patients are now actively experimenting with and transforming through that experimentation. As Susskind and Susskind's (2015) analysis reveals, the very possession of that online-based information is transforming the delineations of which medical practitioners are engaged and at what level in the process of validating information and providing advice to patients. Online culture is serving to redefine professional medical practice into new zones of activity.

Our analysis of individual agency across the three professions helps explain the way that professionals are performing a new online public identity. Part of that reformation and articulation of online persona is to maintain the centrality of the professions as information becomes available and shared and thereby challenges the professions' leadership. A central driver of this new generation of online professional persona and its agency is recognizing their individual responsibility at maintaining their value in contemporary culture. From this shifted agency and reach for both economic and cultural value, the three professions we are analyzing are also involved in potentially new hierarchies of reputation and prestige. Our final step in our study of these professional online personas is to look at how reputation and prestige are being reconstituted.

Step 4: The Online Transformation of Professional Reputation and Prestige

Conceptually, reputation and prestige are closely related. In our VARP analysis of the emerging online professional personas in medicine, law, and academia, reputation can be understood as the pathway that an individual identifies to determine the status and value of an individual professional. Prestige, at least etymologically, implies some aspect of a mystique or magical glamor attached to the process of gaining reputation (OED Online 2018). With these elements, prestige implies a less quantifiable allure of renown; by contrast, reputation is more closely related to the inherent and ethical solidity of any profession. Prestige is extending that into the realm of fame and, perhaps to some degree, even celebrity. Our analysis of reputation and prestige explores the implications of the online reconfiguration of these professions, as well as considering how to calibrate and judge this new way of constituting elevated identity online.

One of the essential differences between contemporary professional reputation and past professional reputation is the capacity to calibrate and differentiate reputation with more accuracy and with a greater number of quantitative and qualitative comparative tools. For instance, all three of the professions in our study (and, of course, many other professions) have at least part of their reputations related to university systems. With a simple Google search one can find the ranking of the best medical schools hierarchized from one (Harvard) to 101 (Princeton) and beyond (QS World University Rankings, top universities 2017, 2018). Indeed, there are other rankings systems – the Shanghai-based ARWU (Academic Ranking of World Universities) and the world rankings of the *US News and World Report* being two very prominent ranking tables – that identify a slightly different order of rankings, but are remarkably similar when related to our three case study professions. On this basis alone, one can quickly identify which doctors, lawyers, and academics can be presumed to have had the best training.

But ranking and reputation have gone beyond this system of where a professional has been educated. For the medical profession, there is a website called RateMDs.com established in 2004 by the same founder of Ratemyprofessor. com (see above) and in its first decade has raised the ire of medical practitioners across North America (Mackay 2007). RateMDs claims to rank the "best doctors in the world" across the range of specializations (RateMDs.com 2018). Much like an Uber driver is given credibility by past riders and their positive reports, this site collects reviews by patients related to 1.7 million doctors under four criteria of "staff, punctuality, helpfulness, and knowledge" ranked on a one- to five-star scale (RateMDs "Best Doctors in the World" 2018). In addition, past patients are encouraged to provide reviews that describe their personal experience with the physician. The number of reviews – the site lists more than 2.6 million reviews and claimed to have "helped" more than 161 million (RateMDs "Best Doctors in the World" 2018) – and the positive versus negative nature of those reviews, makes it a peculiar mix of both word-of-mouth endorsements and rejections, and a quantitatively calibrated overall rating generated by the website itself. The site itself goes as far as to rank the "best" doctors in the world based on the number of positive reviews. The leading doctor with a five-star rating is identified as Dr. Michael Robins (a chiropractor from Markham, Ontario) with 839 glowing reviews. The top surgeon listed is Dr. José Rodrigues with 203 very strong reviews, while the top urologist, Dr. Melodie A. Denson from West Lake Hills, Texas, has all but one of her 154 reviews rated at five stars. The site replicates the verification check mark from Twitter to demonstrate that the person – in this case, the doctor rather than the reviewing patients – actually is real and exists. Interestingly, although the site provides a pathway for medical practitioners to add biographical details, qualifications, and other forms of background material, very few doctors have engaged in this practice.

RateMDs is far from the only site that allows patients to review their doctors. Along with broader consumer-oriented sites, such as Yelp or Google reviews, where health providers are one of many types of business that could be reviewed, Healthgrades, Vitals, and UCompareHealth focus specifically on the medical professions and are among the most used and popular, particularly in the United States (Daskivich et al. 2018). Increasingly, medical practitioners are realizing their reputations in gaining patients are being determined by these online reconfigurations of their identity. Although one study indicates that these reviews do not establish the value of a physician in any accurate way, research does predict that "it is certain that consumer ratings will play an increasing role in how patients choose their physicians in future" (Daskivich et al. 2018).

Reputational ranking has become a prevalent feature online (see Marshall 2016; Hearn and Schoenhoff 2016), and has played into the new constellations of value and agency in many professions and activities. As we have already detailed, reviews of academics and lawyers proliferate through contemporary online culture and they connect with all-pervasive systems of ranking. The management of online reputation has become something now regularly advanced by lawyers, academics, and doctors, along with countless others who are working out how they manage their boundaries, or lack thereof, of public and private revelations (Woodruff 2014). Professionals are engaging in elaborate systems of monitoring their online self that resembles how we are now all engaged in this element of persona construction (see Marshall 2015).

For lawyers specifically, the actual professional practice of law and their usual defense of clients has made them collectively both sensitive to negative reviews that affect their reputation, and threats to reputation that, even if they are online, move into legal territories in terms of defamation, client confidentiality, as well as a host of other judicial matters. A 2014 American survey found that 38% of respondents would use the Web to find their next lawyer (Goodrum 2015, p. 169) while an unrelated 2013 survey of Americans found that "79% of consumers *trust* the information they read in online reviews" (Goodrum, cited in BrightLocal 2014; emphasis added). The new visibility of lawyer reputation reviews from services such as Avvo and Yelp is palpable for these professionals' livelihood. As professional responsibility, privilege, and risk management advisor Mark Fucile argues, lawyers should avoid engaging in responses to negative reviews for a host of reasons, including that responses could lead to disciplinary action, and he counsels that the best strategy is the Shakespearean: "discretion is the better part of valor" (Fucile 2016, p. 89). As chronicled earlier in this chapter in our review of lawyers and value, lawyers have been generally circumspect in their online engagement even as this proliferation of sites that review lawyers' reputations has expanded.

If responding to negative online reviews is not the best way to build reputation across these three professions, and if negative reviews can lead to a further dismantling of professional reputation and persona, the performing of an online professional self has become increasingly essential. What is emerging is a new kind of professionalism across these disciplines, one that is adept at producing an effective and sage-like advisor through online platforms, while actively controlling, monitoring, and effectively building their public identity.

This building of an online persona involves our three professionals in games of prestige that are beyond the ranking or reputation that is calibrated by consumer-like review and by online entities such RateMD, Avvo, and RatemyProfessor. Effectively, cohorts of academics have built the model for other professions through their now steady labor at building followers, networking their work, and expanding their influence in a manner that links their activities to those of celebrities. These strategies are designed to work in ways that build prestige *intrinsically* and *extrinsically*. All three of our professions are engaged in similar and parallel pursuits of this game of garnering prestige.

Lawyers have a circumspect but gradually expanding relationship to this game of self-promotion. As we have seen in our study of Australian lawyers' Twitter feeds, there are relatively few posting information. In contrast, lawyers are much more comfortable on work-oriented social media sites such as LinkedIn. As early as 2009, a reported 17% of LinkedIn users were from the "legal industry" (Goodrum 2015, p. 167). In general, sites like LinkedIn offer professionals opportunities to build prestige and visibility *intrinsically* within their own occupation communities. Connecting their legal practices to clients – building prestige *extrinsically* – may advance through services like LinkedIn, but legal firms have also invested in the development of Facebook profiles that attempt to give avenues for people to find lawyers. Searches for a legal firm by a Facebook user will generate a series of Facebook pages of firms in relative proximity to the user. No matter where one looks, this constructing of a social media profile by law firms has more or less replaced or replicated the stand-alone website as a means of attracting clients. Augmenting these organizational Facebook identities are the links to lawyers within these larger firms, and to their individualized Twitter, Facebook, and Instagram usernames.

There are a number of ways of analyzing this shifting push by lawyers, doctors, and academics to engage in visible presentations for both extrinsic and intrinsic prestige. Conceptually, these professionals are developing brands and this new labor is **self-branding**. The legal profession is most closely aligned to the model of corporate **branding**, with some of the largest legal firms operating at transnational levels and the top 10 – as listed by Global 100 – earning between US$1.95 billion and US$2.82 billion in 2017 (Zaretsky 2017). The world's top 100 law firms had revenues of US$99.3 billion (Zaretsky 2017). Self-branding defines what we have called **industrialized agency**, which is transforming the individual professional into actively working to build their own influence within a field and among the clients, as individual lawyers work to expand revenue streams for their companies. Although this push to imagine oneself as a brand might inhabit the legal corporate world, it does not quite identify what is happening either in the medical profession or among academics. To identify accurately the game of prestige that is working across the three professions as lawyers, doctors, and academics contribute on Facebook, Twitter, Instagram and LinkedIn is to recognize that they are pervasively engaged in the online attention economy that is similar to what are now "influencers" (Abidin 2015; Marwick 2016).

Influencers, as Alice Marwick's work has explored, exemplify a particular pattern of self-presentation on social media designed to attract "instafame" (Marwick 2015). Similar to Marwick's research into the emergence of **microcelebrities** in different contexts (Marwick 2013, 2016), Hearn and Schoenhoff have effectively linked the ways in which social media influencers are extending a long lineage of popular culture **celebrity** and its efforts at "garner[ing] attention, reputation, and, potentially, profit" (2016, p. 202). This reading of the contemporary moment and the new emotional labor of exposing the self has been further explored by Khamis, Ang, and Welling, who conclude that "social media [platforms] like Facebook, Twitter, YouTube and Instagram facilitate not just participation but practices of self-branding" (2017, p. 205). Khamis, Ang, and Welling go on to describe the breakdown "of what were once 'knowledge monopolies ...'": "quasi-experts ... assume the role historically reserved for highly trained specialists (such as doctors, dieticians [*sic*] and scientists)" (2017, p. 205). What we are observing as the professions move into social media is active play in this world of Influencers, where lawyers, doctors, and academics are engaging in a process of having their expertise and their value heard, shared, and (potentially) given some sort of contemporary or online version of prestige.

Conclusion

The online transformation of professional persona is a rich and complex terrain. Because the deep history of professional identity is aligned with the privileged knowledge monopolies and institutional occupational hierarchies, the destabilization of these professions through social media culture and the often algorithmic-inspired tectonic shifts of online, attention, and knowledge economies highlight the competing and contradictory tensions of our new systems of public personas. This analysis of the medical, legal, and academic professions, and their construction and reconstruction of professional persona, demonstrates the need for further investigation. Our work here privileged a VARP analysis in its explorations of the transformations in the contemporary professional persona in value, agency, reputation, and prestige. We established evidence of a new pathway for the production of value, the enacting of individualized and visible agency, the engagement with new, accessible, quantitatively verified and shared reputational rankings, and an increasing push to produce a form of prestige and connection that was derived from celebrity and brand culture and now is part of the pervasive prestige system of social media. Future investigations need to look further at these and other professions through closer analyses of how professionals are comporting themselves online, as well as **prosopographic** online research (see Marshall, Moore, and Barbour 2015; see also Chapter 5 of this volume). A prosopographic study would identify the way in which connections and meanings move through the professions to establish individual and collective professional identities as well as the connections to clients, patients, students, customers, and other groups that use professionals for particular needs. Although we have worked through a great deal related to the five **dimensions of persona**, further studies need to investigate the way that various professionals play in and across the **public**, **mediatized**, **performative**, **collectively constructed**, and **intentional** dimensions in constructing their online reconfigurations of their professional persona. This chapter begins this journey into understanding contemporary professional persona and its reconfigured structure of work, identity, and play in our cultures.

References

Abbott, A.D. (1988). *The System of Professions: An Essay on the Division of Expert Labor*. Chicago: University of Chicago Press.

Abidin, C. (2015). Communicative ❤ intimacies: Influencers and perceived interconnectedness. *Ada: Gender, New Media & Technology* 8: 1–16.

Academia.edu. (2018). Join 58,980,041 academics. Academia.edu. www.academia. edu (accessed January 19, 2018).

Barbour, K. and Marshall, P.D. (2012). The academic online: Constructing persona through the World Wide Web. *First Monday* 17 (9): https://doi.org/10.5210/fm.v0i0.3969.

Becker's. (2016). 50 healthcare apps for clinicians and consumers to know. *Becker's Health IT and CIO review* (July 19). https://www.beckershospitalreview.com/healthcare-information-technology/50-healthcare-apps-for-clinicians-and-consumers-to-know.html (accessed January 18, 2018).

Black, N. (2016). How are lawyers using social media in 2016? [INFOGRAPHIC]. Mycase. https://www.mycase.com/blog/2016/02/how-are-lawyers-using-social-media-in-2016-infographic (accessed January 19, 2018).

Brightlocal. (2014). About us. http://www.brightlocal.com/about-us (accessed September 24, 2014).

Brown, J., Ryan, C., and Harris, A. (2014). How doctors view and use social media: A national survey. *Journal of Medical Internet Research* 16 (12): e267. https://doi.org/10.2196/jmir.3589.

Bruns, A., Burgess, J., Banks, J., et al. (2016). TrISMA: Tracking infrastructure for social media analysis. http://trisma.org (accessed October 29, 2018).

Daskivich, T.J., Houman, J., Fuller, G. et al. (2018). Online physician ratings fail to predict actual performance on measures of quality, value, and peer review. *Journal of the American Medical Informatics Association* 25 (4): 393–400. https://doi.org/10.1093/jamia/ocx083.

Fucile, M.J. (2016). Discretion is the better part of valor: Rebutting negative online client reviews. *Defense Counsel Journal* 83 (1): 84–89.

GMC. (2017). Like a pro [commercial]. https://www.youtube.com/watch?v=yeHV0Ws7ZEw (accessed October 15, 2017).

Goodrum, A. (2015). How to maneuver in the world of negative online reviews, the important ethical considerations for attorneys, and changes needed to protect the legal profession. *Information & Communications Technology Law* 24 (2): 164–182. https://doi.org/10.1080/13600834.2015.1042568.

Hanks, P., Coates, R., and McClure, P. (eds.) (2016). *Oxford Dictionary of Family Names in Britain and Ireland*. Oxford: Oxford University Press.

Hearn, A. and Schoenhoff, S. (2016). From celebrity to influencer: Tracing the diffusion of celebrity value across the data stream. In: *A Companion to Celebrity* (ed. P.D. Marshall and S. Redmond), 194–212. Malden, MA: Wiley Blackwell.

Henry, A. (2008). ESQChat: A social network for lawyers. *PC* (April 30). https://appscout.pcmag.com/social-networking/275388-esqchat-a-social-network-for-lawyers (accessed January 19, 2018).

Johnson, T.J. (1972). *Professions and Power*. New York: Routledge.

Khamis, S., Ang, L., and Welling, R. (2017). Self-branding, "micro-celebrity" and the rise of social media influencers. *Celebrity Studies* 8 (2): 191–208. https://doi.org/10.1080/19392397.2016.1218292.

Koon, W.K. (2016). The complex origins of Chineses names demystified. *South China Morning Post* (November 18). http://www.scmp.com/magazines/post-magazine/long-reads/article/2046955/complex-origins-chinese-names-demystified (accessed October 29, 2018).

Lu, Y., Wu, Y., Liu, J. et al. (2017). Understanding health care social media use from different stakeholder perspectives: A content analysis of an online health community. *Journal of Medical Internet Research* 19 (4): e109. https://doi.org/10.2196/jmir.7087.

Macdonald, K.M. (1995). *The Sociology of the Professions*. London: SAGE.

Mackay, B. (2007). RateMDs.com nets ire of Canadian physicians. *Canadian Medical Association Journal* 176 (6): 754. https://doi.org/10.1503/cmaj.070239.

Marshall, P.D. (2015). Monitoring persona: Mediatized identity and the edited public self. *Frame: Journal of Literary Studies* 28 (1): 115–133.

Marshall, P.D. (2016). Listicles and the play of Klout. In: *The Celebrity Persona Pandemic*, 41–47. Minneapolis: University of Minnesota Press.

Marshall, P.D. (2017). Kommodifizierung von Celebrity: Industrialisierte Agency und ihr Wert in der gegenwärtigen Aufmerksamkeitsökonomie [Commodifying the celebrity self: The peculiar emergence, formation and value of industrialized agency in the contemporary attention economy]. *Zeitschrift für Medienwissenschaft (ZfM)* 16: 49–60.

Marshall, P.D. and Atherton, C. (2015). Situating public intellectuals. *Media International Australia* 156 (1): 69–78.

Marshall, P.D., Barbour, K., and Moore, C. (2018). Academic persona: The construction of online reputation in the modern academy. In: *The Digital Academic: Critical Perspectives on Digital Technologies in Higher Education* (ed. D. Lupton, I. Mewburn and P. Thomson), 47–62. London: Routledge.

Marshall, P.D., Moore, C., and Barbour, K. (2015). Persona as method: Exploring celebrity and the public self through persona studies. *Celebrity Studies* 6 (3): 288–305. https://doi.org/10.1080/19392397.2015.1062649.

Marwick, A.E. (2013). *Status Update: Celebrity, Publicity, and Branding in the Social Media Age*. New Haven: Yale University Press.

Marwick, A.E. (2015). Instafame: Luxury selfies in the attention economy. *Public Culture* 27 (75): 137–160.

Marwick, A.E. (2016). You may know me from YouTube: (Micro-) celebrity in social media. In: *A Companion to Celebrity* (ed. P.D. Marshall and S. Redmond), 333–350. Chichester: Wiley.

Mills, C.W. (1951). *White Collar: The American Middle Classes*. New York: Oxford University Press.

Mostaghimi, A. and Crotty, B.H. (2011). Professionalism in the digital age. *Annals of Internal Medicine* 154 (8): 560–562. https://doi.org/10.7326/0003-4819-154-8-201104190-00008.

Nijman, J.E. (2004). *The Concept of International Legal Personality: An Inquiry into the History and Theory of International Law*. The Hague, Netherlands: T.M.C. Press.

OED Online. (2018). s.v. prestige. *Oxford English Dictionary*. http://www.oed.com/view/Entry/150864?redirectedFrom=prestige& (accessed October 29, 2018).

Parsons, T. (1939). The professions and social structure. *Social Forces* 17 (4): 457–467. https://doi.org/10.2307/2570695.

RateMDs. (2018). Best doctors in the world. https://www.ratemds.com/best-doctors/ (accessed November 12, 2018).

ResearchGate. (2018). About us. ResearchGate. https://www.researchgate.net/about (accessed January 19, 2018).

Sundararajan, A. (2016). *The Sharing Economy: The End of Employment and the Rise of Crowd-Based Capitalism*. Cambridge, MA: MIT Press.

Susskind, R.E. and Susskind, D. (2015). *The Future of the Professions: How Technology Will Transform the Work of Human Experts*. Oxford: Oxford University Press.

Urbis. (2015). 2014 Law Society National Profile: Final Report. Prepared for The Law Society of New South Wales. https://urbis.com.au/app/uploads/2015/05/2014-Law-Society-National-Profile.pdf (accessed October 29, 2018).

WebMD. (2016). Transcript of Q4 2016 WebMD earnings conference call – February 16, 2017. http://files.shareholder.com/downloads/WBMD/4075514959x0x929898/89CBE95F-8CF1-4234-B809-D93060391CE5/WBMD_Q4_16_TRANSCRIPT.pdf (accessed January 18, 2018).

Woodruff, A. (2014). Necessary, unpleasant, and disempowering: Reputation management in the Internet age. *Proceedings of the SIGCHI Conference on Human Factors in Computing Systems*, 149–158.

Yutopian Enterprises. (2000). Origins of Chinese family names (surnames or last names). https://yutopian.com/names (accessed March 9, 2018).

Zaretsky, S. (2017). The global 100: Fracture futures at the richest law firms in the world (2017). Above the Law (September 25). https://abovethelaw.com/2017/09/the-global-100-fractured-futures-at-the-richest-law-firms-in-the-world-2017 (accessed February 22, 2018).

Conclusion

Over most of the second decade of the twenty-first century, a particular British-originated program series entitled *Black Mirror* (2011–) presented a compelling but distinctly dystopian view of our relationship to modern technology. In many of its episodes, we are invited to explore the near-future use of technology and its transformation of the public and private self as information is generated, mediated, and reconfigured toward surprising and usually disturbing consequences for the individuals involved. The series' title, *Black Mirror*, identifies the mixed meanings of our screens (which are usually black until they are turned on), from phones to computers that are, in this futuristic transformation, sometimes further embedded into bots, brains, and eyes. The idea of this technological mirror is that the screen reconstructs ourselves for different ends and different purposes.

In an episode from Season 1 entitled "The Entire History of You," the characters have an implant that can review their complete past from their perspective. The implant is used to re-experience the recordings of one's own life and can be shared on other screens: these activities of the self are called "re-dos." The wonder of the technology, however, can also produce an odd new generation of what is real. In the episode, a husband begins to doubt his wife's intentions on all sorts of events in their shared lives. In his relentless re-doing of moments, his anxieties of her infidelities are confirmed and reconfirmed until he destroys the very possibility of their current life together: a screen becomes a pathway for the emergence of a paranoid and ultimately destructive self. A related episode in Season 3, "Nosedive," constructs a world where every action is rated by anyone who observes us or interacts with us and these ratings are immediately shared across a visible networked system on everyone's phones. This crowd-sharing surveillance by rating shapes the characters' future behavior – a kind of social and public disciplining that makes the characters act to achieve higher ratings as they work to maintain their status for the rewards its provides them in all aspects of their lives.

Persona Studies: An Introduction, First Edition. P. David Marshall, Christopher Moore, and Kim Barbour.

In many ways, the series *Black Mirror* can be thought of as the antithetical – but nonetheless useful – doppelgänger of what we have advanced in this book. We have developed the concept of persona to help us understand the way in which we negotiate our movements through a public and collective world. In making persona an object of study, and even in calling it a research field, we are both trying to come to terms with the new levels of comportment that define our public selves in the contemporary era through deep description and analysis, *and* providing a kind of literacy of how to negotiate this transformed path. Our online or digital persona literacy is an attempt to make us more aware of the potential risks and issues that could lead to the negative *Black Mirror* consequences of our new blending of the interpersonal dimensions of our lives with the patterns of public communication. After all, our public communications, facilitated through the platforms and applications we use – the intercommunication industries – and the implications of the tracking of those patterns of communication by the intercommunication industries, is being increasingly, and publicly, questioned in light of the scandals surrounding the activities of Cambridge Analytica and their ilk.

Along with the possibilities of this changed constitution of identity, we have identified the risks associated with this new mediatized and intensified formation of contemporary persona. Our lens for understanding these risks has been through the very visible formation of persona provided by celebrity culture for the last century. Collectively, we have observed through our previous legacy media the movements of these public personalities that emerged from film, radio, and the various formations of the press, who reached a zenith in the era of television in the latter half of the twentieth century. The work of paparazzi, along with other platforms including talk shows, newspapers, gossip magazines, and websites such as TMZ, capturing celebrities (see McNamara 2015) exposes these public individuals with the intent to produce something revealing about their private lives publicly.

The surveillance of celebrities was part of our elaborate and quite successful representational media and cultural regime and system. A constructed mediatized representation of significant individuals helped provide a working pattern of significance and value that moved in and through our entertainment, economic, and political cultures. The level of surveillance was connected to a system of legitimation of value. Celebrity culture provided a clear hierarchy of public persona that may have not always built consensus, but it provided a working hegemony of what issues/people/topics/entertainment were worthy of discussion.

Our work on persona identifies an expanded network of surveillance as we detailed in Chapters 2 and 3. Online culture has shifted our formations of attention away from representational media and a previous cultural regime that controlled the dispersion and distribution of cultural value. Our surveillance is now populated with billions of mediatized personalities, as most of those who have access to the requisite technology have constructed online versions of themselves. Persona – its publicness and its pervasiveness – has a new face in the contemporary moment; and more than just a new face, it has billions of new faces. The implications of this new level of persona, and persona making and sharing, are what we have investigated in this book.

The issue with this expanded and mediatized proliferation of persona is that people feel they understand what they are doing; in many ways, there is a general need to comprehend the production of personas further and in ways that better support our personal and collective interests and directions. To help explain this further, it is perhaps useful to compare our online experiences and the forms of surveillance we now inhabit to those that are present in our everyday spatial worlds. At one of our universities, Deakin University in the suburbs of Melbourne, the following sign (see Figure C.1) at least warns us that we have moved into a different territory that is not private and not really public.

Figure C.1 Deakin University – Security and surveillance warning sign at its entrance. *Source:* Photo: P.D. Marshall.

Like shopping centers, the university is heralding through this image of a camera and its identification of surveillance that you are entering a space that is ultimately controlled – and monitored – by others. However, the look and feel of this space resembles something that is not monitored: there are trees and walkways between buildings, places to sit and read, and we can see that the uses made of this "space" are filled with free and open conversations. It feels for those navigating on foot through the grounds of the university as if it is public, but it is not and this sign reinforces that. A particular combination of public feel and private ownership allows university students, employees, and visitors access and controlled freedom. The term that we have developed that tries to embody this spatial configuration is "privlic" – a combination of private in economic terms and private in terms of individual activity while the use of the space in its apparent openness is linked with our various interpretations of public (Marshall 2016). This kind of privlic space – like a shopping center – has become normalized, naturalized, and extended in our contemporary world. Similarly, New York City's Bryant Park is a private-enterprise-driven city park that is supported by a series of businesses and sponsors and makes a wonderful space (see Figure C.2). You can sit and play various games such as chess, table tennis, or mini-golf with "free" equipment, while others can access reading material and yoga classes. The bathrooms are as pristine as one can imagine for a public park, with a large flower bouquet in its foyer. Coffee and refreshments are available in kiosks run by the businesses who control the park. What can be

Figure C.2 Bryant Park New York City. *Source:* Photo: P.D. Marshall.

seen in Bryant Park is another privlic environment in its naturalization of public and private space, place, and activity.

It is important to see that our online worlds where we construct our public identities are variations of this privlic space. As our research has revealed, the intercommunication with which we engage via the various social media platforms – with its combination of interpersonal, networked, mediated, and shared disposition – are privately controlled intercommunication *industries*. As we develop our personas to navigate this "space," we are vaguely aware of the user agreements to which we have agreed – but not really. Through social media spaces, such as Facebook, Weibo, WeChat, Twitter, Instagram, and others, we have naturalized this privlic existence of ourselves, others, and the various mediatized and shared content that flows around our digitally ambulating selves. Facebook, along with other social media platforms, has to be seen as a privlic park.

Dealing with this complex digital spatial environment has enormous value for us because of the way these intercommunication industries now are part of the flow of information and communication, from the most massively mass and mediated communication processes and materials, to the most interpersonal forms of connection and sharing. As we detailed in Chapter 1, we subscribe to a cultural studies posture for contemporary persona: we are advocating in Fiske's words and building from de Certeau that we explore "the art of making do" within this environment (Fiske 1989). This art of persona construction and comportment is not easy, but we recognize that it is one of the key locations of agency in our contemporary culture. It is a negotiated public presence of the self that recognizes that we are dealing with a mixed private and public world, and that our individualized online persona must work effectively.

Our engagement has to be aware of the regular and algorithmically organized and congealed harvesting of our persona-derived information online. As our methods and approaches to persona studies underline, it is vital to see the visual constructions of our connections and sharing in terms of personalized infographics as they provide a path of seeing the patterns of interconnection. These connections and sharing patterns also visualize the ways in which the intercommunication industries can mine our production of information and its reformation in a variety of pushed forms such as click-bait style promotions, alerts, and online advertising that are integrated into our use of the most prominent social media platforms. The more we can work through these reformations of how our persona is mined and used online, the better we can engage in this new generation of online agency. As we have identified, some scholars have highlighted that contemporary online culture is producing a new generation of capitalism that has produced a precarious neoliberal individuality. Our position is that the new generation of precarity absolutely requires a better and more knowledgeable engagement and active digitally literate play in its predominant spaces. The new public identity offers possibilities with its new requirements of selling the self. It is, as some authors such as Sundararajan (2016) and Susskind and Susskind (2015) have contended, arguing that new public identities are disruptive to the now traditional corporate and related professional models of capital and work. Our persona research reveals the need to engage in a new type of negotiation with our online world and make informed decisions about the relative value of these changes that have emanated from technological transformation of the public display of the pandemic and visible self.

The Research So Far

Our research and writing in this book identifies how far the field of persona studies has advanced and specifically how our own collective research has allowed for the development of new insights and directions. In our book's early chapters, we have worked to establish the prehistory of our own study of persona. It is important to be aware that persona is certainly not unique to our contemporary era; what is clear from our work is that within different cultures and distinct eras, there were markedly different relations and pathways where personas were active. With persona being neither purely individual nor collective but rather the visible articulation of the way in which individuals negotiate an identity into collectives, each different cultural setting produces different constellations of persona.

Although the historical dimensions of persona are important and need much further exploration, this book had as its core intention an investigation of how online persona operates and transforms our culture. The work so far has admittedly been focused on areas of our own expertise and past research. We cannot deny that our public roles as academics has been disrupted by online culture, which has become one of our pathways into making sense of this transformed public identity world. Connected to this reading of persona are the case study chapters related to our own knowledge: the range of alternative artist identities online, the investigation of gaming culture, and our emerging study of professionals. Lurking around our conceptualizations of these areas are the longer related studies of celebrity and public personality systems that help us identify the pedagogical connections to highly visible versions of public entities, as well as elements of online persona that are advancing in quite different directions.

Our methods and approaches to the study of persona are our most valuable contribution to this nascent field, advancing our understanding and helping to make sense of our contemporary world. These methods and approaches have two forms in our work. Because of the challenge of trying to understand this way of thinking of the self as a strategic public figure that was formed in the different environments of online games, social media platforms, online surveillance, and self-comportment, we are seeking, with some frustration and excitement, to name it effectively. Thus, one of the features of this book is a new lexicon of terminology to help explain persona and its formation of agency. Some of them are neologisms – our description of "privlic" we hope is useful to describe the online mix of private and public despite its not so beautiful sound. Other terms such as intercommunication, representational and presentational media and cultural regimes, micro-publics, autosurveillance, gâmeur, our registers of persona, and the acronym of a VARP analysis are perhaps not all new terms and not all our own, but they have been redeployed for very particular research ends. When wedded with our approaches that have been adapted from existing research methods such as IPA (interpretative phenomenological analysis), action research, visualization, prosopography, online listening, and VARP analysis, we can with confidence say that we have built the tools for further analysis and exploration of contemporary persona and its myriad online configurations. Perhaps with less confidence, but some hopefulness, we would like to claim that this terminology will help historical investigations of persona as well. The value of these tools of terminology is also aspirational: we have built a common research language for the investigation of persona so that future collaborative projects will have a core group of valuable concepts to organize their studies for comparative purposes.

In an overarching direction, we also hope that the book helps people build their own persona literacy. Online pandemic persona and its production of personalized and shared information is something that requires new ways to work out its value for the individual. This book serves that wider purpose of expanding our understanding of the significance of persona and the implications of this shared and sharing culture, its digital reformations, and deployments of persona work. Our methods of investigation (see Chapters 4 and 5) highlight our twin desire to help others think through this new public visibility world where the divides of public, private, and intimate are under constant self-negotiation. We are providing some tools for the management of the contemporary public persona and the new forms of digitalized/emotional labor of comportment that it entails.

We Are Not Alone: Other Research and the *Persona Studies* Journal

Research related to what we have imagined as a new field is, of course, never completely new. The journal, *Persona Studies*, has become a beacon for other researchers to make connections to the study of persona. Since its launch in early 2015, work published in *Persona Studies* has expanded the field in interesting and related directions. Well before we have published this work with its case studies of personas, the journal attracted a range of scholars who addressed work(ing) persona that have certainly helped develop our three example-driven chapters. For instance, Sharyn McDonald's valuable work on academic professional persona reputation management provides an interesting survey of the constitution of this particular form of public identity that we explored in Chapter 8 (McDonald 2015). Likewise, Beaton's (2015) study of self-presentation personas of 1970s petroleum geologists in San Diego challenges the boundaries between private and work identities in their expressed revelations in work-related memorials.

There has been extensive research advanced on political persona with a particularly engaging reading of Donald Trump in terms of film noir-related personas by Virginia Rademacher (2016), as well as a reading of the persona of Barack Obama (Totman and Hardy 2014), and an analysis of a peculiar politician and former paparazzi known as the Geelong Mohawk mayor (Casson 2016). Writers in other issues have provided insights into the way the software industry has for years privileged the concept of persona to "predict how certain types of users ... will interact with the system in a given situation in order to complete a certain goal" (Coorevits et al. 2016, p. 97), a direction that was further explored in a highly significant creative intervention for the journal by Aaron Humphrey (2017).

Contributors to the journal have made important intersections with other emerging disciplines, such as game studies. For instance, there is Mata Haggis's (2016) video essay contribution exploring the growing trend in the video game industry in which independent video game developers are producing unique, personally driven, and emotionally powerful experiences for players. Stefan Werning (2017) examines this trend of autobiographical game making as a powerful mode of conceptualizing and expressing individual identity within game media. Together with Oskar Milik's (2017) analysis of the construction of player identity as the presentation of the self to others in online worlds, these advances in theorizing player persona have greatly influenced the historical approach taken in Chapter 7.

The journal continues to expand the territories now explored through persona studies: one of the most recent issues (2018) reveals the historical constitution of scientific public identity through a series of biographical profiles of scientific personas from the nineteenth to twentieth centuries.

We have not been able to capture all of the directions that the journal has advanced in this too brief précis; nonetheless, the building of this research hub through the journal has permitted the field to expand in ways that have made the entire research endeavor more intellectually rich. Along with this work, we should acknowledge that our approaches to persona studies are very much linked to the scholarship that is proliferating around online influencers. These influencer researchers – led by scholars such as Crystal Abidin (2015) and Florencia García-Rapp (2017) among other scholars whose research intersects with those of Alison Hearn (Hearn and Schoenhoff 2015) and Alice Marwick

(2016) – are exactly where celebrity studies intersects with persona studies as these researchers explore the micro-public/microcelebrity world via usually youthful online and highly visible figures/personalities.

What Still Needs to Be Done

We designed our exploration of persona through the chapters in this book to provide the groundwork for future study. As we advanced on our writing and research, and as we worked through our case studies to exemplify how persona works in the contemporary moment, what became evident was the vital need to expand our analysis of persona and its operation both historically and in our relatively new online-implicated and culturally transformed world. As a way of pulling all our thinking together, we thought it would be useful to conclude here by identifying the directions we would like to take in our future work. However, we also have to acknowledge that the sheer volume of interesting directions for persona studies research needs an entire network of researchers to be involved. This book and this conclusion is an entreaty to engage you, our readers, in our intellectual journey.

Everyday Persona

Our book has certainly elaborated conceptually on the idea of persona literacy, and how essential it is to navigate with this kind of knowledge in contemporary culture. However, we still need a great deal more research on what we would call ordinary or everyday personas; that is, people who are less visible, less desiring of some version of celebrity or micro-celebrity, but are trying to manage a strategic identity in all sorts of domains and directions. Our research does not identify one ideal type of persona and the very idea of an ideal is ludicrous. What we have tried to advance is that constructing the public mediatized selves for some collective setting leads to all sorts of possible configurations. So, one of our basic future directions in research is to investigate more examples of everyday persona, where individuals in all sorts of relations to work and leisure, private and public presentations, are managing their mediatized online personas. Fundamentally, this work informs our future understanding of the cultural gestalt manifested by our relations to social media and its formations of intercommunication. A key concern we hold with the more tightly focused field of celebrity studies is that it *gives even* more attention to those who already hold a disproportionate level of privilege and power. While acknowledging that attention to those in the public eye is important work, we believe that as much, if not more, can be learned from engaging with the everyday. The reemergence of a focus on audience in media studies, matched with the considerable attention given to produsers (see Bruns 2008), and the continued development of fandom studies can all provide interdisciplinary touchpoints for a persona led approach to the study of the everyday user.

Professional Persona

All three of our case study chapters provided investigations of professional personas. Whether players, artists, and craftivists or doctors, lawyers, and academics, it was *work* identities that were present in the online formation of persona that we visualized, tracked, and listened to, with many claiming what they do as a profession. Our own research in these areas is in its initial stages. We would like to look further into the constitution of mediatized and online public identity construction, sharing, and networking in each of these environments. For doctors and academics, we would like to dig into the data and textual patterns of their social media use to determine further the transforming identities and roles in their work areas. In terms of artist personas, it would be interesting to work through the communicative repercussions of musicians and singers as they construct their online identities for the slightly reconfigured audience, networks, followers, and fans, building on the excellent work of Nancy Baym (2007, 2013, 2015). Ultimately, it would be valuable to expand to other forms of work and determine the way in which online persona is transforming these formations of credibility, trust, and connection. Of course, this kind of ambition demands collaboration with others, and particularly those familiar with these occupations and the way that online culture is shifting their individual and collective personas.

Comparative Persona

Although we have not emphasized this work in this book, one of our emerging projects is to develop effective ways of comparing persona across, between, and within cultures (see Marshall 2017c, pp. 19–31). Patterns of public expression of mediatized identity are most visible and potentially influential through the actions of the celebrities and other public personality systems. Each culture – sometimes defined by a nation, sometimes by region, language, and/or ethnicity – produces these visible celebrities that structure patterns of public comportment in their construction of their personas. Our research endeavors to work out the tropes of persona construction that are what we call "intrinsic," only making sense within the culture, and "extrinsic," translating well transnationally. These identify why some personas are international celebrities. Through a study of these celebrities' on and off-line personas through these categories, we hope to produce a way to compare personas. The second stage of this analysis is to consider social media personas within the culture more widely, to determine whether these celebrity personas produce patterns of online public identity for the millions of people in those identifiable cultures.

The comparative persona project is designed to be large and, through using similar terminology across potentially many countries over time, produce a system for continuing and expanding the research into more countries and regions. The work demands a familiarity with research such as "face-work" that has developed in intercultural communication (Ting-Toomey 1994), Todorov's psychologically directed first-impression facial analysis (Todorov 2017), and some of the successful studies that have worked with the individuality that is part of corporate branding and self-branding. As is evident from its breadth, it also calls out for researchers across the planet who can delve deeply into particular cultures and the potentially categorical patterns that are visible in each of these cultures.

Political Persona

The strategic public presentation of the self has many objectives in different collective settings. One of the most intriguing is how a political identity comes into being, gains visibility, and becomes a combination of issues, projection of personality, and an embodiment of a collective. Understanding these processes is an investigation of political persona. Our initial political persona research has focused on how online culture and pandemic persona are contributing to the production of a new generation of political instability. This work builds from what we have identified in this book as the migration from a representational media and cultural regime to a presentational media and cultural regime. Although far from completely explaining the rise of Donald Trump and Brexit in 2016 and 2017, our direction of analysis points to how the online shift with pandemic persona creates a different formation of power that circumvents and weakens the representational political support structures of legacy media (see Marshall and Henderson 2016). We are just beginning to extend this research to help explain what could be described as the (in)attention economy and its structure of sharing interpersonally has also created a new – and surprising – "word of mouth" culture that resembles models that operated in antiquity (Marshall 2017a). Our work on political persona is developing in interesting directions that will ideally lead to new collaborations with scholars in political communication.

Expanding the Data Analytics of (Online) Persona

In this book, we have isolated the data related to personas through a number of analytical lenses. Most prominently, we have emphasized that personas are the self-production of personalized information that moves into the exigencies of the intercommunication industries as much as they present our shared public identities and related interests in our micro-publics of followers and friends. Closely related to our discussion of persona information and its transformation, we have underlined our need to be better aware of how our network is operating online. This reading of the mediatized and online self is perhaps best illuminated in Chapter 7 and its study of "indie" game developer personas, but is also visible in our social media analysis of lawyers using TrISMA data, as well as our studies of doctors and academics in Chapter 8. Our future work will further expand our efforts at visualizing persona networks and interrelations as we make sense of different formations of micropublics and how they intersect with the formation of individual – but connected – personas. In addition, we hope to work through how we can calibrate VARP analysis with links to the ways in which individuals share and relate to each other. This form of text and data analysis of posts, likes, and/or retweets on Twitter, or similar analysis of the movement of images on Instagram will form the basis with which we would like to extend our online analysis back in time in a data-inspired way. The construction of historical persona could be calibrated and visualized through the relations via objects and forms of communications that individuals engaged with in different pre-Internet eras. All of this work in elaborating our use of data analytics is just developing; like our other emerging projects we are hopeful it will be aided by future research collaborations.

Emoji and Avatars: The Persona-Fication of Emotion and Gestural Communication

As our research in this book and elsewhere has demonstrated, the transformation of the self into persona has manifested itself in many and unforeseen directions. The shared and public dimension of what persona expresses has created applications and platforms that, despite their apparent openness, have structured our formation of mediatized and strategic visible online identities. One of our future projects is to study the way in which we convert ourselves into other recognizable entities and forms. Online gaming and its standard reformation of the game player into an avatar has been one of our objects of study and it intersects with some important related emergent research (Banks and Bowman 2016; Frow 2014). In the future we seek to examine the continued evolution of media audience participation into new niche and paratextual industries, including the fan labor of cosplayers, the persona work of Twitch. TV streamers and the extra-informational layering of contributed meaning via YouTube video blogging (vlogging), podcasting, and eSports commentating. We are also beginning research into our regular use of emoji and stickers on social media and its frequent deployment for interpersonal texting and group chats (Marshall 2017b). Emoji has developed into a proto-language and communication system for emotion supported strongly by an integrated and authorized accrediting authorization that resembles the original authorization of URLs on the Web. Augmenting these developments are the commercial applications such as bitmoji and zmoji, designed to personalize our online expression of emotion. These various structures are producing a kind of *persona-fication* of our online emotive communication. Our avatar research calls out for collaboration across fields such as linguistics, psychology of emotions, visual graphics as it relates to fabricating a personal character, game studies, branding, and self-branding in online culture and marketing, and new generations of studies in communication. It represents a fascinating and complex direction for our future studies of persona.

Conclusion

What we have presented in this book are the building blocks for further research, contemplation, application, and study. For all the work we have developed and advanced, the field of persona studies is taking its first intellectual steps. It has revealed an expanded and intensified reforming of our various collective worlds through this now mediatized persona. We hope this book helps you navigate this transforming world and perhaps assist us and others to take the next steps in persona studies.

References

Abidin, C. (2015). Communicative ❤ intimacies: Influencers and perceived interconnectedness. *Ada: Gender, New Media & Technology* 8: 1–16. https://doi.org/10.7264/N3MW2FFG.

Banks, J. and Bowman, N.D. (2016). Avatars are (sometimes) people too: Linguistic indicators of parasocial and social ties in player – avatar relationships. *New Media & Society* 18 (7): 1257–1276.

Baym, N.K. (2007). The new shape of online community: The example of Swedish independent music fandom. *First Monday* 12 (8): http://journals.uic.edu/ojs/index.php/fm/article/view/1978 (accessed October 29, 2018).

Baym, N.K. (2013). Fans or friends? Seeing social media audiences as musicians do. Matrizes 7 (1): 13–46. https://doi.org/10.11606/issn.1982-8160.v7i1p13-46.

Baym, N.K. (2015). Connect with your audience! The relational labor of connection. *The Communication Review* 18 (1): 14–22. https://doi.org/10.1080/10714421.2015.996401.

Beaton, B. (2015). Crafting a work persona in 1970s petroleum geology. *Persona Studies* 1 (2): 31–41. https://doi.org/10.21153/ps2015vol1no2art468.

Black Mirror. (2011–). [TV program] (exec. prod. C. Brooker and A. Jones).

Bruns, A. (2008). The future is user-led: The path towards widespread produsage. *The Fibreculture Journal* 11: http://eleven.fibreculturejournal.org/

fcj-066-the-future-is-user-led-the-path-towards-widespread-produsage
(accessed October 29, 2018).

Casson, R. (2016). Gas, grass or ass, no one rides for free: The Mohawk mayor.
Persona Studies 2 (2): 42–56. https://ojs.deakin.edu.au/index.php/ps/article/
view/614/598 (accessed October 29, 2012).

Coorevits, L., Schuurman, D., Oelbrandt, K., and Logghe, S. (2016). Bringing
personas to life: User experience design through interactive coupled open
innovation. *Persona Studies* 2 (1): 97–114. https://ojs.deakin.edu.au/index.php/
ps/article/view/534/581 (accessed October 29, 2018).

Fiske, J. (1989). *Understanding Popular Culture*, 2e, reprint. New York:
Routledge.

Frow, J. (2014). *Character and Person*. Oxford: Oxford University Press.

García-Rapp, F. (2017). Popularity markers on YouTube's attention economy:
The case of Bubzbeauty. *Celebrity Studies* 8 (2): 228–245.

Haggis, M. (2016). Creator's discussion of the growing focus on, and potential of,
storytelling in video game design. *Persona Studies* 2 (1): 20–25. https://ojs.
deakin.edu.au/index.php/ps/article/view/532 (accessed October 29, 2018).

Hearn, A. and Schoenhoff, S. (2015). From celebrity to influencer: Tracing the
diffusion of celebrity value across the data stream. In: *A Companion to
Celebrity* (ed. P.D. Marshall and S. Redmond), 194–212. Malden, MA:
Wiley Blackwell.

Humphrey, A. (2017). User Personas and social media profiles. *Persona Studies* 3
(2): 13–20. https://ojs.deakin.edu.au/index.php/ps/article/view/708/653
(accessed October 29, 2018).

Marshall, P.D. (2016). When the private becomes public: Commodity activism,
endorsement and making meaning in a privatized world. In: *Contemporary
Publics: Shifting Boundaries in New Media, Technology and Culture* (ed. P.D.
Marshall, G. D'Cruz, S. McDonald and K. Lee), 229–245. New York: Palgrave
Macmillan.

Marshall, P.D. (2017a). The new word of mouth culture: Pandemic fame/persona/
rumour/reputation and the production of contemporary instability. Public
lecture, Centre for Digital Media, Vancouver (October 25, 2017). https://prezi.
com/m/ths87uiywhgr/?utm_campaign=share&utm_medium=copy (accessed
October 29, 2018).

Marshall, P.D. (2017b). Gestural communication and emoji culture: Strains
of connection in an era of confused and false information. Public lecture
presented at the Social Media Lab, Ryerson University, Toronto
(September 12, 2017) http://prezi.com/iza9l0ubxbze/?utm_
campaign=share&utm_medium=copy (accessed October 29, 2018).

Marshall, P.D. (2017c). Comparative persona: From cross-cultural "celebrity"
analysis to the transformations of the public self in online culture.
In: *New Media and Social Transformation* (ed. J. Xin), 17–31. Beijing:
Communication University of China Press.

Marshall, P.D. and Henderson, N. (2016). Political persona 2016 – an introduction. *Persona Studies* 2 (2): 1–18. https://ojs.deakin.edu.au/index.php/ps/article/view/628 (accessed October 29, 2018).

Marwick, A.E. (2016). You may know me from YouTube: (Micro-) celebrity in social media. In: *A Companion to Celebrity* (ed. P.D. Marshall and S. Redmond), 333–350. Chichester: Wiley.

McDonald, S. (2015). Responsible management of online academic reputations. *Persona Studies* 1 (2): 54–63. https://ojs.deakin.edu.au/index.php/ps/article/view/462 (accessed October 29, 2018).

McNamara, K. (2015). *Paparazzi: Media Practices and Celebrity Culture.* Cambridge: Polity Press.

Milik, O. (2017). Persona in MMO games: Constructing an identity through complex player/character relationships. *Persona Studies* 3 (2): 66–78. https://ojs.deakin.edu.au/index.php/ps/article/view/672 (accessed October 29, 2018).

Rademacher, V.N. (2016). Trump and the resurgence of American noir. *Persona Studies* 2 (2): 90–103. https://doi.org/10.21153/ps2016vol2no2art617.

Sundararajan, A. (2016). *The Sharing Economy: The End of Employment and the Rise of Crowd-Based Capitalism.* Cambridge, MA: MIT Press.

Susskind, R.E. and Susskind, D. (2015). *The Future of the Professions: How Technology Will Transform the Work of Human Experts.* Oxford: Oxford University Press.

Ting-Toomey, S. (1994). *The Challenge of Facework: Cross-Cultural and Interpersonal Issues.* New York: SUNY Press.

Todorov, A.B. (2017). *Face Value: The Irresistible Influence of First Impressions.* Princeton: Princeton University Press.

Totman, S. and Hardy, M. (2014). The charismatic persona of colonel Qaddafi. *M/C Journal* 17 (3): http://journal.media-culture.org.au/index.php/mcjournal/article/view/808 (accessed October 29, 2018).

Werning, S. (2017). The persona in autobiographical game-making as a playful performance of the self. *Persona Studies* 3 (1): 28–42. https://ojs.deakin.edu.au/index.php/ps/article/view/650 (accessed October 29, 2018).

Glossary

Key Words in Persona Studies

Persona Studies: An Introduction, First Edition. P. David Marshall, Christopher Moore, and Kim Barbour.

Key word/concept	Definition	Examples and exemplification
action research **first person action research** **second person action research** **third person action research**	An applied research technique that is designed to include the subjects in the learning, knowledge, and value process in feedback loops as the project advances.	**First person action research** involves the self in an exploration of the subject's own persona. It is designed for study, but also a determination of whether the persona is achieving ends for the self. It is used to further investigate changes and amendments to the persona that are implemented and trialed. **Second person action research** acknowledges an intention among a group of subject/researchers for improvement of certain conditions. The researchers work collaboratively toward this common and shared goal. It may involve something like a group of professionals who want to all construct appropriate online personas for themselves. The process of sharing with others in the project is beneficial to all. These are generally small qualitative projects with a recording of transformations, outcomes, and awareness by individuals of improvement in their personas. **Third person action research** implies a larger cohort of subjects and a study of their engagement with the process of making their public identities (personas). Subjective feedback and an interactive process is the method for the research, as opposed to keeping an objective distance from the subjects of the study. The key object of this process is to produce a step change, perhaps in an entire association or professional group, that might be spread out geographically.
affect	An area of study that investigates how emotion moves through an individual or a culture.	Affect is the opposite of cognition; it refers to a subject's feelings and emotions, as opposed to intentional thought and reason. Affect is "felt" in the body, and the mind then processes the sensation and formats the experience as emotion.
agency	The capacity to create change in society and culture; the catalyst for a transformation or shift politically, culturally, or economically.	Agents are often thought of as individuals. Identifying which individuals can produce the greatest change is one way to think of agency. Thus, political leaders are agents, business leaders are agents. Famous celebrities can be agents because they have a new type of agency that originates in the personalization of media. Individuals have agency when they bring about change or produce an effect.

agency – industrialized/industrial agency	The new comfortability of a formation of engagement in the world where the individual is commodified and derives capacity to affect change through this commodified status. It is similar to neoliberalism and its definition of individualism, but it is not necessarily a critical definition because it recognizes that this agency can affect change and describes a new situated and strategic position in contemporary culture.	Industrialized agency is most evident in celebrities. They are commodified individuals who, through their commodified status, are able to affect change in contemporary culture in many ways. Some are brand ambassadors of products; but others represent political, social, and environmental issues, and shift the attention economy and the culture in different directions.
application programming interface (API)	A computer programming term for a standard series of protocols and subroutines designed to make communication between different software elements compatible.	The Twitter API is accessible via the developer's website to enable anyone using Twitter to understand how the service works and provide a series of tools for integration with other applications and products, such as mobile phone apps or websites.
artist/artistness	Most simply, an artist is a person who makes what is understood as art. Artistness consists of those personal and professional qualities that make up the sociocultural discourse around being an artist, and draws from the **"myth of the artist"** as well as the artist as an economic producer of **creative labor.**	Artists play a range of roles in our society. They can challenge existing discourse, or support social, political, and environmental positions, or simply add color and beauty to our homes, workplaces, and public spaces. The arts are understood to contribute to social cohesion and economic progress, but individual artists often support their practice with work in other industries.

(continued)

Key word/concept	Definition	Examples and exemplification
asynchronous media and communication	A media form that allows communication to occur not at the same time between sender and receiver.	Most online media can be watched when the individual chooses and is therefore asynchronous. You also choose when to answer a text on Wechat: it is sequential, but also asynchronous. A call on a phone is synchronous, however. Reading a book is asynchronous.
attention economy	The conceptualization of human attention as a scare resource, and the processes by which digital media in particular attempt to gain and sustain that attention.	YouTube operates as an attention economy. The platform provides its content creators with a detailed analytics package that reveals user views, comments, ratings, as well as the gender and age groups of viewers with whom the video is popular. YouTube rewards content creators with a share of advertising revenue based on the attention, duration, and number of viewers each individual video retains.
audience	A group of people watching, listening, reading, playing, and/or consuming a particular text.	Mass, theatrical, event, networked, online are all types of audiences. New terms to describe how an audience is different online have developed: **users** is one of these; another is **produsers** to identify that the online audience is both a viewer and a maker, someone who produces and shares related content with others. YouTube is a site where produsers share reviews, remixes, parodies, and other paratextual content, often oriented toward fan cultures.
autoethnography	Autoethnography is a portmanteau of "autobiography" and "ethnography." It is a research method that attempts to make sense of the experience of culture through attention to the individual. It offers a deep connection to the anthropological reading of ethnography with the researcher focused on him or herself as the object of study. It is aligned with **first person action research**	In some ways, autoethnography is the starting point for persona studies: we explore the different ways in which we construct our identities through texts, images, and comportment. From this vantage point of the analysis of the self, we can begin to see how others are producing personas.

avatar	An icon or figure that represents an individual – often an animated drawing or image.	Avatars are a particular type of online persona that is used in games, but also in some aspects of social media where the picture used expresses the individual – as in WeChat for instance.
backstage	A theatrical term used by Erving Goffman to identify those areas that are not publicly visible, but nonetheless areas where certain people witness a different construction of the presentation of the self.	Backstage can describe preparation for the performative frontstage. In online culture, it may describe those elements that are not exposed, but remain offline. However, the exposure of backstage where the real person inhabits is one of the impetuses behind the surveillance of the media of celebrity culture – to see the backstage and thus more authentic version of the star.
branding and self-branding	Originally a way to describe ownership, the term has come to embody the individualization of corporate identity. Self-branding is the incorporation of the sellable self into the understanding of a particular individual's value.	The branding of cattle is still a useful way to understand branding as fundamentally about ownership. In the contemporary moment, the brand has become more valuable economically than the real assets of a corporation. For the individual, online culture has produced a culture where there is normalization and naturalization of self-branding. Influencers work hard in this environment and develop a related industrial agency.
celebrity	A celebrated individual who has visibility in the media over and above their primary professional activity.	There are film stars, TV stars, sports stars, even business stars; they become celebrities when we watch them for more than their professional activity and follow their lives and perhaps their thoughts. Celebrities are powerful because they can be used to promote causes, can draw attention to events and activities, and they can make certain products visible and popular.
collective	A conceptual way to identify groupings of people that are connected in some socially shared way without privileging other political or cultural norms and imperatives that are connected to words such as "public" or "community." Persona is a way to negotiate one's self into various collectives.	The range of types of collectives is infinite; it is the imagined community of social networks online *and* the quantitative and data configurations of those same collectives.

(continued)

Key word/concept	Definition	Examples and exemplification
commodity/commodification	A commodity defines an object by its value in the marketplace over and above any other form of value. Commodification identifies the way our world is increasingly focused on market definitions of value until everything becomes a product.	Everything in a supermarket is a commodity. It is designed to be sold. A celebrity is an individual who has been commodified by our culture. Their meaning has been made into a product that can be bought and sold. An athlete and a film star both allow themselves to be commodified, and online culture is pushing us all to commodify ourselves and accept it as normal and natural.
communication	Communication comes in many forms. It is the exchange of information across a medium. The techniques employed for communication sometimes occur through different media technologies to convey meaning and messages.	Communication can be written, oral, visual, audio, face-to-face, symbolic, gestural, and so on. Communication can also imply temporal relations, such as synchronous and a-synchronous forms of communication.
convergence	The blurring and blending of media technologies and the diminishing distance between the role of audience and the functions of the producer.	Video games are a converged media: they have narrative direction like a film, but they also have interaction with other audience members as well as the individual building their own narrative. Several different kinds of media are blending in video games. Social media is another example of convergence – it produces text, images, moving images, animation, and interpersonal communication as well as networked and more widely shared "mass" communication.

craft (in arts)	Craft making is often defined in functional terms, where a highly skilled individual makes an object with use-value, whereas art must exist on its own terms without being a functional object. Ceramics, fibrecraft, woodwork, and so forth are generally considered craft as opposed to art, unless through their production they are made "useless" – such as a ceramic "vase" which cannot hold water, or a wooden form resembling a chair which cannot be sat on.	Some forms of craft traditionally associated with women, such as needlepoint, knitting, quilting, and banner making, have been used for activism, as in **craftivism**.
craftivism	Using **craft** as a form of activism in an effort to effect change gently with personal contact and individual effort. Craftivism stems from a dissatisfaction with more combative forms of activism, such as attending rallies and marches, and privileges practices traditionally associated with women, such as needlework.	Knitting groups who combine sit-ins with craft, such as Knitting Nana's, may use the practice of knitting to disrupt the expectation that protestors are aggressive or confrontational. Mini banners, made using cross-stitch, provide small reminders to act ethically or to reconsider purchasing new clothing or other consumer goods that may not be produced in a sustainable manner.

(continued)

Key word/concept	Definition	Examples and exemplification
creative labor	Stemming from the introduction of the creative industry discourse in government policy in the 1990s, as well as Richard Florida's influential work on the creative class, creative labor redirects attention to the economic potential of the arts through income production and taxation, as well as contribution to the social and political well-being of a community.	The term "creative industries" refers to an industrialized version of creative labor, which is highly dependent on different forms of intellectual property. The development of software, games, social media platforms, and other Internet-based products and services are now included alongside traditional media industries (print, cinema, television, and radio), and the arts by governments with an increased focus on the "creative economy."
dimensions of persona	We have identified five dimensions of persona: public, mediatized, performative, collective, and having intentional value, agency, reputation, and prestige (summarized as VARP).	See Chapters 3 and 7 for detailed examples of the dimensions of persona in action.
dividual	Deleuze's term that cleverly identifies the division of the individual in what he calls the "control society" where we can be divided up into endless data points, markets, statistics, and other representations made possible by technologies such as computer-based systems and algorithms.	The dividual – unlike the individual – is not coherent and singular, a unified body. The dividual has multiple formations and it has been a useful term to identify the interesting way in which we manage ourselves and the versions of our identity that are allowed to emerge in social media. A Facebook profile looks coherent, but it is a dividual as the data it generates is used and reconstructed for another version of a potential consumer, typically advertisers looking to market a product to specific consumer "types."
exposure	A concept used in persona research to describe the relative levels at which an individual reveals him or herself publicly.	Our sharing of photos online identifies a type of exposure. Similarly, a celebrity figure or politician has to regulate the nature and amount of exposure to maintain their value or their particular message. It is a condition of contemporary culture to expose; but exposure identifies a new form of regulation.

facework	A concept used in intercultural communication specifically to describe how one can read the different visual and gestural cues of communication that are specific to a given culture. It is also a term that Goffman used to describe a visual presence of the self through facial cues.
	Facework implies a kind of impression management of first impressions. Metaphorically, it is linked to persona studies on two levels. Individuals try to construct their facial images for certain effects – clear strategy of moving into a collective world. Also, individuals construct mediatized faceworks – possibly most clearly presented on Instagram – that establish recognizable first impression personas for those who are connected to these online entities or are perusing to ascertain their value or online reputation.
frontstage	A theatrical term of the location of the actor on stage; it was appropriated by Goffman in his work that emerged from symbolic interactionism.
	This describes the visible work of persona: it is most closely linked to the performativity dimension of persona. When we walk out of our living space into the street, we are moving into a frontstage; similarly, when we post something about ourselves on social media, we are moving into the performance mode or on to the virtual frontstage of our social media persona.
gamer	Gamer is a person who plays games. It is a term used by Mackenzie Wark to describe an individual that comes to an understanding of the world through quantifiable failure.
	Although somewhat synonymous with the term "player," the term "gamer" is currently contested through links to hypermasculinized toxic behaviors online, such as homophobia, sexism, racism, and other antisocial conduct.
gâmeur	The gâmeur is a new persona type present among developers, players, and paratextual workers in the video game industry. The gâmeur is a presentational media figure, signaling a capacity to challenge normativity in the mainstream.	A description based on the concept of the flâneur, a gâmeur is someone signaling the capacity to challenge the dominant forms of expression commonly found in the video game industry. A gâmeur might be a Twitch.tv streamer who plays indie games that represent non-normative gender identities or an **indie** game developer who seeks to include characters of different body types or cultural representations.

(continued)

Key word/concept	Definition	Examples and exemplification
global village	McLuhan's term for the way in which electronic media – television and radio in particular – metaphorically produced a different relation to time and space that "shrunk" the world. The diminished proximity created by the resulting complex of networks produced a "village" effect.	The orality of media is at least part of the idea of the global village for McLuhan, which makes it "cool" and not "hot" like print: this permits a different constitution of a collective connection that resembles a village. The global co-viewing of live broadcast events such as the Olympic Games, produced the effect of the global village. Another example might be the live responding to events via platforms like Facebook, Twitter, and WeChat.
impressions	An online term to identify the number of times a particular website has been "visited."	Impressions do not identify whether the user engaged with the website, but merely measures the numbers of visits. It is a simple and crude way to establish online reputation and value. Impressions are used to calibrate whether a particular YouTube channel or blog reaches a threshold of attention that may attract advertising through the intercommunication company that curates the overall application or program.
indexical communication	A form of communication and sign that points to the value and presence of other forms of communication.	Indexical communication dominates our reading of our online worlds. In its simplest structure, we are drawn from our reading of one source to click on to a link of a related source of information. Advertisements online operate in this way, but another variation of this form of communication is what is often called "click-bait." The clustering of related information is part of the structure of the intercommunication industries that service our uses of social media in particular. A very useful way of understanding this indexical communication is to read the relation of information as it is structured on the shared news social media site of Reddit, where the "upvote" is an indexical indication of engagement with the content.

indie
Short for independent, the term indie suggests a capacity for publication outside of the mainstream. Originating in the garage punk movement of the 1960 and 1970s, and adapted to the film industry in the 1980s and most recently to the video game industry.

Indie video games are developed and published outside the major studio system and without financial support from large companies. Indie games are made available via community run websites such as Itch.io and self-published via digital distribution platforms such as Steam. Indie games have the freedom to offer alternative representations and non-normative depictions of race, class, and gender.

industrialized agency
See agency

information visualization
Also known as data visualization and visual data analysis. The process of producing visual representations of information in order to communicate specific values from the data.

Visualization portrays data in different ways in order to observe patterns and make meaning in alternative ways. Tables and graphs are traditional forms of data visualization. More recently, network visualization tools have become popular means of communicating links between users in social groups.

intercommunication
The new generation of online platforms allows for the individual production, reception, and sharing of different media and communication forms. The term implies interpersonal exchange as being a form of intermediary between these different ways of communicating.
Intercommunication also implies a hybridized interpretation of the flow between representational and presentational media.

Social media identify intercommunication and can be defined as the intercommunication industry that encourages individuals to communicate in all these various forms in order to generate more data about the individual to feed back into the advertising industry, which is very interested in monitoring what we do online.

(continued)

Key word/concept	Definition	Examples and exemplification
internetworked	Persona is internetworked, which comes from the way that online culture is individualized and yet continuously aggregated. Internetworking extends from relations between individuals to networks of connections between platforms.	The internetworked movement of information of the self generates personalized content that is aggregated across networks. It involves movement and connectivity between groups of interests and communities of practice. Fan cultures, for example, are not conducted in isolation online, but rather are an expression of personal interests that are connected to the collective expressions of similar individuals.
interpersonal communication	On a basic level, interpersonal communication is the direct conversational communication between two or more individuals. It can be either unmediated (that is, face-to-face) or mediated (that is, online as text, phone, or other one-to-one forms).	Social media is comprised of a variety of interpersonal communication systems. The language of the current generation of social media sites and services is based around interpersonal communication networks. For example, Facebook offers direct and indirect interpersonal communication through the Messenger application, comments, and "likes."
interpretive phenomenological analysis (IPA)	IPA is a research method that is designed to understand that reality is comprised of interpretation. Integrating hermeneutics into the investigation, it deals with the constructed nature of reality and our subjective role in those constructions.	A persona is a constructed version of the self, which means that IPA is a useful method to look at how the individual interprets their constituted public identity formation. It is a close listening to the subject's process and ultimate formation of persona.
intimate	Part of the private world, but defined by activities that are designed as even more private – intimate usually implies physical closeness and sometimes sexual relations.	Like privacy, the boundaries of intimacy are also being challenged by the personalization of media. The visibility of the most intimate elements of human life are changing our cultures.
legacy media	A term that is now used to describe media before the Internet, in particular.	All media that predate the Internet – but there is a tendency to refer to the powerful ones of the last 100 years: television, radio, film, magazines, and newspapers.

legacy politics	A term that describes the legitimation link between the institutions of political representation and the institutions of the mediatized representation emerging into dominance in the twentieth century.	In Western cultures, a certain naturalization and normalization of acceptable politics emerged in how media represented politics and privileged both issues and personalities. Although different in different systems in terms of timeframe, the era of persona has challenged legacy politics.
legacy political persona	A term to identify the way that political power and its formation of leadership is connected to media forms of representation – exemplifies the representational media and cultural regime.	At its zenith, the legacy political persona would have been key leaders in Western culture – Ronald Reagan, Mikhail Gorbachev, George H. Bush, Margaret Thatcher, and Francois Mitterand. In the contemporary moment, it is those most connected to forms of legitimation of political parties, mainstream media, and established system of politics and power. In 2016, Hillary Clinton, in the United States, was as close to a legacy political persona that we now have.
massively multiplayer online role-playing games (MMORPGs)	*See* role-playing games	
media	The technologies that we use to move or transport information, messages, ideas, stories. Media *mediate* between senders and receivers of information. The singular form of the word: medium	Examples of media include print (books, newspapers, and magazines), visual (photography and film), electronic (radio and television), and digital (mobile telephony, computer, and Internet).
media genre	Patterns or forms of communication that have developed through the medium and its uses. Genres are not fixed and change over time due to evolving codes and conventions.	Books developed into novels, biographies, nonfiction, fiction, and so on. Newspaper media genres include news, editorials, advertisements, reviews, and sports reports. Movie genres include action, romance, historical, fantasy, science fiction, comedy, and musicals as well as hybrids or blends of these genres. Television media genres include situation comedy, drama, news, sports, music, and others.

(*continued*)

Key word/concept	Definition	Examples and exemplification
mediatization	The transformation of our lives and our culture into some media form. Instead of seeing things directly, we interact increasingly through screens. **Mediatized** is one of the five dimensions of persona.	Online culture is mediatized. When we use a mobile phone to post an image via a social media platform, our personal lives are mediatized. Another example of mediatization is the process of politics happening in the presence of cameras, such as the White House media briefing, or the broadcast of parliamentary question time. We begin to determine the significance of something only if it has been shared in some mediatized form online. Mediatization allows for the collection of more and more information and data about us.
meme	Described by Richard Dawkins as the smallest unit of cultural reproduction, a meme is an element of culture or system of behavior that is shared and transformed within and between different collectives. The meme has found a particular voracity in cultures connected by online media. The transformation of a meme often identifies knowledge and information that defines an in-group as much as those that cannot read the meme and its various permutations.	Memes often turn into extended visual jokes online and in social media. One of the most visible memes of late 2016 – and therefore a very wide in-group – was one devoted to the transfer of power from Obama and Biden to the Trump Whitehouse in Washington in late 2016 and early 2017. Different images, with transformed captions, played with the key objects of power in the American executive, including – in humorous ways – how Obama and Biden could tease or confuse the incoming president.

microcelebrity

Microcelebrity is a self-presentation technique. It means an individual who is at the center of their own modes of production. A microcelebrity is not surrounded by managers, handlers, agents, and representatives, and is directly interacting with fans with a focus on attention to authenticity. They are particularly well known by a group of followers in specific online communities.

Microcelebrities define the new commodified persona online. Video blogger Casey Neistat is a microcelebrity with 9.22 million followers and 2.13 billion total views. He is able to support his vlogging through direct advertising and YouTube advert revenue. Young women, such as Chriselle Lim, Ingrid Nilson, and Michelle Phan, have started out as social media influencers presenting reviews and how-to videos on makeup, fashion, and lifestyle, and now earn significant sponsorship money and have a dedicated fan following. Other microcelebrities might be famous as Twitch.tv streamers or YouTube personalities but remain largely unacknowledged in legacy media formats.

micro-public

In the era of online culture, smaller publics can develop around an individual or a particular interest.

The formation of a cluster of followers, users of a hashtag, or commenters on a video can be thought of as a micro-public. It is a network of activity that can include linking, liking, tagging, meme use, and other forms of mediated expression.

myth of the artist

Through this myth, the artist is constructed as a solitary genius whose creative abilities are inherent. Along with this is the necessity of suffering, either personal or professional, an expectation of (and likely disregard for) financial difficulties, and a bohemian, transgressive, or left-wing sensibility. The **creative labor** discourse challenges this conceptualization of the starving artist by focusing on economic contributions.

This artist's myth is being increasingly challenged, but we can still see elements of the myth being performed through artist's personas. The so-called 27 Club, musicians and actors who died in (or close to) their 27th year, is a good example of the myth in action, where the artist's brilliance is cut short by drug addiction, alcoholism, poverty, or tragic accident.

(continued)

Key word/concept	Definition	Examples and exemplification
neoliberal individualism	A transformation of the notion of individualism that implicitly embraces a sense of personal responsibility in relation to work and contribution to an economy. It has generally been a critique of the breakdown of the structures of collective support around work, labor, and employment that had emerged in the first half of the twentieth century in forms of social democracy.	The best exemplars of neoliberal individual can be seen in online culture among vloggers and Instagrammers who are claiming to be "influencers." This range of usually young people have constructed sites/channels designed to draw interested viewers and subscribers to their spaces. They labor intensively on being producers of their public selves or personas for a type of valuation. Their success is determined by their number of views/followers/friends and how/ whether this enumeration of their influence and power can somehow be monetized through sponsors and advertising.
new media	New media refers to the blending of media or the *convergence* of media made possible by its digital transformation and its digital and electronic transmission, reception, collection, and recirculation.	Social media describes a new media form with its blend of past forms and its use on multiple devices.
new media genre	Patterns or forms of communication that have developed in the converged digital media.	There are many examples of new media genres that have emerged in the last 30 years that are beyond our notions of legacy media and its uses: Texts, stickers, and emoji via Wechat, Twitter, and Facebook; how-to videos and other vlogs; selfies and their form of communication in Instagram; video and online games.
panopticon	Originally Jeremy Bentham's term to describe how a form of potential surveillance can discipline a prison population to control their behavior. Foucault advanced this idea to describe the patterns of self-discipline that operate in cultures that take the wider notion of surveillance and internalize it into a structure of action.	In contemporary culture, with the ubiquity of cameras, the sense of surveillance is ever-present. Similarly, with our use of social media, our public identities – our personas – are a shared version of ourselves that move into the dataflows of the intercommunication industries.

Term	Definition
parasocial	The sensation of virtual connection between the famous personas (celebrities) and their audiences.	Parasocial is often used to describe kinds of interactions between fans and stars. The type of correspondence and engagement in these exchanges might appear and sound quite interpersonal and in the realm of the private. However, it is a constructed relationship and affective connection that is likely not fully shared in any face-to-face relationship or any one-to-one correspondence. The lines of the parasocial have been crossed with the uses made of stars/celebrities and their fans via various social media.
paratext	Paratext was described by Gerard Genette as the liminal devices and conventions both within and outside of a text that form a complex mediation between text and audience.	A fan paratext could include a cosplay of a favorite character. The choice of costume items, symbolic paraphernalia, and role-playing gesture are all paratextual and presentational forms of play. Mia Consalvo refers to the paratextual industries in her account of game "cheats" which include websites, mod chips, and fan sites, as well as other content in the form of cheat codes, game reviews, walkthroughs, and online player discussion boards.
performative	One of the five dimensions for the analysis of persona. The performative dimension refers specifically to persona as a form of acting and enactment by the individual for particular purposes. It underlines the role-playing quality of persona.	Think of how we produce slightly different identities for different purposes. Individuals who are parents will often adopt their parent-persona when they and their children are the focus of outside attention. Similarly, we take on roles as a consumer or customer when we approach a sales agent or a fast-food counter. Online we perform different identities – sometimes our work identity, sometimes our gamer identity, sometimes our dating identity: these strategic and performative personas sometimes cross and converge and sometimes are hermetically sealed as best that we can to maintain such a status in a data-mined social media space.

(continued)

Key word/concept	Definition	Examples and exemplification
persona	A strategic public identity that is neither the true individual nor a false individual. It is an identity that is used to navigate the social world and only exists to manage collective connections. It is a performance of the self for strategies to be used in some public setting.	All of us construct identities and profiles online – these are personas. In real life, we also take on strategic public identities. Politicians and celebrities are the original personas – strategic identities for their particular political or perhaps economic ends. In addition, personas are used in software development and business and marketing: persona identifies the kinds of identities that are the target of a particular program, service, or computer application. One imagines the "persona" of the end-user to help design the product.
persona literacy	An awareness of our own activities in constructing public identities as well as those of others. In digital and online culture, it means understanding what we have created and how it is shared.	Persona literacy often demands visualization techniques to see the interconnections and networks each person creates. It also is understanding how one's data is created and how it is shared and used for the larger intercommunication industries purposes: often for commercial and surveillance.
persona studies	The academic field that investigates persona in all its forms of public presentation of the self.	Persona studies understands that we are performing our public identities and explores this through qualitative and interpretive research of online and everyday culture as well as quantitative studies of social media activities by individuals. *Persona Studies* is also the title of the academic journal that helps define the field.
personal public	A term that refers to the followers of an individual in an online setting. See also micro-public.	Followers and friends in a social media network define a personal public. Personal publics intersect with other personal publics through intercommunication and this allows for extensions of personal publics and the possibilities of some activities to go viral and become very popular online.
personalization	The reduction of collective life through the filter of the individual; the transformation by consumer culture into an appeal to individual tastes, usually through purchasing products.	The online and social media world is organized around the individual – individuals are the gatekeepers – and thus they represent the best example of the personalization of culture.

presentational media and culture	Defines the emerging direction where we are encouraged to present ourselves publicly through online and social media platforms. It is a challenge to the way our worlds were comfortable with representational media and culture in which a small, publicly visible group would represent our political, cultural, and economic interests.	This is a major cultural shift – more of us are public and mediatized and we are more comfortably presenting ourselves in this way. Politics is probably under the biggest threat by this change as our politicians have to find new ways to connect to citizens. Presentational media is much more dispersed into intersecting micro-publics as opposed to a coherent national public.
prestige	A term used in VARP analysis that identifies a perception of influence arising from success and achievement. It is a longer-term structure of reputation that on occasion can move across cultural fields and social networks. The word, from its origins, is magical in nature and intersects with conceptions of charisma for personas.	Prestige operates as an extended word-of-mouth reading of particular personas that is visible and is felt over an extended period of time. It is supported by networks of other prominent public personas to give the prestige lasting legitimacy and extensive geographical and temporal reach.
private	Two meanings are important here: private means not visible to the public and thereby behind the closed doors of a family's household, or domestic. Private can also mean individual property as opposed to public or collective property.	With our increasing mediatization of ourselves through online culture and social media use, we are having to define new boundaries of private and public and intimate as well. This is one of the great challenges of contemporary culture. It also means that we are becoming increasingly comfortable in making ourselves "commodities" of private value.

(continued)

Key word/concept	Definition	Examples and exemplification
privlic	A way to characterize our blending of private and public experiences where both the private (domestic), economic and industrial entrepreneurship are blended with shifting notions of a public domain.	Real examples of privlic space included shopping malls, the way that celebrities embody a cause but incorporate the support of corporations, and some parks that blend their openness with private enterprise. In online culture, this blend is best characterized by the way that we use social media sites (Facebook, Instagram, Weibo) as both public and private and how companies who "own" the spaces we inhabit comfortably mine those uses for data.
prosopographic field study (PFS)	The adaptation of prosopography to the particular directions of persona studies. A prosopographic field in its original usage may relate to a village and a particular moment of time; in online cultural analysis, it is piecing together the array of virtual objects/texts that are valuable for a particular online collective.	PFS is a critical method of analysis developing for persona studies. In online culture, this may be articulated through visualization of informational patterns and sharing; it may be a pattern of liking, sharing, or tweeting on a particular social media site; it may be texts and images that are privileged within a sharing community or collective that have particular value and potentially a hierarchical structure of significance that needs deeper analysis.
prosopography	Traditionally, an historical method for linking information related to people in a community to make sense of the cultural patterns, hierarchies, responsibilities, and forms of exchange in those communities. The term identifies the use of the portrait and the accouterments attached to the facial image as an organization of cultural and political value in a particular time and place.	The actual word derived from the ancient Greek, which meant face or mask. Thus, prosopography is looking for those aspects/features that people visibly present. This kind of study has gone beyond the face or mask and can include other objects with which we surround ourselves.

public	A nineteenth- and twentieth-century conception of collective identity. A strategy to identify common ideas and directions. Connected to representational media and culture. Often referred to as a public sphere for debate and discussion – the basis of our politics and the nation-state and even international conceptions of a world public. In persona studies specifically, public refers to one of the five dimensions of persona that define our strategic identity and its movement into a visible space and populated territory.	News tries to produce a public and a public interest; politicians also try to generate a coherent public direction. Public is also used to describe all that is not private. It is what is common. In online culture, more is public and visible and this changes how we think of our public world. Our persona is designed to be visible and for public use and thus it is an identity that is public or at least how we individually project ourselves into our idea of a public.
public self	Sometimes used as a synonym for persona in persona studies. Because of the complex range of meanings associated with both public and self, it is usually a term that simply implies the movement of the self into some public or collectively constructed world.	A mediatized persona can be thought of as a public self of an individual; more visible public selves may be celebrities and politicians. In essence, the public self is how we might imagine our way of negotiating our movement through a collective and be perceived in the world.
representational media and culture	The structure of media, politics, and culture that have worked together at producing a coherent – though negotiated – sense of a visible leadership in politics, culture, and the economy. Legacy media have helped us both to identify and to focus on particular individuals as important and so the systems of representation are reinforced by the media.	The way television and politics have worked for the last 70 years is the best example of the representational media and cultural regime. With new systems of presenting publicly, this system is under threat and is breaking down. Online culture and social media are fundamentally presentational and, as massive numbers of individuals present publicly, they are the threats to representational media and culture – although power is still contained within these older institutions of representation across the globe.

(*continued*)

Key word/concept	Definition	Examples and exemplification
reputation	Reputation is traditionally understood as beliefs or opinions associated with an individual's character. In presentational media culture, it is quantified through social network metrics. Reputation is a term utilized to describe the calibration of (intentional) value related to personas. It is one element in VARP analysis.	Reputation is increasingly calibrated in online culture. The number of views of a YouTube channel is always up to date and is thus a way that reputation can be quantified. The likes and shares associated with an account, along with numbers of followers and friends, or the number of retweets are important reputational factors in the status of online influencers.
role-playing games (RPGs)	A game in which players assume the roles of characters in a fictional setting. Pen-and-paper role-playing games emerged in the 1970s with Dungeons and Dragons. Video game RPGs enabled individuals to control a "party" of characters exploring virtual worlds.	Non-fantasy settings were popularized in the late 1980s with the rise of the cyberpunk genre. Multiuser domains (MUDs) were the first online RPGs that enabled users to take control of an individual characters and interact with other players in a live setting. These evolved into massively multiplayer online role-playing games (MMORPGs) which have a persistent game world. The most famous MMORPG, *World of Warcraft*, by Blizzard software, had a peak of 12 million subscribers in 2010.
smart media	The capacity of individualized information to be constructed and used by both users and the intercommunication industries.	Autocorrect is a smart media form that tries to predict our usage; over time, smart media will predict our individual patterns and assist through probabilities in our texting/writing. Smart home devices, such as Alexa and Google Home, allow us to engage with smart media. Many applications are providing information but also collecting information about users; Google matches our interests with its searches and is "smart"; Facebook anticipates from our posts a range of possible products that might be of interest to us. Our "liking" is a particular technique used as information to generate parallel likes back to the individual user. In the era of persona, we are encouraged to share information to allow the smart media of the intercommunication industries to provide more accurately to our wants.

social media	A generally acknowledged expression of online social network applications designed to connect networks of people through sharing of their interests and pathways to acknowledge their links with others.	The examples of social media emerged from original platforms such as MySpace and perhaps the blogging site LiveJournal; in some ways the expansions of email services, such as the free Hotmail, were linked to networked connections which formed the basis of social media power and value. The current use of these applications – Facebook, Instagram, Snapchat, Twitter, Wechat, Weibo, and others – describe some of the principal ways in which we create mediated personas in the contemporary moment.
surveillance	Surveillance is the systematic collection and analysis of observed data. It involves the practice of monitoring and technologies for the observation and recording of activities.	Humans have used surveillance technologies in perpetuity. Journals, maps, and biographies have been important tools for recording historical observations. Spyglasses, telescopes, and semaphores provided the means to observe the movement of people, troops, and objects at a distance. Metadata, GPS, and social media activity are contemporary technologies used to document movement, location, and networks of association.
synchronous media and communication	A form of mediated communication where the sender and receiver are experiencing the mediated form at the same time.	A telephone conversation is synchronous; a film and its audience are synchronous; radio and television are examples of synchronous media and communication.
value	The first part of the fifth dimension of persona, *value* flows through the other dimensions in its organization of economic, cultural, and often idiosyncratic personal value of the public formation of an identity. It is central to the components of a VARP analysis.	Engaging with others and determining the varying levels of investment regulates what is significant and what connections are valuable to an individual's own sense of worth. Various types of online activity are also ways of expanding value; the choices that individuals make about what they show, with what they connect, what they like or favor, are all further signs of value to a persona. Prestige and reputation are complex constructions in this online space, but they are linked to the reach and depth of the forms of connections that people hold in esteem.

(*continued*)

Key word/concept	Definition	Examples and exemplification
VARP	VARP is an acronym of four components related to the fifth dimension of persona identified as having intentional value. VARP identifies a connected series of related notions of "value, agency, reputation, and prestige."	VARP analyses of the academic, law, and medical profession are explored in greatest detail in Chapter 8. It explores how value is established for certain visible personas – in this case derived from the history of particular professions.
viral	The movement of information through a process of (rapid) sharing in online culture.	Viral media are objects and patterns of behavior which are replicated across multiple platforms. The metaphor suggest audiences are passive carriers that spread the media content. Memes are a good example of communication patterns that have a degree of viral spread. Henry Jenkins has proposed the alternative idea of "spreadable media" which returns individual agency to the act of sharing content.

Index

Note: Page numbers followed by "n" indicate a reference list entry.

Persona Studies: An Introduction, First Edition. P. David Marshall, Christopher Moore, and Kim Barbour.
© 2020 John Wiley & Sons, Inc. Published 2020 by John Wiley & Sons, Inc.